A Conversation about Economics

Richard Werner CMA/CFM

Edited by Dawn Werner

Illustrations by Amy Michalares

Contributing Editor Alissa McMannis

ISBN-13: 978-1508493204

CONTENTS

Dedication

To my parents Omer and Frances Werner who provided me the opportunity to grow up with a comparatively open and inquisitive mind and whose hard work and good example have remained as a solid guide to me throughout my life.

Introduction

We have all had them, that conversation at work around the coffee station or with family on a holiday visit. We discuss, we listen, and we learn. Certainly it's not like a school setting but nonetheless we are in a situation where we are immersed in an interesting conversation that often ends up teaching us something. The conversation might be about politics, cars, restaurants, or why your employer's business is or is not doing so well.

You may have conversations that regularly touch on the subject of economics, or maybe you have overheard others discussing economic concepts, or perhaps you just have a natural and healthy curiosity about a subject that impacts every aspect of your life. Whatever your reason, and in the hope of developing a better understanding of how economics impacts your world, you scoured the earth *(or internet)* to find this informative, yet entertaining, book. On the other hand, you may have accidently tripped and stumbled nose first into this book and you may be thinking… *"I might like to read up on economics sometime after I have finished watching the paint dry or have counted all the sand grains on the beach*". If you are harboring any thoughts along these lines then I suspect I had best pique your interest quickly.

Much like a car enthusiast might want to engage another person in talking about what makes their car exceptional or someone who has a medical issue may want to delve into a discussion about their condition, someone who is affected by the economy *(and that would be all of us)* might want to spend some time trying to understand what makes our world tick. All of us have a vested interest in the economics of our world, we are all involved in our economy and through our decisions *(including our choices at the polls)* we all play a leadership role in how effective our local, national, and world economies perform.

Most of us, at one time or another, have played a game *(be it football, golf, or a board game)* and at some point in time we chose to learn the rules and strategies of that game. The reason we made the effort and found the time to learn is obvious... we wanted to understand what we needed to do in order to be successful. No reasonable person would want to spend their time doing something without knowing the rules or at least having some semblance of what it takes to win the game. And, just like you wouldn't play a board game without reading the rules first, it's important to develop an understanding as to how economics affect you in the game of life especially since you're already playing the game… every day when you go to work, make a trip to the store, or choose where to invest your retirement savings you are interacting with the economy.

Economics is fundamental to living in a free society and it's important to understand it in order to know how and why you should try to preserve it. Every day there are reports in the news citing economic concepts and no shortage of talking heads engaging in debates related to them, yet the concepts remain a mystery to many of us. We hear terms on the news such as *"the economy grew 0.5 percent in March"* or *"consumer confidence is down which forebodes a potential recession"* but few truly understand what they mean and how, or in what ways, they affect us. My hope is to help you understand basic economic concepts, help you put them into context, and help you to understand how any number of factors in our economy often, but not always, can lead to certain resulting economic conditions.

If you are still toying with counting the sand on the beach you may be asking yourself about now, "Why should I, or anyone, else take the time to learn more about economics?" or more importantly "Why did I buy a book on the subject?" Well, if you watch any amount of news or engage in political debates with friends and family, you will not be able to avoid the topic of economics for very long and chances are pretty good that you would like to come across as knowledgeable and well informed and, while economics is too complicated to glean a competent understanding and knowledge level of from a talk show or from a commercial, you don't need a Ph.D. on the subject to be an informed citizen. Going a step further, a significant part of our political decision making process is driven by economics which means understanding the basic processes of economics is essential to performing that most important of civic responsibilities… informed voting.

Economics, at least the parts we expect our government to influence, is in many ways like tinkering with an old car or developing a better cooking recipe. More of the same is unlikely to fix a problem, like adding more salt to a favorite dish, at some point more becomes too much and you need to reverse direction. A mechanic working with an old car might start by adjusting the fuel mixture to make it richer but at some point it becomes too rich. Economic topics like taxes, jobs, and entitlement programs *(to name just a few)* cannot be addressed by the same answer every time. But by understanding the interworking of factors within the economy and how one affects the others, you can then be better able to make sense of the news and intelligently engage in political debates about economic matters.

Like many complex subjects, economics is one that most of us tend to develop opinions about based on what experts tell us. As an example, one such expert and a noted economist, made a comment that he thought it was impossible to effectively prosecute white collar crime. If you know more than a little about business, or have worked in situations where you have come into direct or indirect contact with any type of white collar crime, you might be appalled by the thought that an expert would propose that we cannot hold white collar workers to any kind of legal standard. As a society, whether we realize it or not, we all support or oppose beliefs, such as the one put forward by this economist, and through our voting we either support or reject these concepts. Knowing a little more about economics can help you make informed judgments and the better informed our voting population is on matters affecting economics the more likely we are to enjoy a better economy. Among the objectives of this book will be to explore concepts embodied in statements, such as the one about regulations and white collar crime, in order to give you a better understanding of the workings of our economy.

Why should you or anyone else take the time to learn more about how the economy works? There are many reasons but I am of the opinion that the two most important are (1) *to be a more competent consumer* and (2) *to be able to make better decisions as a member of the voting population*. The reason for the first is fairly obvious, (*if you don't know just smile and nod your head, I'll explain it in a second*), and the reasons for the second are as varied as the population *(I'll get to this too, just give me a minute)*.

What does being a more competent consumer mean?

If you, as a consumer, are aware of how prices are set and why prices rise, you can better judge the value you are giving up *(your cash)* in exchange for the value in the good or service you are buying. By educating yourself on what works and does not work in economics, can clue you into what is real value and what is hyperbole. I will provide an example of this later in the book *(chapter sixteen)* when we delve into why marketing people earn very good livings convincing consumers *(us)* to spend money buying what may be just an image of greater value. This image of value conflicts with what is best for the consumer whose focus should be on the more tangible attributes of the good being purchased. For example, as a consumer buying a chair, would you be better served to buy a product based on a sexy commercial or based upon careful research of the chair manufacturer's quality record? *(and don't say "sexy commercial")*.

Throughout this book I will use examples to demonstrate how understanding economics can help shine light on what may be faulty thinking. So as not to keep you in suspense let's get started with my first example. Suppose you are shopping for a can of chicken soup and you have two choices, a nationally recognized brand name and a lesser known brand that costs 50% less. When you do your homework you may find that both products have been made at the exact same factory using the same formulas and quality controls. So in this case what are you getting for the added cost, nothing, right? Or, maybe you might find that the cheaper soup is exactly that a cheaper, lower quality, and a less satisfying product. Now while you might not want to spend a lot of time researching soups, there are purchases that do warrant a consumer taking the time to evaluate which purchase choice is a better use of their financial resources.

Making better decisions as a member of the voting population

Earlier I mentioned that we each play a leadership role at the polls… as voters we choose which leaders to hire to manage our society. Being a knowledgeable person in the voting booth is probably the best way we can avoid our country becoming another Nazi Germany, Soviet Union, or some other failed society. This truth is probably something that extends well beyond economic knowledge but, within the confines of this text, we will stick to the economic reasons.

Opinions are strong and varied on this point, but arguably many voters do not go to the polls armed with sufficient facts and therefore cannot reflect and make decisions based upon the facts. Having moved around a bit in my career I have had the benefit of living in districts that leaned in opposing political party directions. I have personally thought that in some overwhelmingly Christian districts, Jesus himself could run against Satan and, if Jesus was of the district's minority party, he would maybe generate the closest race in the district's history but would still lose by a comparative landslide. Look, it's normal to become indoctrinated into one party or the other due to family leanings or that of the city, town, or county in which you live and it's just human nature to adopt the values of those close to you. The goal of this book is not to try to make independents out of Democrats or Republicans, but instead to help develop an understanding of what economics is and how the system works. In this way, as a voter, you can come to a more informed decision when listening to a candidate's position on the various economic issues.

Further to the point, let me share a brief personal observation about politics, economics, and some possibly less informed voters I have known. A relative of mine is very vocal about his political leanings, his history has been one of frequent unemployment, lengthy stints on workers compensation, and prone to often be on public assistance. Another family member, who is also very politically vocal, is church going, hardworking, has never taken a dime of the government's money, and staunchly defends the other political party. If you think the first one leans democratic and the second republican guess again. By all accounts both of these individuals are good people, never ones to cheat another and equally likely to help a stranger who has a disabled car. The point is not that either one is wrong but that neither one really understands fully what their party of choice tends to support as economic or social policy.

I am not trying to say that strong supporters of one party or the other are ignorant or that they blindly vote based on what they grew up with as children, I'm just saying that many subjects, including economics, are more mysterious than they need be. Just like the cave men of 10,000 BC, because the knowledge was not yet available to them, did not understand the movements of the Sun and the Moon in the same way if we don't have the knowledge of basic economics the workings of our society will be just as mysterious to us. So let's focus on taking the mystery out of economic concepts.

My intention throughout this book is to steer away from political arguments and stands on the many economic issues such as taxes *(on who and how much)* and whether government should or should not have a role in healthcare. Instead my goal will be to put into view how economics, within a free nation, can work in a pure state and provide insight into what really happens and why. With that said I believe everyone is subject to some form of intellectual blindness on any subject and, while I will try to keep my prejudices from tainting the descriptions here, you should keep in mind that I, like every other writer, have preconceived notions as to what is correct and as a result it is possible that facts I present may be twisted by those influences. That warning not only applies here but it also applies every time you tune into MSNBC, Fox News, or CNN and while you may not frequently hear that warning elsewhere please remember it as you go forward through this book and beyond.

In providing insight into the world of economics I will share with you stories from my life where I was confronted by economic concepts in action, description of historic events and how they demonstrate an economic concept, and the story of a fictional island where the economic concepts come to light through working examples. Often seeing the humor in a situation can be an aid to understanding and hopefully you will be amused occasionally along the way.

In terms of opinion, I will share many but in doing so will endeavor to keep my explanations closely aligned with recognized economic theory. I will only intentionally try to sell the reader on one concept… that free enterprise is a powerful economic model, one that has beaten out all challengers thus far on the planet Earth. Understanding free enterprise economics is everyone's responsibility whether you are a voter, a parent, or a participant in an economy. I hope you will find reading this book both enjoyable and informative.

Chapter One

(The Beginning)

Most Americans do not have a good understanding of the workings of our economy or how the global economy interacts with the United States' economy. This is unfortunate because the important concepts of economics do not require an advanced degree in this science; our basic education, as provided in the United States, along with a little outside reading will provide what we need to know about economics. This book will help put the concepts in terms that will take away a good part of the mystery.

While understanding economics, or at least the basics of economics, is within the grasp of most Americans, developing that understanding does require a little study and the willingness to consider dependent activities. Much of economics in action is just simple common sense… a matter of considering what logical choices people will make when trying to fulfill their wants and needs. If you keep in mind that the root of economics is based on that simple concept you will have set for yourself the foundation for understanding economics.

Each day you play a role in the United States' economy whether you are a producer or a consumer of products and/or services. Your contribution to the economy can be obvious *(as in a worker producing a product in a factory)* or less obvious *(as in an ad designer who, though not directly connected to making a good, works to facilitate the sale of that good)*. The economy is a complex web of people producing goods and services for each other's consumption.

Obvious contributions to the economy can be easy for us to understand, such as how the person who makes the proverbial indispensable widget adds something of value for the rest of the population to consume. However the value of other roles in the economy, such as finance and marketing, can be more difficult to understand because the connection between what is being produced and the end value to the consumer is not as obvious. I will attempt in this text to provide the context necessary to understand what makes the economy go, what causes the economy to not work so well at times, and how interconnected jobs and resources all work together.

Economic terms, such as inflation and productivity, are used every day in the news and are as much misunderstood as they are understood. Throughout this text we will attempt to help you develop a working knowledge of what is meant by many basic economic terms. The approach we will use is to provide both real world and fictional examples using easily understood language to walk you through a demonstration of the economic concept.

Since we all participate in the economy *(by helping to guide our economy through the choices we make at the polls and by producing and consuming resources)* it is crucial that we understand economics and develop the knowledge we need to make wise decisions. As a contributor to the economy, understanding your role will enable you to make better choices in your life whether you are a top level executive or an entry level worker.

Anyone who has ever spent time among entry level employees knows that there is no shortage of stories describing mind boggling missteps by management. These perceived missteps may simply be a case of the story teller not understanding the bigger picture but it is also just as likely that management, not having a clear understanding of what happens on the front line, made decisions that have led to a waste of economic resources.

Why should we care about economics as it relates to our work? Does it really matter if entry level workers mistake good management decisions for foolish actions? Among the selfish reasons to care about economics is any waste of economic resources diminishes the quality of life for everyone.

After graduating from high school I spent my last year as a teenager working in a high end, small lot production, furniture factory, which meant most of the jobs we ran only consisted of a couple dozen pieces up to a few hundred pieces. This factory used a job costing system that involved each employee, who performed a step in the production process, to fill out a time card for that job. To explain by example let's say there is a job to make 30 chairs. One person in the process has the responsibility for making the chair legs; this person retrieves a rough cut board from the lumber pile and cuts it to the appropriate length. For 30 chairs this person will make 120 cuts. In our example it takes this person 30 minutes to complete the 120 cuts *(four chair leg pieces per minute)*. This employee then fills out a time card for the job reporting he spent 30 minutes on the 30 chair project. This data leads factory management to assign a cost of one minute of work by this employee to each chair. As the chair passes through all the steps in the factory the dollar cost of each of these manufacturing operations are added together providing a cumulative labor cost per chair. The cumulative labor cost plus the cost of materials *(i.e. wood, fabric, finishing chemicals, and etc.)* are then totaled together to give us the final cost of the chair.

I, as the factory newbie unschooled in the ways of the factory world, was assigned to work with a very large man, who went by the nickname of Mule. Mule ran one of the most complex machines in the factory called a sticker machine. This machine took in the cut-to-length and -width pieces of wood and made all four sides' smooth and uniform and, in some cases, applied an additional shape to one or more sides of the wood. My job was to take the finished pieces coming off the machine and stack them on a factory production cart. In this arrangement I could only work as hard as Mule chose to run the machine. Mule was very good at what he did so he could get a lot of production out in a short time. I grew up on a family farm so for me work meant getting the work done as quickly as possible and staying at the job until it was complete. Mom and Dad drilled into the heads of all of the kids in my family this approach to work, which I was soon to find out ran into conflict with this factory's generally accepted approach to work.

From our first day in kindergarten we have had to learn to adapt to our social environment and I quickly learned that a big part of fitting into the environment and the socialization process of my new job was learning the "art" of time card completion. As you might suspect, what was reported on the cards was not a true reflection of what actually happened on the factory floor. On any given day, Mule and I would run ten to twenty jobs each requiring a separate time card. Our day would start at 7 am and for an hour an fifteen minutes we would run several jobs. Mule would then sit down with me to fill out our time cards and would account for a full two hours of work *(including the 45 minutes between 8:15 and 9 am that we hadn't worked yet)*. Mule would assign that 45 minutes to the various jobs we had just completed and then head off to the restroom for about a half hour, spend the next 15 minutes visiting some of his buddies around the factory, and then start his 9 am general factory break.

Mule was an intimidating guy who was nearly twice my size so I guess I could maintain that it was out of fear that I adopted a work style that was very foreign to me but, in all honesty, my true motivation came from the desire to fit in with this sub element of the local society. Unfortunately, this work style was not unique to Mule *(and now me)*; it was a plant-wide behavior that only varied based on the creative ways individuals could come up with to waste time. The cumulative result was 25% to

50% of wasted time was absorbed into each day's work. What I didn't realize, and I am sure Mule didn't either, was that by our actions we were making the cost of furniture produced by that factory more expensive. For simplicity's sake, let's assume that one chair had a manufacturing cost of $100 and that the final cost included 20% materials and 80% labor *(a good part which was wasted time)* then taking the math forward some $20 to $40 dollars of each chair's cost was due to this socially enforced "art" of time card completion.

Because of these shenanigans you might think that the company where Mule and I worked would have gone out of business fairly quickly but it continued producing expensive high quality furniture for more than twenty more years. Now you may be thinking, "This was probably a union plant where the union was the cause of the bad work habits". Well you would be partly right, it was a union plant but, from the best that I could tell, the union had nothing to do with these costly work habits. I can say this because this particular union was pretty weak and all it seemed capable of achieving was securing the lowest pay and worst benefits in the area… I might go so far as to say that, at its best, this union could not get its members sunlight on a sunny day. So to blame the union environment for the inefficient use of the factory labor is most likely wrong.

What causes this type of mentality among workers, management, and others within our society? The most likely cause… a lack of understanding amongst workers as to the connection between low productivity and employee rewards, the next most likely reason is poor management. But, at the root of both, is the lack of understanding economics.

Let's focus on the workers first, is it reasonable to assume the workers in this plant, in 1975, were not taking actions to deliberately put the plant out of business or lessen the company's ability to give raises to its workers? Obviously neither of these goals was driving the workers to act in this wasteful way. So why did this happen?

In order to answer this question let us first examine the motivations of management; we assume that management would have more information than the plant's non-management workers on the effects of lower productivity. Anyone who has ever managed people knows how difficult it can be to motivate people to work harder. So how do we do it" Well, the easiest means to motivate people is to get them invested in the results. This is not necessarily invested in the company, in terms of stock ownership, but, in general terms, invested in working to insure its success. This brings us to a basic and well known principle known as the carrot and stick motivation approach.

Almost every company seeks to employ the carrot and stick approach in order to achieve company objectives. During my short youthful stint with this furniture company I was able to see both techniques in practice with a heavy focus on the "stick".

On a daily basis the plant manager and foreman would look to discipline poor performance, verbal and written warnings, suspensions without pay, and firings happened frequently. One of the most talented employees, we'll call him Jerry, went through all the discipline processes twice during his career, including being fired. Jerry was brought back about the time I was hired so I got to see him start the process all over.

Jerry taught me how to run a machine that was probably forty years old at the time and in doing so I was able to learn more than a little about what made him tick. Jerry primarily wanted to take care of Jerry. He was a man of action however his actions seldom benefited the company or his standing within the company. Jerry would prioritize his work based on which jobs he liked to run the most, he was as adept as anyone at taking the long bathroom breaks during the day, and he felt entitled to use company equipment, time and materials to complete personal projects. At different times, Jerry used the company equipment to convert company lumber into finished pieces for home projects. At one point he found some rosewood in the lumberyard and decided to use it for knife handles and we spent the better part of a couple days using the wood along with some metal from the factory to make ourselves two knives.

Jerry had the skills and intelligence to be a major contributor at this plant, he was talented and capable of doing great work and could be very productive when he wanted to, he just seldom wanted to unless of course it was for one of his personal projects. Jerry just never stayed focused on using his skills, talent, and intelligence to the benefit of the company and ultimately he chose to leave and work for another local company, a company that was known for offering the best wages and benefits.

At this point in my career I was already studying accounting and I found it curious that this free spirited and intelligent man went to work for a company that had a reputation for running a tight ship *(an employer that would on the surface seem ill suited for Jerry and his propensity to avoid productive work)* while at the same time the furniture company, which desperately needed a person with his skills, seemed incapable of retaining him.

The underlying reason for an individual and company mismatch, like in the case with Jerry and the furniture company, is a lack of understanding of what each needs from the other. Just like in the workplace, our role in the economy is often not clear to us and we are not able to see a clear correlation between doing well at work and being more financially successful. Understanding the workings of economics is the key to remedying this, for example, if Jerry had a clear understanding between how working hard and efficiently affected his pay and/or job security, Jerry possibly would have been more likely to perform better. Additionally, if management had been better educated in the psychology of the worker and the workings of economics they might have been better able to construct an effective method of managing and motivating Jerry. Absent this Jerry consistently underperformed and the company lost valuable production output and ultimately a very skillful employee.

As an example of this let's say that Jerry, working at his optimum capacity, could generate an extra chair's worth of production each day. If that chair sells for $200 then the economic cost of this lost productivity is $200 minus the cost of any direct materials going into the chair, in this case and let's say that is $50. If you told the workers that their lack of effort was costing the company $150 each day per employee I doubt you would have heard much of an outcry from the workers. If, however, you could convince the company and the employees that the $150, if earned, would benefit both the company and employees then the collective team would view this lost productivity differently.

The company, at one point, contracted with outside consultants to create the proverbial "carrot" to provide motivation for employees to improve productivity. Unfortunately, the "carrot" that the consultants developed and implemented, a gain sharing plan, was so complex that no one, other than a finance guru, had any chance of understanding it. At that point I was well into completing an accounting degree, and though still far short of a guru, I would like to think I had enough knowledge to at least see some vague connection between my performance and a potential financial reward but the dots just weren't there for me to connect. But let's not digress into a commentary on the design and implementation of gain sharing plans. The important point here is that even though management knew, to some degree, it needed to gain the cooperation of the workforce in order to drive better performance, and despite knowing and attempting to do the right things, they were still unsuccessful in gaining the workers' cooperation.

The struggle described here is a common one within working environments across our planet but, even though the goal is simple enough, you seldom hear of companies who are successful in gaining optimal employee participation in the company's success. You can make an argument that there are simply not enough workers who have a strong work ethic in our economy. It's certainly true that some people would not work hard on a consistent basis even under the threat of physical harm, but this does not accurately describe all or even most American workers. Generally speaking, people in this country desire to work for successful companies and want to be a success at what they do.

We all have a universal desire for many of the same basic things, food, security, and love. Within the sciences of psychology and economics these are described as a hierarchy of needs. Each person has their own weighting for these needs and because of this it makes finding a single solution to universal motivation difficult. For our purposes here it is simply important to recognize the fulfillment of these needs is desired by most people and concurrently most humans are willing to work to satisfy their various needs.

Opposing desires and needs coexist within people, among these is the need for leisure time, and it's this need for leisure time that often comes into conflict with the need to be productive. It is this desire for leisure that prompted workers at the aforementioned furniture factory to spend hours each week in the bathroom sleeping, resting, or reading rather than working. Most would agree that few people would choose to spend hours in a restroom as their first leisure time destination. Given the choice Mule, Jerry, or I would have worked our butts off to get to go home twenty minutes early or to make an extra ten bucks. The collective failure of employees and employers to align their economic and social desires caused the loss of the productivity to be spent, among other places, in the company restrooms resulting in a waste of resources. Given the incentive of going home early or making a few extra dollars, versus taking the half hour all expenses paid vacation in the john, most employees *(there will always be the exception)* would have willingly forgone extended bathroom breaks in order to put out the production of an extra job or two.

Our purpose in this text is not to do an exposé on the waste at a factory several decades past but, instead, to enable you to develop an understanding of how the science of economics works. Possibly the next time you read a news story regarding a drop in factory productivity in the United States, you can now envision what that loss looks like and more importantly what that means to our economy. *(I offer apologies to any reader who has just had the disturbing vision pop in their head of several thousand workers sleeping seated in innumerable company bathrooms throughout the United States).* If you can, after finishing this book, better understand the connection between higher productivity and a better lifestyle for society, then the time you spent reading and the time I spent writing this book will have been worthwhile for both of us.

Chapter Two

(The Island Economy)

Imagine there is a small island, we will call it Adam's Island named for a famous Scotsman, Adam Smith, who visited the island during the time it was being first settled in eighteenth century. On Adam's Island there live three families, Farmer, Sheppard and Fisher who, in the beginning, made up the entire population of the island. These families split the island into three parcels, Farmer's parcel is rich farm land, Sheppard's parcel is made up of rolling grassland, and Fisher's parcel has a bay with the best fishing access on the island.

This island represents a complete economy that has everything needed to sustain the simple needs of these three families. For a number of years each family has subsisted only on what they have been able to produce on their part of this island. Each family has 180 hours a week that they are able to devote towards producing products for their family's consumption and, by working very hard, each family has been able to be met their basic needs without any dependence on the other two families.

Each family's part of the island has very different capabilities in terms of producing the basic goods needed to survive.

- The Farmer parcel has six hundred acres of land, the best of which can produce forty bushels of wheat per acre, requiring eight hours of work per week per acre to farm. The parcel can also be used to raise sheep however, the land is not well drained so it cannot be used for pasture much of the year and, in order to raise the sheep, the land must be used to grow hay which then needs to be harvested, stored and feed to the sheep. The family can raise three sheep per acre and each sheep requires the family to spend twelve hours per week per acre caring for them. The Farmer parcel also has access to the sea but it is a challenging walk that involves going down a steep path to the sea. The Farmer family can catch one fifth of a pound of fish per hour spent fishing.

- The Sheppard family also has six hundred acres of land most of which they can use to either raise sheep or grow wheat. The family can raise five sheep per acre and the labor required to care for the sheep is twelve hours per week per acre. The land is well drained and the family must irrigate the land part of the year in order to produce wheat. Even with irrigation the best yield possible is thirty bushels of wheat per acre and requires ten and half hours of work per week per acre to produce. There is also access is to water for fishing however, the waters have difficult currents resulting in poor fishing and the family is only able catch one sixth of a pound of fish per hour fishing.

- The Fisher parcel, also six hundred acres, is mostly in a low lying area of which only forty acres are suitable for farming or pasturing sheep and another twenty acres can only be used for pasture. The forty acres can produce thirty-two bushels of wheat per acre but it requires fourteen hours per week per acre to grow the wheat. The land, if used for sheep pasture, can support four sheep per acre and requires eleven hours of labor per week per acre. The family has the best fishing access on the island enabling them to catch one quarter pound of fish per hour spent fishing.

To survive on this island each family needs to have a minimum of two hundred bushels of wheat, wool from twenty sheep, and five hundred pounds of fish each year. Each family can, on their own, produce enough of each of these essential goods. The following table shows the number of hours each family will spend to obtain the minimum amount of wool, fish, and wheat needed to survive.

Minimum Need	Wheat 200 Bushels	Twenty Sheep	Fish 1,500 Pounds	
Family	Hours of Work Required Each Week to Produce			Hours Worked Per Week
Farmer	40	80	50	170
Sheppard	70	48	60	178
Fisher	80	55	40	175

Each family, based upon their need for the three products, is working almost every available hour and still is only just meeting their minimum needs for each of these essentials.

Much of the early history of man was spent as subsistence hunter-gatherers where each person, or family, sought to find what they needed in order to feed and clothe only their selves. Trading, which no doubt developed over time, most likely came about when one family, who found themselves with an excess of one type of good, offered to exchange the excess for another good held by another family. You can possibly imagine a family ten thousand years ago who successfully hunted a wooly mammoth offering their near term excess supply of meat to a family who had an excess supply of dried berries.

Later in the history of mankind, humans began making a habit out of being inter-reliant. For example, tool makers provided hunting supplies to hunters and in return the hunters provided meat to the tool makers. This reciprocal type of relationship led the way for individuals to focus on improving their skill set and to become experts at generating a specific commodity that they could then trade to an expert who specialized in another type of commodity. So, as in our example, our expert tool maker could craft, not only more but, more effective weapons and then trade them to our hunters who could then spend more of their time hunting. This arrangement allowed both groups to live better than when they lived their lives completely independent from each other. Even our ancient ancestors were likely to have had special skills that set them apart from each other. If you lived in the days of our cave dwelling forefathers, you may have been the person who could rapidly make a very sharp and deadly arrowhead but could not hit a deer with a bow and arrow if it was standing still ten feet in front of you. If this was your situation, to survive in ten thousand BC, you would have needed to find a great hunter whose ability to quickly make a quality arrowhead was less than stellar.

As humans our natural tendency is to continually work towards improving our lifestyles and the same is true for our islanders.

On our little island, the heads of the Farmer and Fisher families met one day to discuss the struggle to meet their family's respective needs. Farmer recognized that Fisher was able to catch fish faster and in greater quantities because his family's parcel offered easy access to great fishing areas that were only available on the Fisher side of the island. Fisher, on the other hand, realized that the Farmer family was able to more easily produce greater quantities of wheat than his family could produce on their parcel. To take advantage of each family's core commodity, Farmer offered to raise an extra eighty bushels of wheat in trade for five pounds of fish per week. Fisher gladly accepted and the two heads of family shook on the deal. Farmer returned home to her family to boast of her deal making prowess, the results of which will have the family working an additional sixteen hours per week producing wheat but, in exchange, the family will save twenty-five hours per week previously spent fishing. At the same time Fisher tells his family that by spending only twenty extra hours per week fishing they will save thirty-two hours the family would have spent each week raising wheat. Both families were very pleased with this new arrangement.

You can probably think of a time when you struck a good deal where you thought you got the better end of the bargain because the other party overvalued the good being sold or traded to them. In this case did Farmer take advantage of Fisher or vice versa? You can do the math because you have the benefit of knowing the intimate details of both families' production capabilities but, in most trading situations, those trading or selling goods would generally not have knowledge of those details. In the case of the Fisher and Farmer families, both believed they cut a great deal and neither knew exactly how good the deal was for the other party. The important thing in trading is not that one or the other got the better deal but that both parties are better off following the trade than either was before the deal.

After the first year under this arrangement the head of the Sheppard family inquired how the other two families could have so much free time without any apparent reduction in their quality of life. After a little prodding Farmer could no longer resist telling Sheppard of the shrewd deal she had made with the Fisher family. Sheppard, being particularly sharp, recognized that Farmer had better farmland and Fisher had better fishing access and that somehow the two families were capitalizing on their respective strengths. After some thought Sheppard suggested to Farmer that his family had some unused pasture land which was superior to Farmer's and they would be willing to use a portion of this to produce additional wool to exchange for wheat. After a bit of haggling, Sheppard agreed to produce wool from five sheep in exchange for eighty bushels of wheat from Farmer each year.

Farmer once again told her family of her negotiating prowess. By working two additional acres of wheat, adding sixteen wheat production hours per week, they could have Sheppard raise five sheep for their family. This new trade would save the Farmer family twenty hours per week. Sheppard too, thrilled his family with the news that they will save twenty-eight hours per week they would have spent growing wheat and to do so they would only need to work an extra twelve hours per week raising the five additional sheep, or a net savings of sixteen hours of work per week.

At this point all three families are trading with one another resulting in a reduction in time spent working each week… the Farmer family has saved thirteen hours each week, the Fisher family twelve hours, and Sheppard family sixteen hours. This savings will initially become an increase in the amount of leisure time each family gets to enjoy increasing the quality of life for everyone on the island.

Trade on the island continued to develop until Farmer grew all the wheat, Fisher caught all the fish, and Sheppard raised all the sheep. Under this arrangement, the following table shows the average hours per week each of the families worked in order to meet the islander's needs.

Family	Wheat	Wool	Fish	Total Hours
Total Island Need	*600 Bushels*	*Sixty Sheep*	*500 Pounds*	**Per Week**
Farmer	120	0	0	120 *(previously 170)*
Sheppard	0	144	0	144 *(previously 178)*
Fisher	0	0	120	120 *(previously (175)*

The families each reduced their work week by more than thirty hours so, at least initially, all three families were very happy with the trade agreements and the resulting lifestyle improvements. However, despite the universal improvement not every family benefited equally. As you can see by the table, the Sheppard family is working twenty-four hours more per week than either the Farmer or Fisher families. Later we will see how this disparity in the benefits from the trading arrangement will come to cause problems for our island families.

Once trading on the island had fully evolved each family began to use a portion of their free time to produce more of what they were most efficient at. They used some of their additional production for their own consumption and the remainder they traded to the other families. Farmer grew more wheat, Sheppard produced more wool, and Fisher caught more fish. Each family began to consume more, worked less than before, and had a higher quality of life. The result was growth in the collective wealth of the island and this is exactly how the world economy has benefited since the dawn of trade.

Unfortunately throughout history most nations, and more importantly the individuals within those nations, failed to grasp the benefits of trading. If you consider what has happened on the island and how logical this move to trading appears to be, why then in the real world do people resist trading? Doesn't it seem obvious to have the people who can create goods most efficiently do so and then trade those goods for other products the people need? Let's return to the island to consider why this kind of change might not be welcomed.

One of Fishers son's, Sam, was the family expert in raising wheat on their property and as such was held in high regard up until the families began trading. Once the Fisher family began to trade for its wheat instead of growing it, Sam had to join the family on the boat each day. While Sam enjoyed a shorter work week and more food and clothing as a result the intra-family trading, he did not feel like it was worth it to him personally. Sam enjoyed working the land, when he was out on the fishing boat he would often get seasick and then dockside at the end of the day he found cleaning fish to be disgusting. Sam lobbied his father constantly to allow him to resume growing some of the family's wheat and to get out the fishing work. Ultimately Fisher relented and allowed Sam to grow wheat thereby reducing the trading with Farmer and forcing Farmer to do some of their own fishing.

What happened on our island is what happens in the real world when a good, let's say shoes, are imported from a foreign economy at a lower cost. Most people are happy to be able to buy shoes at a lower price. But what about the shoemakers, how does this benefit them? Unfortunately they quickly lose their jobs and lobby their representatives to put a stop to the foreign shoe imports. You, as a well educated economist, meet with the shoemakers in order to convince them not to resist the new shoe import agreement because they, along with everyone else, will benefit from the increase in trade. You explain to them, using well laid out charts and graphs, how all shoemakers will have the opportunity to go to work in a new industry and that this will allow our country to operate more efficiently. If you are successful in doing so, stop studying economics and begin your career in sales you will make a fortune! The reality is the shoemakers will not see how importing shoes will do them any good. In the real world changing careers is scary, costly, and difficult and those forced into changing careers, as a result of cheaper imports, are almost never happy about having to do so.

Today we have the benefit of some education in economics being included as a part of our high school and/or college experience; however, early in the history of trade, economics education was not prevalent in most of the population and honestly, in the earliest years of trade, even the best educated people did not understand how the mutual benefit of trade worked. Most trade occurred based solely on the desire to achieve a profit and the benefit to the respective economies was accidental. Even today most nations focus on managing the balance of trade rather than seeking out ways to increase trade in a fair and sustainable way. Later in this book we will delve deeper into why sustainable trade is critical to the long-term success of our modern society.

Throughout this book I will try to show the various sides of the arguments around economic concepts especially those concepts which are controversial. Let's start with looking at an example of a managed trade program and the negative aspects of a long-term imbalance in trade. At the start of the twenty-first century, China rose to be the preeminent area of low cost manufacturing. China has been accused of trading unfairly with the West by manipulating exchange rates of its currency *(which appears to be a fair criticism in that China is managing to grow its exports and minimize its imports).* The product of this manipulation resulted in the accumulation of foreign funds rather than allowing the Chinese consumers to use the currency received in trading to purchase goods and services from the West. By doing this, China has held down the cost of goods coming out of China thereby enticing further foreign investment and accelerating the movement of manufacturing from the western economies and into China. The result of China's managed trading program has been a more rapid development of the Chinese economy and industrial base at the short-term expense of the quality of life for the consumers in China. Opponents of free trade are often quick to point to this example and others like it where trade with a foreign partner hurts one partner and benefits the other *(very unlike the example I used with Adam's Island)*.

One of the goals of this text is to examine why overly manipulating trade in the long-term hurts the overall world economy. Admittedly trade and the underlying economic effects are not simple enough to understand without some education on how this complex exchange works best. As we proceed, keep in mind how sensible the trade gains achieved by Farmer and Sheppard were and how that concept often works for us every day in the real world.

Chapter Three

(The Introduction of Money)

While benefiting from the trading between families, the three families on Adam's island found that the timing of their needs and the supply availability of the three commodities *(wool, wheat and fish)* did not always match up well. As an example, Sheppard's sheep would only be sheared once a year and it was best if all the sheep were sheared at about the same time each year. On the other hand, Fisher could catch fresh fish every day and, if the family had a particularly good day, the excess fish could be dried for future use. Farmer's wheat harvest was dictated by the seasons which only allowed for one harvest a year from which Farmer could maintain a store of wheat until the next season's harvest. Like us, all three of the island families preferred to eat on a regular schedule and on our island making clothes from the wool was done when time permitted. The result was that often our island families did not always have their commodity available when one of the other families wanted to trade. This made trading inefficient particularly when one of the seasonal goods was involved.

Now one day, the enterprising Farmer family decided that trading would be easier if they could use paper certificates that were payable in each families' commodities rather than waiting until both parties had the goods to trade. These paper certificates would be known as Greenbacks. After much discussion between the families it was agreed that each Adam Island Greenback would be assigned a worth as outlined in the table below. Each family was given 100 Greenbacks and agreed that they must each accept the paper money when presented in exchange for the goods each family specialized in producing.

Wool	One Pound	1 Greenback
Wheat	One Bushel	2 Greenbacks
Fish	Two Pounds	1 Greenback

The new means of exchange made trade between the families much easier and for some reason it also made the families feel wealthier. And, since the families no longer needed to carry the goods with them that they wanted to trade or trade for *(and store goods that they didn't need yet)*, it allowed each family to focus their time and effort on managing their production and storage in a way that allowed them to most efficiently meet the demands of their customers… the other two families. As a result, the families found they could spend more time producing their product which meant that more goods were available for sale and trade. Initially each family had an ample supply of goods to meet their needs and sufficient Greenbacks to purchase new supplies when needed.

Farmer took great pride in the improved island economy, attributing everyone's enhanced life styles to the addition of Greenbacks as a means of exchange. Still she was surprised by the extent to which this change added to the wealth of the island.

Even though the population of the island remained the same, all the families were now able to spend more time working on production and Farmer surmised that the improvement in island lifestyle was due to having made trade more efficient... everyone produced more and therefore the island's wealth had simply increased as a result. What Farmer missed considering was that the one hundred Greenbacks each family initially received actually did add to everyone's collective wealth since the one hundred Greenbacks were additive to the goods each family held when the Greenbacks were issued. Admittedly the families could not eat or wear the Greenbacks but knowing these pieces of paper could be used in exchange for the essentials of life gave each family a sense of added wealth. Money, of any type *(Dollar, Peso, or Greenback)* is only as valuable as its ability to be used to buy things we want and our island Greenbacks were effectively backed up by the products each family wanted and each family committed to provide. This concept, in conjunction with all the families having a strong work ethic and honest business practices, resulted in the addition of the paper money simply adding wealth to the island's families.

Efficiency in the exchange process within an economy is a critical factor in the success of an economy and is probably among the least understood elements of economics. A perfect economy would have everyone working in their field of strength and utilizing the resources to which they have easy access. You could think of this ideal economic state as being similar to a well lubricated and perfectly tuned engine in your car. Everyone in the economy would be at work on time and willing to work overtime on a minute's notice to meet any increase in demand for their product or service. In this perfect economy the balance between production needs, conservation for the future, and the protection of the environment would be perfectly struck.

When Farmer conceived the idea of adding Greenbacks into the island economy as a medium of exchange, what she was effectively doing was lubricating the island's economy. As an example, whenever the Fisher family wanted to increase their wheat stores, instead of waiting until they had fish to trade, they could use Greenbacks to purchase the wheat from the Farmers. Utilizing Greenbacks as a medium allowed Farmer to sell his product based on customer needs while allowing Fisher to fish when the fish were biting. As a result, demands were met in a way that allowed both trading partners to operate at peak efficiency.

In our own economy we have gone through two major "lubricating" cycles… the first was when money was added as a medium of exchange and then again when credit cards were added as a means of payment. Dating back to before recorded history many different forms of money have been used and it has evolved over time to become more efficient. Gold was used as an early form of money but traders had to be concerned about irregular shapes, weights, and purity. These concerns are examples of the lack of faith in the value of money. In today's world, travelers experience this concern when they travel to other countries and try to buy goods with their country's money or when they exchange their money for the local currency. Most people are not as comfortable using or holding a currency they are not familiar with. This lack of comfort tends to inhibit trading… in other words it makes trading less efficient.

Based largely on a country's stability *(defined in both political as well as economic terms)*, our world will view each country's currency with a different level of credibility. To personalize it a bit, let's assume you have, or will someday have, a retirement fund. Chances are you'd be reluctant to have your retirement savings kept in a fund that is based solely in a third world country with a history of political instability, Haiti for example. You would probably also be hesitant to use Haiti's currency, the Gourde, as a medium of exchange because you lack faith in its stability. A currency is only an efficient medium of exchange when there is great faith in that currency.

By using a trade example we can gain a better understanding of this important concept. Let's say you have a customer who wants to buy your product and only has access to Gourdes, would you simply take today's exchange rate and sell them your product? You might, if the transaction could be safely processed immediately. But let's say you had to make the commitment today for delivery sometime in the future. In this case you would try to build into your price the risk of the Gourde losing value. This price difference creates friction in the exchange which makes selling your product to your Haitian customer more difficult. The higher price creates friction with your Haitian customer and for you it's the time it takes to come up with a price that covers your added risk.

Economic friction occurs whenever the economy performs below the optimum level. Something as big and complex as the world economy can have any number of friction elements within it. Political leaders throughout history have come to understand the concept of friction and have, in some cases, devised systems to try to improve the efficiency of their country's economy. Later in this text we will examine some of these attempts in greater depth but for now we will review some of the broader concepts that have been used.

In our history, political and business leaders have come to see trade between nations as both good and bad. It's always good when you're selling your country's goods or services to a foreign land because the added sales tend to grow your country's economy bringing with it more jobs and increasing the profits of business owners. On the other hand, when a country imports goods, it often times creates unwelcome competition for the domestic businesses that provide those same goods or services.

Most economists would agree that trade between countries is good and should be encouraged and that it is the path to making the world more efficient and growing the world's collective wealth. Historically however, countries have not acted in accordance with economists' views on encouraging trade. Even today, most people react negatively to an industry dying in their country as a result of foreign competition... a consequence of a foreign economy being able to more efficiently produce a good or service.

Countries, in response to unwanted trade, have erected barriers to the entry of goods from foreign countries. Some of the most commonly used barriers are called duties and tariffs which effectively make the import of foreign goods more expensive. In the next chapter, using an example involving our island economy, we will see how this concept of import duties and tariffs might play out.

Chapter Four

(Trading Wheat with Fertile Isle)

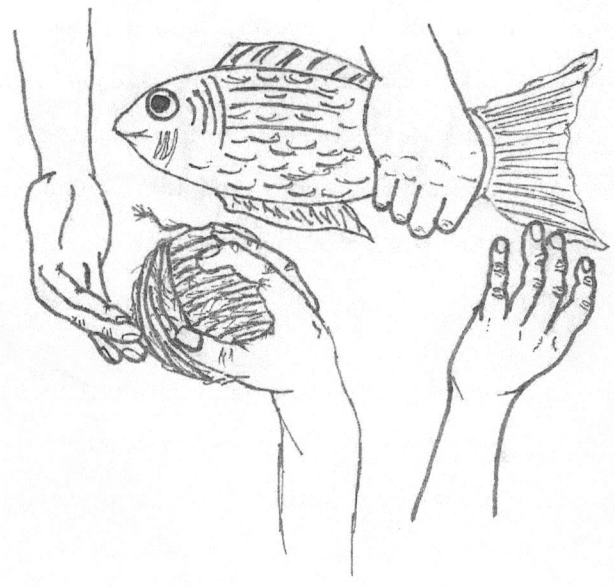

Not too far from our Adam's Island community existed another island known as Fertile Isle. Fertile Isle was richly blessed with outstanding farm land that allowed the local farmers to raise wheat in great abundance. The inhabitants of Adam's Island and Fertile Isle would occasionally come into contact with each other while fishing. The two communities were on friendly terms and spoke a common language and it was not uncommon, during these chance meetings at sea, for conversations to eventually turn to what life was like on each other's island. The inhabitants of Fertile Isle were very interested to learn how the three families on Adam's Island had established a system of trading with each other and they were very intrigued by the stories of how the trade agreements had improved life for all three island families. After much consideration, the leaders of Fertile Isle decided that, if they could establish a trade agreement with the Fisher clan, they too could improve the quality of life on their island.

Fertile Isle knew that the Fisher family *(due to their superior location and fishing techniques)* was much more productive at catching fish than they were. The Fertile Isle clan *(having much richer farm land)* also knew that they could produce and provide wheat twenty-five percent more efficiently than could be done on Adam's

Island. So, the Fertile Isle folks proposed a wheat-for-fish trade agreement with the Fisher family… forty-five bushels of wheat per year in exchange for five pounds of fish per week. Fisher thought this was a great deal since, for the same amount of fish, they were currently receiving only forty bushels of wheat per year from the Farmers. Fisher and the Fertile Isle people shook hands and agreed to start this new deal at the next harvest season.

Fisher, being an ethical trader, told Farmer not to plan on producing extra wheat next season for his clan because he had entered into a wheat supply arrangement with people from the neighboring island. Farmer immediately told her family the news and, as families tend to do, they began to lament how this would affect their lives. They realized that, without the Greenbacks they received at harvest time from selling wheat to Fisher, the Farmer family would not be able to afford to buy the fish and wool they would need.

Farmer met with Sheppard and told him that, as a result of Fisher's new trade agreement, beginning with the next season her family would need to decrease the amount of wool that they would have normally purchased from Sheppard. Both families were very frustrated by this turn of events… because of the Fisher's deal with Fertile Isle their two families were going to endure significant hardships.

Farmer and Sheppard decided that they could not sit back and accept a change by one island family that would cause economic suffering on the other two and, while our little island did not have a political system to speak of, Fisher would quickly come to understand the meaning of political pressure. This came in the form of a meeting between the three families where Farmer and Sheppard convinced Fisher that the Fertile Isle deal had to be canceled. In exchange for Fisher's concession, Farmer agreed to lower the price of wheat and provide forty-two bushels a year in exchange for the five pounds of fish per week.

This new agreement amongst the Adam's Island families would keep the Fertile Isle people out of the trading arrangement while still providing Fisher family at least some of the benefit they would have enjoyed had they followed through with importing the less expensive wheat from Fertile Isle. Other than Fisher getting more wheat, without working any harder, neither of the other families on Adam's island benefited from this new agreement.

The United States has faced the effects of low cost imports numerous times throughout the country's history and frequently these imports were not universally welcomed. When, as a result of imports, an industry would begin to suffer local political pressure would begin to pick up *(similar to what happened during the meeting of the three island families)*. As local political pressure built in the United States, the government would frequently take action to keep out the unwelcome competition. These actions, often in the form of tariffs, would be levied on the imported goods making them more expensive thus taking some of the competitive pressure off of the local industry.

Let's say, for example, that a shovel produced in the United States sells for ten dollars but a shovel imported from England sells for eight dollars. To keep the domestic shovel industry from suffering, the United States might impose a twenty percent tariff on English shovels. This tariff would increase the price of an English shovel from eight dollars to nine dollars and sixty cents. This would still leave domestic manufacturers at a price disadvantage and might force them to lower their prices, just as Farmer had to do on Adam's Island. In this example, the domestic manufacturers might be able to lower their price per shovel to nine dollars and fifty cents and still survive whereas a price decrease to eight dollars may have caused many of the less efficient shovel manufacturers to close their shovel factories.

Resisting or preventing trade, like the residents of Adam's Island did, tends to hurt the consumers in both the importing and exporting economies. Later on we will work through a more evolved trading arrangement where Adam's Island and Fertile Isle are both able to benefit from Fertile Isle's ability to produce lower cost wheat.

Free trade between two free enterprise driven economies allows the free flow of goods based solely on the desires of the consumers in the respective economies. In a true free trade environment there would be no artificial constraints on the flow of goods. Had this been true on Adam's Island it is likely that both Fisher and Sheppard would have struck deals with Fertile Isle and Farmer would have been left to figure out how she and her family would meet their needs. This might have meant that the Farmer family would have to return to a subsistence existence where they would, as before, raise their own sheep and catch their own fish or, alternatively, cut the price on their wheat in order to maintain a portion of their wheat market that they would now have to share with Fertile Isle. This would continue until someone in the Farmer family came up with a new product or a better way of producing their existing product, wheat.

Free trade can be, and often is, a messy business where there are winners and losers. Losers, in this case, can become unemployed or otherwise lose some or all of their accumulated wealth. Some losers move on quickly to the next opportunity while others stick doggedly to the only thing they know how to do. In most of today's western economies, there are social safety nets that mitigate the effects of economic turmoil *(such as the shrinking or even the loss of an industry)* that can result from changes in trade. Social safety nets involve things like unemployment benefits and retraining for displaced workers. As you come to understand the economics of free trade and free enterprise it is important to keep in mind that progress often comes with a short-term social cost. While some people will benefit immediately from the results of change others may end up being worse off until they and their local economies are able to adapt to the change in circumstances.

Chapter Five

(Hard Times for the Fisher Family)

In our island community, there came a time when the addition of wealth for two of the families *(Farmer and Sheppard)* hurt the wealth of the third family, the Fishers. This happened when both the Farmer and Sheppard families decided they wanted to spend some of their leisure time on the water, so the two families each bought a boat and built docks on their part of the island *(in the Farmer's case this included building steps down to their dock)*. During their leisure time on the water the two families eventually decided to spend some of their time fishing.

With easier access to the sea the Farmer and Sheppard families became better at catching fish and, as a result, bought less fish from Fisher. The Fisher family however, continued to buy the same amount of goods from Farmer and Sheppard which caused their supply of Greenbacks to quickly diminish. The Fisher family had no choice but to cut back on their lifestyle. They began to work longer hours in order to grow the wheat and raise the sheep they could no longer afford to buy and, because they were not as efficient at these tasks as the other two families were, they ended up working long hours and had less to show for their extra work.

This is not unique to life on our island, it also happens during recessions in the United States. For example, our own families, when they feel less wealthy, tend to cut back on consumption. This could show up as not going out to dinner as often, which then causes the owners of restaurants, the wait staff, and the restaurant's suppliers to all have lower incomes.

Let's say your brother works for one of the suppliers, who as a result of the depressed restaurant business, reduces your brother's hours. The result of this reduction in the family income makes your family feel collectively poorer… your family might spend a portion of their income helping your brother, which then negatively impacts their ability to consume, or maybe your brother's plight creates the fear that you too could suffer a reduction in income so, as a precaution, you and your family choose to cut back on the consumption of goods or services.

Back to our island… as a result of the Fisher family's decision to grow some of their own wheat and raise some of their own sheep, the other two families began to see a decrease in the wealth coming into their respective families and, even though both families had more Greenbacks in their possession then before, this made them reluctant to spend them because of the *(economic)* fear caused by the decrease in new revenue coming into their respective families.

This loss in confidence in the island economy caused both Sheppard and Farmer to be more careful in what they bought from each other which further decreased the amount of trade between these two families. Both Sheppard and Farmer continued to do much of their own fishing but no longer as a leisure activity, instead they were now fishing as a way to save their precious Greenbacks. The loss of confidence in the island economy caused these two families to change their buying habits and draw back into the old self sustenance economy where they grew their own wheat, raised their own sheep, and fished for themselves instead of being able to use their time efficiently by sticking with what they did best.

What has happened in our island economy is the result of a decrease in consumer confidence. This is a case of where perception precedes the result. More specifically, the assessment by consumers that times are bad, when they really aren't, which results in changes in consumption patterns that then leads to a broad economic downturn. This is a key concept to keep in mind and represents one of the levers our political leaders attempt to pull periodically to avert or lessen the impact of a recession.

As an economic tool, our government's leadership will often try things like a tax rebate to push money into the hands of the consumers. The intended result is for consumers, who now have more money at their disposal, to feel better about their personal economic condition. Money in the bank, so to speak, causes many consumers to spend more which then drives demand and leads to more factory orders and the need for more services. The result of this increase in economic activity tends to improve consumer confidence. Keep in mind there is a difference between consumer confidence and business confidence. Management of businesses will not necessarily react in parallel with consumer confidence, nor be motivated by the same levers which may predictably work on consumers.

Following the recent changes in the island's trading relationships everyone on the island is glum about their financial situation. The majority of the island's money supply *(the three hundred Greenbacks)* is now primarily being held by two of the three families… the Sheppard and Farmer families have one hundred forty-five Greenbacks each and the Fisher family has only ten. The families all have to work longer hours which means that they all have less leisure time. The fact that the islanders are still producing and consuming roughly the same amount but having to work harder to do so clearly reflects a deterioration in the island society's quality of life.

At this point it's important to consider what happened to the three families and what brought about the hard times to Fisher and then to the other two families. At the same time it is important to recognize what did not happen to cause this economic malaise on Adam's Island. *(While doing this keep in mind that what happened to the island economy has also happened, on a much larger scale, to the United States' economy and world economy at different times in the past).*

Let's start with what did not happen. The island did not suffer a natural disaster... such as a storm, blight on its crops, or the loss of its good fishing. Furthermore, the Adam's Island people did not suddenly become less industrious nor did their skills diminish. So then what did happen? There was simply a shift in economic preferences.

Just like on Adam's Island, the United States' economy has experienced shifts in consumer spending that have resulted in economic downturns. For example, in the late twentieth and early twenty-first centuries, a staple of the United States economy was manufacturing jobs and when these jobs were rapidly shifted to other economies *(Mexico and more substantially to China)* it had a broad effect on the economy because most people in the United States had some connection to someone impacted by the change. These types of shifts, at a minimum, tend to make individuals, families, and communities less confident in the economy and more frugal in their spending habits.

In our example, there were no significant physical disasters that pushed the United States into a recession but, like in our island community, it was due to a loss of consumer confidence. At this juncture we will not go into how governments address the loss of consumer confidence but instead will return to our story and see how Adam's Island recovered from their depression.

The island, still locked into a severe economic depression, suffered a natural disaster... a severe storm that did significant damage to the island. Among the damage were the boats owned by Farmer and Sheppard. Neither family had been proficient sailors and therefore missed the warnings signs of the impending storm and, due to their lack of sea faring knowledge, did not appropriately secure their boats prior to the storm. Fisher, having had greater knowledge of the water and the dangers storms posed, had their family's boat securely stored.

All the families felt even more depressed following the storm, but recognized they had little choice but to make the best of things. Both Sheppard and Farmer continued to need fish for their families so they began to carefully dig into their Greenback supply to buy fish from the Fisher family. Fisher, now having a few more Greenbacks, began to buy a little more wheat and wool from the other two families. After a few months each family began to resume a more normal process of trading then, as the next crop cycle began, Fisher and Sheppard decided to raise less of their own wheat and resumed buying what they needed from Farmer. Concurrently, Fisher and Farmer decided to leave the wool production to the Sheppard family. After another year of economic transition, the island economy came back into the equilibrium it had enjoyed prior to Sheppard and Farmer beginning their leisure boating and fishing activities.

The way in which leisure fishing led to a depression on Adam's Island provides us with valuable insight into one of the ways an economy can be driven into a recession and the sometimes counterintuitive measures that can bring about a recovery. Once an economy moves to the point where there is discretionary spending and leisure time, consumer confidence becomes an important, if not the key factor, in moving the economy in one direction or the other. Another factor in economic well-being is the smooth workings of the free market economy. Later in this text we will delve into the various things that can disrupt the workings of the economy but for now we will explore the disruptive influence example that we saw in this chapter and dig deeper into why it had the effect it did.

Since the root cause of the recession was a reduced demand for fish purchased from the Fisher family, the question is why that change had such a significant impact on the economy. Our island has, at this point, only three main products that drive the economy, so when the demand for one family's product diminished, it resulted in a snowball effect on the rest of the economy. In formal economic text books there are the terms *elastic* and *inelastic* demand. Without going into text book mode let's talk about what these terms mean and then explore how to judge which *(elastic or inelastic)* applied in the case of our island economy.

The term elastic demand means that the economy will be inclined to absorb or consume added quantities of a product when it's available in the market. Inelastic demand refers to a product where the market only desires a limited quantity of that product and will not consume added supply when it's put into the market. It's important to keep in mind that few products have perfectly elastic *(meaning that the economy will take in unlimited additional product)* or perfectly inelastic *(where the economy will use only a finite quantity and will not consume any more of that product regardless of availability or price)*.

In our island economy fish would appear to be a product with a largely inelastic demand… whatever fish Sheppard or Farmer caught themselves they used in place of the fish they would have previously purchased from the Fisher family. In actual practice the inelastic demand conclusion would still be reached *(even if the Farmer and Sheppard families modestly increased their overall fish consumption)* as long as the decrease in fish bought from Fisher was enough to reduce the cash the Fishers normally had available to purchase goods from the other two families. This scenario would ultimately leave the Fishers with only a small amount of Greenbacks which would then trigger the recession and ultimately, when the economic situation becomes more severe, a depression.

What if however, the Fisher family had another area of production where they were able to employ their efforts just as efficiently as they did when fishing? In that case, when the other two families started catching their own fish, the Fishers could have simply channeled less effort into fishing and more into the other productive task. This would have kept the Greenbacks flowing and the Fishers would not have been as severely affected by the downturn in demand for their fish. Taking this thought a step further, the added diversity in the island economy could have averted the island's recession completely. The lack of diversity is what brought the fictional Fisher family to economic hardship.

History has plenty of real examples of how the lack of diversity can lead to economic disaster. One such example is the island of Naru[1]… Naru, an island located in the Pacific, had a large

---

[1] 1. Naru information in part taken from

deposit of phosphate located close to the surface and, as a result, was a primary exporter of the mineral for a number of years. The mining began in the early years of the twentieth century and continued into the early nineteen eighties when the phosphate deposit was exhausted. The island flourished during the mining years and in the sixties and seventies boasted the highest per capita income in the world. However, once the mines closed the country's economy fortunes fell quickly and drastically and Naru became an impoverished island nation.

Naru, in the most dramatic way, reflects the risks of having an economy dependent upon a single product or service. Since before World War II, the Middle East has enjoyed the benefits of being the primary supplier of oil to a world economy that has a nearly insatiable desire for oil. Suppose, however, that suddenly the world no longer needed petroleum products. The results would be similar to what happened in Naru but on a much larger scale… instead of the roughly ten thousand people who were affected on Naru more than a hundred million people would be impacted in the Middle East.

http://en.wikipedia.org/wiki/Nauru

The governments of the Middle East have been trying to diversify their economies but, it is my belief, that the oil producing nations of this region are a long way from being able to maintain their economies without the billions in petro-dollars. As a consumer you can gauge the region's progress when you begin to associate the region with something besides oil and the investment of oil revenues. Today this region is politically unstable and most would agree that an extreme change in economic circumstances would likely, at least near term, make it more so. Like the situation of Farmer and Sheppard, it would not be long before the economic hardship of the Middle East would bring negative impacts to the other nations of the world just as Fishers' economic hardship eventually caused hardship for the other two families on Adam's Island.

Chapter Six

(Economic Lubricants and Economic Friction)

An economy has two particular attributes that it shares with an automobile… lubricants and friction. For an automobile to run smoothly it needs to be maintained with fresh quality lubricants. Keeping the same analogy if friction comes into play either intentionally *(applying the brakes)* or unintentionally *(when a bearing runs out of lubricant)* the automobile will begin to work inefficiently usually causing it to slow down or to stop working completely.

In application the economy's lubricants and friction are a little less obvious. Anything that helps the economy move goods and services smoothly, in order to meet demand, would be considered a lubricating factor. As an example suppose you, as a consumer, want to buy a new electronic wonder device that can only be purchased through a retailer. To sell you this device the retailer needs to special order it through a faraway wholesaler who, in turn, orders it from the manufacturer who happens to be located on the other side of a great ocean. In all, the process will take about three months and will, due to markups from both the retailer and wholesaler, significantly increase the cost of the product. In this case the manufacturer sells the wonder device for $100.00 but after 100% markups from both the wholesaler and the retailer your cost will be $400.00.

How efficient does this economic process seem to be in getting the wonder device from its maker to you the consumer? Let's further suppose there was a great deal of demand in your town for the wonder device… in fact so much, that if the devices were available for immediate purchase at a cost of $200.00 each, five thousand could easily be sold each month. The factory, recognizing the profit opportunity, decides to setup a local company store. They rent a retail location in your town *(ten thousand dollars per month)*, hire ten employees *(salary and benefits fifty thousand per month)*, and ships five thousand devices to the store. Is this new process of delivering this wonder product to your community more efficient than the earlier method? To keep the math simple we will ignore any increase in units sold as a result of cutting out the wholesaler and assume that wholesaler would also have been able to sell 5,000 units, now let's do the math…

Wholesaler process
(Consumer cost, $400 per unit)

5,000 units sold per month @ $100.00 each

5,000 x $100 = $500,000 monthly net revenue

Direct to Consumer process
(Consumer cost, $200 per unit)

5,000 units sold per month @ $200.00 each minus monthly rent & salaries

(5,000 x $200) minus ($10,000 + $50,000)

$1 million - $60,000 = $940,000 monthly net revenue

With the new process the manufacturer will make four hundred and forty thousand dollars more in net profit while providing the product to the consumer at half the price. Obviously this is an extreme example of improving the efficiency of moving goods from manufacturer to consumer. Without question the opening of a factory store removed a great deal of unnecessary economic friction and improved the efficiency of getting the wonder device into the hands of the consumer. In the real world things seldom change so rapidly and change, when it happens slowly, can itself be a form of economic friction.

It is important to keep in mind that a change, like we described above, is not without some negative fallout. In our example the distributor and the original retailer both lost revenue when the manufacturer changed *(in this case streamlined)* the process of getting the product into the hands of the ultimate customer. Even if a process is more efficient for the economy as a whole, the change almost always impacts some group negatively. Consider the changes Wal-Mart has had on small local retailers in the latter part of the twentieth century. Thousands of retailers across the United States were either hurt or completely put out of business. Not everyone would agree that the lower price and the convenience of being able to complete your shopping in one store was a positive change. Personally I would argue that, in pure economic terms, the change was positive to the economy… it enhanced the efficiency of distribution and made purchasing a wide variety of goods more convenient for to the consumer. Whatever your personal feelings are towards Wal-Mart, the application of the concept is good for consumers in that it makes the distribution of goods more efficient. You can argue the peripherals of Wal-Mart's methods but the concept, of taking steps out of the distribution chain and using Wal-Mart's buying power to drive down costs, delivers more value for the dollar to Wal-Mart shoppers. The change in distribution, while more efficient, is not an argument for Wal-Mart's business practices, wage scales, or approach on employee benefits.

It's no secret that retail jobs tend to pay wages that, not only qualify most employees as low income but also, provide little to no access to affordable medical and dental care. Even though this might be a pejorative statement about retailers, in reality it has more to do with being effective. A big box retailer can't provide middle class type wages and benefits. That is a societal fact of life rather than an economic argument against retailers including Wal-Mart.

Suppose our society's laws were such that all employers were required to provide a standard set of benefits to employees and that the minimum wage was such that a Wal-Mart clerk would achieve the same economic status as an auto worker. With these improvements to employee compensation retailers *(all retailers including Wal-Mart)* would need to increase the markup on goods in order to remain successful. This change in compensation for retail workers would not in any way change the economic savings that would have come from replacing the small retailers and related distributors. The economic benefits accruing to the Wal-Mart's of the world would be largely the same in this higher wage environment and the smaller retailers would suffer from their competitive disadvantages and ultimately be unable to compete with the larger retailers.

Arguing that Wal-Mart is bad, because there are a lot of low paid retail employees as a result of its existence, is a false argument since all businesses must follow the existing rules of the society *(regulations)* in which they operate. If we, as a society, decided that we should no longer have big box retailers the result would be an economic efficiency loss *(in the form of higher costs)* without a significant change in the compensation going to retail workers. The return to a world of small retailers would reduce executive pay and possibly increase the number of middle class store proprietors but it will not result in much of a change in store clerks' compensation.

Moving forward, let's accept the premise that making any process in the economy more efficient is better for us as a whole, despite the fact that efficiency improvements may hurt some participants along the way. Change within manufacturing and distribution, even though it may benefit society as a whole, will hurt more than a few John and Jane Q Publics along the way. Change, even good change, can be hard and, as you have heard often, you can't make an omelet without breaking some eggs.

In some cases friction is introduced to achieve other economic objectives. As an example, patents are granted to the developers of prescription drugs giving them a monopoly on that drug's sales for a set period of time. This is an example of where the United States' economy is not a pure free enterprise economy but instead a regulated economy. Let's consider what would happen if the United States government would eliminate all drug patent restrictions. Immediately numerous companies would begin flooding the market with less expensive generic drugs to compete with the brand named drugs. The cost of healthcare in America would drop drastically in a matter of months. Sounds like it might be a good idea right? But what happens to drug research and development within the big pharmaceutical companies? Without the government mandated protection of patents the big drug companies, who invest heavily in developing new drugs that save, improve and prolong life, would lose their incentive *(profits)* for developing these new medications and research and development of new drugs would come to an end.

Clearly, at some point in time, our government decided that an effective way to stimulate new drug development was to give a limited term monopoly to drug development companies. In this way drug companies could enjoy a period of monopoly driven profitability in exchange for investing in intensive research and development. How efficient does this system work is a topic beyond the scope of this book and is as controversial a topic as any in our society. It is however an excellent example of governmentally applied economic friction that in fact may be good for our society.

What is less easy to see is the friction that is not mandated by law but is a product of the free enterprise economic system itself. Most of the advertising campaigns you experience are intended to influence buying decisions so that consumers do not make their purchase decisions based solely upon price or the information on the product label. The goal of most advertising is to convince the potential consumer to buy the advertiser's product, or more specifically, to buy the advertiser's product based upon the information conveyed in the advertising. This often means buying the advertised product despite the fact there are lower priced alternatives available. If the advertiser is successful, the advertising will create friction by lessening the effectiveness of the consumer's buying decision process. In fairness, some advertising contains an element of product education and there are also regulations that prohibit making blatantly false claims within a product's advertising… nonetheless, the primary *(if not sole)* motivation for advertising is to promote sales. As a consumer it is important to consider both elements and the intent of the company spending the money on the advertising.

As an illustration, let's use the purchase of a television to help us gain a better understanding of advertising and its potential for creating economic friction. The Coach Potato family wants *(no must have)* a sixty inch flat screen TV before the "big game" and it must be high definition. The night before the big shopping expedition, the Couch Potato family, while watching one of their favorite shows, sees an advertisement from a nationally known company that claims their sixty inch, high definition set is the best product on the market *(it also, incidentally, happens to be the highest priced brand on the market)*. In this case there is a competitors' model that, with the exception of being one hundred dollars less expensive is, by all measures, equivalent to the model that was advertised. As planned, the Coach Potato family goes to the electronics' store and after shopping decides to buy the more expensive flat screen. Even though the TVs were equal, in terms of value, the Coach Potato family paid *(some may say foolishly)* a one hundred dollar premium for that brand while receiving no visible additional benefits.

You might assume that the cost to the overall economy is the added one hundred dollars the Coach Potato family paid. However there is an additional element to this transaction… the advertising itself. From an economic standpoint the extra money is not wasted because the consumer is receiving TV programming that was paid for in part by the advertising. Since the TV programming was also consumed by other viewers you cannot say the incremental one hundred dollars paid for this TV *(and by other families making this same choice)* is really wasted. These are the types of things that make it difficult to say with certainty that some activities in an economy are either good or bad. As a student of economics all you can do is study the cause and effects and make your own judgment.

In the introduction to this book I mentioned that to understand economics would require understanding dependent activities. In our example with the Coach Potato family the dependent activities are the advertising and the TV programming the advertising makes possible. One could certainly make the argument that without the advertising the TV would be less expensive and the consumer and the TV manufacturer would have a more efficient delivery process. However, if advertising were eliminated consumers would either have to pay to watch programming, which might reduce the demand for TVs or there would be no programming, which would eliminate the need for a TV altogether. We are not going to provide an answer to this set of dependent activities as it is akin to the age old question of which came first the chicken or the egg.

Efficiency in supplying goods and services to consumers has, in the past one hundred years, undergone more changes than what had occurred in all prior recorded history. Specialization has been a key to this progress and has enabled the quality of life to improve drastically in a relatively short period of time. Specialization in this context is a broad type of economic efficiency improvement.

In the preceding example the TV manufacturer, the TV retailer, and the TV channel are all illustrations of specialization at work in our economy. These however are relativity recent advances. Two hundred years ago manufacturing was a much more intimate affair and tended to be done at the local level. Even then there was some specialization in that the blacksmith made your tools and the mill owner ground your grains, all were specialists who usually did one thing for their community and traded the product of their specialty with the rest of the village or town.

Circling back to our little island families, you will recall it was specialization that first brought economic improvements to the island. By having Farmer farm, Fisher fish, and Sheppard raise sheep; the island had more goods available and the islanders worked less to get those products.

We compare this clear example of efficiency brought to an economy to the very gray elements involved in the purchase of the higher priced TV, purchased by our hypothetical Coach Potato family, and we can see why most people ultimately give up trying to understand the complex workings of national and international economics.

Rather than being intimidated, by not being able to clearly see the answer to a set of economic circumstances, it's better to try to understand the elements of an economic transaction set. In almost every situation you can gain insight just by identifying the role each participant plays in the process of fulfilling the end product that is in demand. Once you have identified each participant's role it's easier to look at the end cost to the consumer and those who share in the price paid by the final customer from the first step in the supply process to the final step of putting the product into the consumer's possession. With this information in mind you can then begin to assess from an economic perspective if the process is doing an efficient job of supplying that product to consumers.

Returning to our island, our three families were once again trading regularly and were also communicating on a much more frequent basis. The Farmers were back to focusing on growing wheat and the Fisher and Sheppard families were using their Greenbacks to purchase the wheat they needed from Farmer. Now let's suppose that even though all the families needed the wheat, what each actually consumed was flour. A member of the Fisher family, the one responsible for grinding his family's wheat into flour, in a quest to make his job easier developed a grinding wheel. With the use of this grinding wheel the Fishers could make better flour and could do so in a fraction of the time it had taken using the old mortar and pedestal method.

During one of many conversations the Fishers mentioned to the other families how their new invention allowed them to make better flour in much less time. After hearing this, the Sheppard and Farmer families wanted to benefit from this more efficient flour producing method. There were two options, each family could try and develop their own grinder or they could make a deal and Fisher could grind the flour for the whole island. Fisher, being on the road to becoming a shrewd trader, saw the opportunity to enrich his family by using their new discovery. Fisher knew by now that one bushel of wheat would produce twenty five pounds of finished flour so the families worked out a deal where they would trade one and a quarter bushels of wheat for twenty-five pounds of flour.

Flour produced by Fisher soon became a customary product for the entire island. The Fisher family felt wealthier, since they were now providing both flour and fish to the rest of the island and, as a result, they increased their demand for the other two families' products. Since the other two families no longer had to grind their own wheat they were able to use this time to grow more wheat and raise more sheep which allowed them to sell more to the now more affluent Fisher family.

The invention of the Fisher grinding wheel and grinding process clearly brought efficiency to the island… all the families' benefited, overall consumption and supply increased, and the quality of life for everyone on the island improved.

Keep in mind the island represents a small economy and therein improving everyone's quality of life is easier to measure and comprehend than it is in a larger economy. Furthermore, in a larger economy, it's not a realistic goal to expect that any one economic efficiency improvement will improve everyone's quality of life. Instead, in a larger economy, the goal for the efficiency improvement would be to benefit more people than it will adversely affect.

Our earlier story about the wonder device is a good example of an improvement to economic efficiency. Even though the new distribution method hurt some people *(the wholesalers and retailers lost revenue as a result of being eliminated from the distribution chain)* a larger group of people *(the consumers)* benefited from the new means of distribution… they can get the product quicker and for half the cost.

Throughout the United States' economy there are actions every day that bring the opportunity of added economic efficiency, some come about quickly while others take more time. As a further illustration of the concept, let's consider a new manufacturing process that occurs in a hypothetical brake manufacturing facility that we will call the Stop Quick Company. We will suppose that this new brake manufacturing process will lower the cost of brake pads by twenty-five percent. Do you think that manufacturer is going to lower the selling price of the brake pads by the same twenty-five percent? Don't hold your breath... it would be rare for any business to pass on all of their new found savings to the consumer.

Stop Quick, like any profit based business, will instead calculate a reduction in price that will provide to Stop Quick the maximum profit increase. If properly calculated, the new lower price will be enough to entice consumers away from other competing brands in favor of Stop Quick's brand. Therefore, not only has Stop Quick's profit margin *(per break pad)* increased but their sales volume has also increased. This change benefits Stop Quick *(maximized sales and profit)* and consumers *(lower cost brakes)* but hurts Stop Quick's competitors *(their comparatively higher manufacturing costs will result in fewer sales)*. So, even though it's not the full twenty-five percent, the economy will still receive some benefit *(lower prices for brakes)* from Stop Quick's new innovation.

Digging a bit deeper into this changed brake manufacturing dynamics, you have one company using less of the economy's resources to produce brakes while the rest of the companies are still using the less efficient process. Until all companies have access to this manufacturing innovation consumers will not receive the full benefit of the new process.

Stop Quick will most likely patent their innovation to prevent other companies from adopting it *(unless of course they agree to pay Stop Quick a fee for the right… known in the marketplace as a royalty)*. Alternatively, they may decide to keep the new manufacturing technique to themselves and work towards developing an effective monopoly in the brake manufacturing business. Either way the natural result will be to have all or most of the brakes made using the new method. But what will work out better for consumers?

Let's forget about government anti-trust laws for a moment and let's say Stop Quick chooses to become a monopoly in the manufacture of brakes. If they choose to do this Stop Quick would ultimately have complete control of supply. Stop Quick, once its competitors are put out of business, could then charge whatever price resulted in the most profit. This option could result in consumers paying more for brake pads than they did prior to the innovation. If however, Stop Quick licensed the process to other suppliers in such a way that they continued to make a profit then Stop Quick would not only make its higher profit on the sale of brake pads but would also earn royalty revenue from the manufacturers who bought the right to use their intellectual property. This approach may not result in all the benefits flowing to the consumers of brake pads but would clearly be a better result for the economy. In addition, by virtue of the lower societal resources being consumed in the manufacturing process for brake pads, the economy also receives a benefit. Higher profits for Stop Quick, lower prices to consumers, and a reduction in consumption of the resources needed to make the brake pads represent added efficiency in the economy and thus an economic benefit.

Throughout the time that Stop Quick owns the rights to this manufacturing process the owners of Stop Quick will receive higher profits which they will use for either more consumption or added investment in the economy. The added consumption could be the expensive mansion the company's owner builds or frequent travel to exotic locations but either way this profit finds its way to others in the economy. You might call this a trickle down result of the efficiency improvement.

Often you will hear politicians and economists talk about the importance of reward for those people who bring innovation to the economy. In this example, had there been no long-term benefit for Stop Quick improving their manufacturing process then the better process may never have been found and the economy would have continued on indefinitely using the old less efficient method.

Since patents expire after a number of years the profits coming into Stop Quick will decrease as it loses its monopoly on this process. Once this happens, and all companies can use the process without paying a royalty to Stop Quick, the benefit of the efficiency will flow to the consumers through lower prices for brake pads and all the companies making brakes will return to making similar profits.

What we have covered in the last few paragraphs is a cycle of economic events that occurs frequently in the world and United States economies. It is probably not well understood and often you will hear companies, like our hypothetical Stop Quick, criticized for their windfall profits. This criticism is short sighted because innovation brings great things to the economy long-term. So, while our economic system may periodically be misused to enrich a few at the expense of the many, if it is governed effectively innovation and lower prices to consumers can follow. The reward of wealth to the innovator is in the long-term a small price to pay for progress.

Chapter Seven

(Inflation)

In the previous chapter we examined the impact of a change in price and how that might impact the larger economy. In this chapter we will continue that exploration and how it might incite a cycle of inflation.

Throughout the global economy there continues to be incidents of inflation within individual national economies. During the United States' history there have been numerous periods where significant and disruptive inflation has occurred. Uncontrolled inflation can, among other things, damage consumer confidence and more importantly make doing business in that economy more difficult. Consider the Argentine economy where the Argentine Peso has suffered from frequent, rampant bouts of inflation. This instability has made it virtually impossible to establish prices based upon the Peso so any international trade in Argentina is generally based on the currency of the trading partner. Even with the protection this provides the trading partner, the Argentine buyer still has no way of knowing what their local cost will be for products they import or what Peso based price they can expect to receive when they export.

In an economy suffering from uncontrolled inflation it is difficult to borrow or lend funds. If inflation is not a quantifiable factor the lender cannot accurately price the loan. Example: assume you are in a stable pricing environment where inflation is within one to three percent, you, as the lender, agree to loan money at a four percent rate. Based on the value of funds at the time of the agreement you will make at least one percent or as much as three percent profit on that loan. In the case of the borrower, the real cost of the interest will be between one and three percent after adjusting for the range of inflation. *(Note the borrower will be paying with funds that will have anywhere between one and three percent less buying power than the funds at the time borrowed.)*

There are entire books devoted to the subject of the real costs of borrowing and we will not go into depth here on those concepts; it is however important to understand the thinking of lenders and borrowers and how their actions are impacted by the amount of inflation and, most importantly, the predictability of the range of inflation. In the preceding example the lender needs to make a profit on their hypothetical loan and, based on their economic data, they believe there is certainty that inflation will not exceed three percent, therefore a one percent minimum profit is certain and the possibility of making as much as three percent exists. In the real world, to calculate a profitable interest rate, lenders use complex formulas where, in addition to inflation, things like the risk of borrower default is factored into the equation.

Most borrowers are often not as sophisticated as lenders in terms of what provisions they require in the loan agreements and are therefore at a disadvantage. Knowledgeable borrowers however are able to negotiate much more palatable deals. For example, a young accountant I worked with years ago went to great lengths to calculate the financial aspects of his new car purchase and the underlying financing before arranging for his car loan. Intelligent and lengthy negotiations occurred where I suspect the auto dealer's salesperson and finance manager and customer were at least equally matched. As a result, my accountant colleague got a much better deal on his new car than the average customer. In this case the dealer's finance manager had a very small margin for error in making sure this auto sale and loan would be a profitable one for the car dealer.

My accountant colleague was not your normal car buyer… most car buyers simply don't have the skills to perform a thorough financial analysis. On the other hand, had this accountant been buying a used car *(where the critical factor would have instead been the mechanical quality of the car)* then his financial acumen would not have been enough to ensure he negotiated a good deal *(unless of course the accountant could somehow guarantee that the car was mechanically sound).* If, on the other hand, the used car buyer was a skilled auto mechanic, he or she would be better equipped to assess the used car and negotiate an equitable deal. While we are straying a little off topic it is important to recognize that there is a broad set of skills that are sometimes needed to make the best personal financial decision and often understanding the effect of inflation is a key component of those decisions.

What we have covered thus far has hopefully explained the basics of how interest rates are affected by inflation. On this foundation what would you suppose might be an auto loan interest rate where inflation is less predictable *(for example where inflation might vary between one and ten percent over a four year period)?* In this case the auto dealer and the lender will have a much more difficult task in establishing an effective interest rate. The dealer knows that selling cars at an eleven percent interest rate is much more difficult than say at six percent rate. If the dealer does not participate in the inflation risk with the lender the lender will establish a loan rate at least as high as the highest possible inflation rate plus some minimum level of profit.

Therefore, in order to accomplish a lower interest rate, the dealer will often share a part of the profit with the lender to help offset their risk.

Often consumers struggle with the concept that lenders can lose money by lending at too low of an interest rate, using a simple example I will show how this can happen. While there are a host of factors lenders need to consider when establishing a lending rate, for our purposes we will focus on a single factor… inflation. Suppose I lend $500 to my niece to buy a computer with the agreement that she will pay me back when she graduates college in four years. Having just bought a basic computer, I plan to replace it in four years with the identical computer my niece just bought. However, I'm pretty sure that the price of that computer will be higher four years from now so in order to have enough money to buy it I will charge my niece four percent interest on the loan. Since she's my niece and I love her I'm keeping it simple and will just add twenty dollars each year to the loan which means at the end of the four years I will have $580 to pay for my new computer.

When the loan comes due my dear and very responsible niece promptly pays me the $580.00 as the agreement required. I take my $580.00 and go out to buy my new computer only to find that the best available price for that model of computer is $600.00. Clearly this has not worked out as I planned since I am effectively out twenty dollars. I lost money in this scenario because I lent money at four percent when computer inflation was running at five percent. It is this same set of facts that applies to the auto lender in that the lender needs to make sure that they receive back, at the end of the contract, funds that will cover the effects of inflation. To over simplify, if the auto dealer knows that it requires ten thousand dollars to finance a car today and they desire to remain in business they must be repaid an amount that at least equals the amount a car is expected to cost at the time the loan is fully repaid.

Keeping our example simple the lenders here are in the business of loaning money for the purchase of a car. In this example, we will assume the lender is using their funds for financing *(versus using an outside source)*. The lender loans their funds to a consumer to buy a car in year one that is fully repaid at the end of year four. If the resulting accumulation of the consumer's payments at the end of the loan term is only enough money to buy ninety-nine percent of a current day car then clearly the lender cannot sustain their business long-term. In addition lenders will need to cover administrative costs as well as provide the owners of the financing business with some element of profit *(their piece of the pie)*. A lender in this situation might price the loan as:

The today price of the car	$10,000
Inflation on the $10,000 over 4 year	2,400
Lenders administration expenses	500
Lender profit	500
Total required loan payments	$13,400
Monthly payment for the car loan of	**$279.**[17] *($13,400 /48 payments)*

Thus far we have examined the effect of inflation without addressing its origins. In a large economy it's difficult to understand what causes inflation so, in order to gain a more intimate insight, let's return to our island economy.

At one point the Sheppard family decided that they weren't being compensated sufficiently for their wool and insisted on a price increase arguing that, in order to produce the wool, they had to work harder and put in more hours than the other two families did to produce their products. After much discussion amongst the family heads, Farmer and Fisher agreed to increase the price of wool by 20%.

Much of behavioral economics is formed around how most humans will react to changes in economic circumstances. In the case of a price increase, consumers of the product that undergoes the price increase will react in a fairly predictable fashion.

The families on our islands, who each held one hundred Greenbacks at the time of the change, will modify how they look at the value of their Greenbacks and will change their spending habits, not just on wool, but on everything they buy.

The logical reaction of the other two families, once they find that wool is more expensive than before, is to suddenly feel poorer... any consumer or buyer would have the same reaction. This is an unpleasant feeling and most humans will seek to find a way to change the circumstances so they can return to feeling better about their economic situation.

Since half of the Farmer and Fisher family's total purchases were wool from Sheppard, both Farmer and Fisher found themselves ten percent poorer. The higher price for wool caused the buying power of their Greenbacks to be diminished or, looking at it in another way, the compensation they received for producing wheat and fish was now ten percent less effective in terms of buying power. With their lower buying power the families' could no longer maintain the lifestyle they had previously enjoyed. In order to buy the same amount of wool as they did before the price increase, the Fishers and Farmers would need to increase the inflow of Greenbacks to their families. Both families knew they wouldn't be able to sell more of their fish or wheat so the only option they saw was to raise their prices by ten percent. What neither the Fisher or Farmer families counted on was the other raising their prices.

If the Fishers had not also raised their prices then the Farmers would have been back to where they were before the increase in the price of wool. But since the Fishers did increase the price of their fish, the Farmers still did not have sufficient Greenbacks to buy the same amount of wool and fish as before. In order to offset the Fishers' price increase the Farmers would now need to raise the price of their wheat by another ten percent. In response the Fishers, in an attempt to have the same buying power as they had previously, will again increase the price of their fish. Next Sheppard realizes that his family is back where they started and so his next logical move would be to increase the price of wool again. This cycle of price increases continued until each family's supply of Greenbacks was insufficient to buy even a few days' worth of the supplies they needed. The families were forced to spend more of their time buying small quantities of products as opposed to before when they could comfortably buy a week's worth of products at a time and, as a result, all the families found that they felt much poorer.

What happened on Adam's Island is an example of rampant inflation where prices went up uncontrollably and, as a result, damaged the trading process. The damage inhibited trading by making the economy's money supply insufficient to support normal commerce. Beyond this there would also be a fear of holding money during the inflation cycle due to a concern that, as time progressed, money held by the families would lose value. So, even if a family had all the goods they needed, they would likely prefer to hold a commodity like wool rather than cash. In today's economy, when there are fears about the stability of the local currency or potential inflation, those who have ready cash may choose to buy a stable value commodity like precious metals. During these periods the price of something like gold tends to not only increase but to increase at least as rapidly as inflation. The problem for the economy is that, as result of the tendency to store our cash in things like precious metals, it effectively moves capital or working money out of the economy. Said in another way capital held in precious metals is capital that is not being invested in productive activities like business growth and product development.

Inflation fears tend to exacerbate the problems that lead to the inflation in the first place especially when those fears drive money *(specifically investment capable capital)* out of circulation through the purchase of stable commodities or through investment in a foreign economy. On our island there is no capital market where investors can choose between investing in economy expanding investments like stocks, investing in offshore interests, or take depressive actions like buying gold but that doesn't mean our island doesn't have capital they can lose. In fact, now that the economy is unstable valuable members of the community may choose to move to another island where they would feel better about their economic prospects. The loss to the island, as a result of the inflationary cycle, would be in human capital. Any capital leaving an economy hurts the economy at large.

Using our island example, suppose one of Farmer's daughters chooses to leave the island because of the uncontrolled inflation? Let us also assume that Farmer's daughter was the only member of the community who knew how to convert wool into a certain type of clothing. In this case the loss of the Farmer's daughter would cause the entire island to lose access to that type of clothing thereby diminishing the entire community's lifestyle.

In the real world we see this when the best and brightest leave an unstable or poor economy in order to work in a society with a better economy. When this happens the poorer nation loses valuable human capital and the wealthier or more stable nation gains the benefit.

Inflation by itself can be managed in a mature economy by controlling the money supply so that, as prices rise, the available cash in circulation is increased in order to maintain the buying power of the cash money in circulation. However, printing money can also increase the inflationary cycle so it needs to be carefully managed by the nations' treasury departments. In the next chapter we will delve deeper into the topic of managing the money supply.

Inflation can drive other behaviors in consumers as well. Another possible reaction on the part of the Farmer and Fisher families, other than increasing the prices on their products, would be to simply accept that wool is now a more expensive commodity and to be more prudent in how they use wool in their day-to-day lives. This change in thinking may include being less likely to throw out wool clothing when they start to show wear and to be more conservative in how they use wool to create new clothes. Recognizing the greater value of wool the families will tend to be more careful in their consumption of this now more precious commodity.

This reaction to the change in the price naturally leads to a decreased demand for wool. Farmer and Fisher bought less wool but paid more for it. We see this type of action and reaction in our daily lives as it relates to pure commodities such as oil and gas. Whenever there is a crisis among the oil producing nations there is an immediate increase in the price of oil and the products produced from oil such as diesel fuel and gasoline. The higher price of gasoline tends to cause some consumers to decrease the amount of gasoline they purchase. As with the wool in our island economy, consumers tend to value gasoline more highly when the price goes up and most will do what they can to reduce their consumption of this now more expensive product.

As presented in the island example we are assuming that the demand for wool would be affected by a change in price… that is as the price increases the demand for wool decreases. Demand for different products often reacts differently to price changes... some products we buy are perfectly elastic in how demand and price interact yet others are perfectly inelastic. If a product's demand reacts significantly to a change in price the product is viewed to have an elastic relationship between price and demand. Gasoline, in our real world example, would be considered to have some elements of elasticity in its demand-to-price relationship. A key factor in determining if a product will behave elastically, or tend to be inelastic, is the nature of the demand. In simplest of terms, to what degree can a customer exercise control over the amount they consume. Two quick examples:

- Antibiotic drugs would be considered an inelastic priced product since, if a person has an infection, they will most likely buy the needed antibiotic regardless of the price. *(This of course would be truer if there were only one antibiotic available to treat the infection and the infection was life threatening.)* The degree to which a person has other options or the likelihood that they will recover without an antibiotic the more elastic the demand-to-price relationship will be.

- A candy bar would have a more elastic relationship between demand and price *(at least for most adults)*. Ignoring brands and advertising influences if you are hungry for a chocolate bar and the price is fifty cents you may buy the candy bar. If the price suddenly went up to ten dollars most consumers would probably not buy the chocolate bar *(unless of course you're my wife)*.

Returning to our island's wool situation, the Fisher and Farmer families are facing a problem where wool is now considered to be more valuable than when the three families setup the exchange values for their three commodities. For a moment let us consider how the islanders might feel about this change in circumstances… in all likelihood Farmer and Fisher feel less wealthy than before the new value was assigned to wool because they now consume less wool which constrains their lifestyle. The Sheppard's, on the other hand, will feel wealthier than before the price adjustment because they now hold sole access to a commodity that has increased in value. Even if demand for wool decreases to where the number of Greenbacks received each month doesn't change, the Sheppard family will not have to work as hard giving them more leisure time with no loss in income.

In the real world a comparable situation would be gas and oil. When there is a spike in demand or a crisis in the oil producing regions of the world the price of gas goes up and virtually all consumers are affected by this change in price. When you examine this situation you will notice, as a result of the price increase, the oil companies will receive more revenue just like the Sheppard family did when they increased the price of their wool. The oil companies however do not fully benefit from the change in selling price because their cost of crude oil is going up on the supply that does not come from the company owned oil wells.

In this example, oil and gas consumers are in exactly the same spot as the Fisher and Farmer families in that they now have to pay higher prices for the oil based products they buy each week. As consumers how do we react to this situation? For the most part we will have to pay the higher price but, at the same time, most of us will all take steps to reduce our use of these products. How much effort we put into reducing our consumption depends on our discretionary income levels. If your family is lower income you may have to cut back on the quality or quantity of other necessities like food or medical care in order to afford the gas needed to go to and from work. A higher income family may reduce the number of trips they take by car and beyond that they might reduce the amount of money spent on entertainment or other discretionary purchases.

At this point it is important to note that simply increasing prices does not increase wealth or productivity. Higher prices will often generate increased production. In the case of oil and gas, higher prices may increase exploration which would ultimately increase supply it can also lead to the development of alternatives such as electric cars *(on our island the alternative to wool might be in growing cotton)*. In other cases higher prices might only result in a transfer of wealth, which is exactly what happed on the island... a portion of Farmer and Fisher's wealth moved to Sheppard in the form of increased leisure time.

Consumers always react in some way to higher prices... usually this reaction is focused on a desire for returning to the standard of life they had prior to the price increase. Higher prices at the gas pump might cause consumers to consider walking or taking public transportation to and from work, school, or other destinations. An increase in the price of broccoli might cause a grocery shopper to pick up cauliflower instead. The high price of a new prescription drug for hemorrhoid suffers might prompt this much maligned patient group to use a generic or an over-the-counter medication instead of the newer drug.

Within the inflation affecting any economy there are factors other than the pure cost of production inputs that drive price increases. When there are price increases most businesses will cite the rising cost of labor, employee benefits, and supplier costs as the culprit but it's important to recognize that some price increases *(or portions of increases)* may also be due to a controlled effort to grow business profitability. Producers actively try to manage prices to improve profitability and no discussion on inflation is complete without examining how this affects the costs of goods and services.

In our economy consumers and producers wage a continuous, but generally quiet, battle over the price of products. Producers have control of supply and will generally use this leverage to try and establish prices that result in the highest profit. In a pure unregulated free enterprise economy both producers and consumers react freely to changes in price and the producers have the opportunity to earn higher profits in the market that has experienced a price increase. The broccoli producers, in a market where there are high prices, will react by ratcheting up production and, when supply catches up with demand, the consumers will buy the added broccoli but only when the price is reduced. This economic dance between consumers and producers over pricing is repeated frequently with supply going up and down as does the price of the product.

There are of course exceptions, sometimes rouge producers will deviate from this practice in an attempt to achieve the highest dollar value of sales regardless of profit, socially conscious producers might choose to sell at a lower price than the market allows, and markets that are regulated, such as the pharmaceutical market, have monopoly rights on products for a designated timeframe and can demand and receive higher prices than would be possible without patent protection. (*Pharmaceutical firms in the United States must constantly fight a publicity nightmare where high profits are viewed with public disdain and consumers perceive them as greedy opportunists. In response, many large pharmaceutical companies have established discount and subsidy programs for low income individuals in an attempt to improve their company's reputation and mute public criticism*).

As a consumer you have a number of choices you can make in response to higher prices *(in some cases more choices than in others)*. For example, you would likely never consider mixing your own drugs but you might try to grow broccoli or select a different vegetable to consume. When facing higher prices consumers will be forced to make decisions on how they allocate their income or how much time they spend working in order to increase their income. Price changes always force consumers to think about what to do to adjust to their change in circumstances. It is for this reason that the increased price of wool on our island will bring about some type of reaction. There may be acceptance for a while however it is likely that the consumers *(Fisher and Farmer)* will be dissatisfied with the new state of affairs and will continue to seek alternatives which may possibly lead to changes that Sheppard, as the producer, might find worse than the old lower price of wool.

As it was Farmer happened to mention their wool plight to a visiting sailor who suggested using cotton instead of wool. The sailor not only knew how to grow cotton but also had a supply of seeds with her. Farmer purchased the seeds and listened carefully to the instructions on how to grow cotton. Fortunately for Farmer the cotton grew very well on the island and soon her family had two commodities *(wheat and cotton)* that they could use and sell.

Once the island dwellers began to understand the attributes of cotton they found that cotton fabric was better to use for many of the island's needs. Farmer's cotton was less expensive than Shepard's wool so very quickly both the Farmer and Fisher families began using more cotton and less wool to meet their needs. With this change in dynamics the demand for fabric on the island was now evenly split between wool and cotton which reduced the Sheppard family's income by half. With fewer Greenbacks the Sheppard family no longer had enough money to buy the wheat and fish they needed to feed their family resulting in a poorer quality of life. On the other hand the Farmer family, by now selling both cotton and wheat, was accumulating more Greenbacks.

The island now had the Farmer family working much harder raising both cotton and wheat and as a result the Farmer family quickly accumulated more than half of the island's wealth. Fisher still held their normal one third of the wealth which left the Sheppard family with only one sixth of the wealth. Sheppard's family was now spending time not only raising the sheep but also trying to grow wheat and catch fish in order to compensate for what they needed but could not afford to buy.

The increase in the price of wool and the introduction of cotton has both the Sheppard and Farmer families working harder than before. Farmer is wealthier, Sheppard is much poorer and both are suffering from a shortage of leisure time. Clearly the plan Sheppard had when they raised the price of wool did not work out for them and at this juncture has inflicted more harm to the island economy than good. Raising the price of wool disrupted the island economy's equilibrium… prior to the price increase everyone's needs were satisfied and the wealth the island was optimally distributed.

The loss of economic stability on the island is akin to the United States economy in the early twenty-first century when some people had to work too hard, some were out of work, and the distribution of wealth became more concentrated[2]. In a large economy this type of problem is hard to solve. If you are one of the wealthier members of society you are not going to readily give up your wealth in order to achieve a more optimal

---

[2] http://en.wikipedia.org/wiki/Wealth_in_the_United_States

distribution nor are you likely to invest in new production or in the development of new ideas when the economy is not performing well. Instead the logical move, in an uncertain environment, would be to invest your wealth in economies that are growing or in something that is more likely to hold its value such as gold. However, either of these actions on the part of investor will tend to further depress the local rate of economic growth

Fortunately it's easier to restore equilibrium to our island economy because it's clear what needs to change. The problem is a miss match between available labor on the island and required production... Farmer can productively grow wheat or cotton and Sheppard can produce more wool than the island now needs. To restore equilibrium more labor should be expended in Farmer's production and less in Sheppard's. If this was a purely socialist society Farmer might deed over the cotton producing land and expertise to Sheppard and let them focus on producing wool and cotton however for a more capitalistic approach let's assume Farmer offers to hire the Sheppard family's excess labor to help work the cotton fields. During the early days of this arrangement the Farmer's keep the techniques for growing cotton carefully guarded in order to maintain their cotton monopoly.

With no other work available on the island, Farmer is able to hire the Sheppard workers very economically. With the low pay the Sheppard's are not able to return to their former wealth but from their perspective things are better since they are now making enough Greenbacks to provide their family with sufficient food and clothing.

Over time, in the new arrangement of economic production capacity, the Farmer family continues to grow in wealth becoming the wealthiest family on the island. As their wealth grows the Farmer family works less and hires more of their labor from the poorer Sheppard family. The economically disadvantaged Sheppard's long for the days when they and the other two families were on a more equal financial standing. As time progresses the Sheppard workers begin to gain full knowledge of the cotton growing process and one of the Sheppard's steals a few cotton seeds to take home.

The Sheppard family decides to try growing some cotton on their land and quickly found that it not only grew, but grew much better in their soil than in Farmer's. The Sheppard's cotton grew with much longer and stronger fibers which made it much more desirable to the island's people. At first the small Sheppard crop was no more than a novelty among the islanders but in the second year they grew a much larger crop and made it available for sale. At once the Fisher family stopped buying their cotton from Farmer and began buying it from Sheppard. Next many in the Farmer family decided they too preferred making things out of Sheppard's cotton. Once again the island returned to equilibrium with Sheppard supplying the island's fabric needs and Farmer and Fisher providing the wheat and fish for all the island's needs.

Admittedly, even in a three or four product economy, problems are not likely to be solved as smoothly as they were on our fictional island but, putting that fact aside, let's make a before and after comparison of our island's economy in relation to Sheppard's attempt to increase the price of wool.

Before: Sheppard was working harder than the other two families but equally enjoyed all the wheat and fish they needed along with wool products.

After: With the addition of cotton to Sheppard's product offerings the family now was working a little less than before and had both cotton and wool to make its fabric. In this respect Sheppard now had the same wealth, more leisure time along with two types of clothing, other fabrics, and thread products. Based on this fact alone the chaos brought about by the price increase on wool eventually made the Sheppard family better off.

The island economy also improved for the Fisher and Farmer families as they too now had cotton products that made farming and fishing not only easier but more productive. While this was a complex set of events with a number of ups and downs for the three island families the result has left the overall island economy in a better place than before.

Chapter Eight

(Managing the Money Supply)

Early in the last chapter the inhabitants of Adam's island were in a difficult state of affairs… a bout of rampant inflation had created a situation where the amount of Greenbacks in circulation could no longer support trade on the island.

Like any currency, the currency on Adam's Island *(Greenbacks)* only has value based upon what it can buy. As you may recall when our islanders introduced currency as a means to facilitate trading they established a value for the Greenbacks based on the value of products the island could produce in a reasonable time period. At that point in time each family was allotted one hundred Greenbacks for a total three hundred Greenbacks.

To briefly illustrate the value of currency let's look at our island's Fisher family. The Fisher family produced and traded fish however, due to the short shelf of fish it was not a practical currency. *(Farmer and Sheppard had their own challenges with the trading of wheat and wool)*. Therefore, in order to facilitate trading for all three families the islanders introduced a more practical currency… Greenbacks. The Fisher family was originally given one hundred Greenbacks on the basis that they would have or be able to produce that value in fish. Utilizing the Greenbacks the Fishers would no longer have to catch fresh fish and transport them to the other side of the island in order to trade for wool with the Sheppard family. Instead Fisher would use the Greenbacks to buy the wool and Sheppard would hold onto the Greenbacks until their family needed to purchase fresh fish.

With this in mind, our island's Greenback shortage problem *(as described in the last chapter)* was not a value of production or output problem, but instead it had become a problem of an insufficient money supply. Once the heads of the families came to realize they held more value in products than the island had in ready cash they decided that they would add Greenbacks to each family's supply *(again based upon the average monthly output of each family)*. After much discussion amongst the family leaders it was agreed that each family would receive an additional one thousand Greenbacks. The enlightened leaders, wanting to avoid another inflationary period, also considered how best to address the root cause that had disrupted their equilibrium and led to the need to increase the money supply. The three heads of the families agreed that the original trading arrangement resulted in the Sheppard family having to work harder than the other two families so, to remedy this imbalance, the families agreed to a five percent increase in the price of wool while keeping the prices for the other existing products unchanged...

at least until the next meeting of the family leaders. At this point the families have restored its economy to a stable state, although in a very much non-free enterprise way.

Let's consider what might have happened if the three families had not agreed to regulate future price changes but instead left the prices to freely fluctuate as they had in the prior price increase cycle which they had just suffered through.

In this alternative scenario the Sheppard family, still rightly believing they were being treated unfairly, immediately raised the price of wool by ten percent. Farmer and Fisher were not happy about this but since the money they held had been increased tenfold they felt they could easily afford the higher price. Over a few months the Farmer and Fisher families noticed their supply of Greenbacks was diminishing as they were spending more on wool than they were receiving from selling their products to Sheppard. Quite naturally the two families increased the price of their products by ten percent hoping to recover the Greenbacks they had lost to the Sheppard family. What will likely happen next is the same sequence of events that caused the original cycle of inflation and our islanders will ultimately end up with another shortage of Greenbacks.

A monopolistic pricing situation existed on our little island because there was no real competition since each family had a monopoly on the product they supplied. Without pricing competition *(which is the natural means of controlling prices)* each family had full control over pricing and supply of their product. Monopolistic pricing limits the natural pricing restraint effect that is typically found within a free enterprise economy and therefore other controls are required in order to keep the economy functioning properly. If there is no control on price increases in an economy dominated by monopolistic suppliers then pricing can easily spiral out of control and damage the efficiency of the economy including causing the fixed money supply to become insufficient.

If the monopolistic pricing on the island is not regulated then the money supply will need to be adjusted periodically in order to keep the economy running smoothly. The families will need to regularly increase the money supply so that the available cash continues to equate to the average monthly output of each family. The bigger the increase in the money supply the more rapidly inflation will be a factor because more money on hand allows higher prices to be accepted. At some point the families would be transporting wheelbarrows full of Greenbacks in order to buy a pound of wool which would be well past the point where inflation would make the Greenback *(based on shear volume)* an ineffective means of facilitating trade. The obvious answer would be to use Greenback denominations of higher values in place of stacks of individual Greenbacks.

Inflation within an economy tends to depress trading as it makes the exchange process of currency for goods more complicated and therefore less efficient. Most families can recall a time when they bought too much of a product or bought it at the wrong time and the product spoiled or went unused. Anytime this happens it is a drag on the economy as it represents waste. For an economy to deliver optimum satisfaction each participant needs to achieve maximum utility out of the products they purchase.

As an example, I purchased a twenty dollar piece of salmon at Costco and put it in the fridge with the intent of fixing it for dinner within a couple of days. Had I made the salmon for dinner as planned my family and I would have received the utility or benefit of a nice meal. Unfortunately my family's schedule got very busy and the salmon was forgotten. After a while my wife noticed a foul odor and we had to take time out of our busy schedules to search for the source and after some time we zeroed in on the refrigerator and found the now spoiled salmon to be the culprit. We then spent additional time cleaning and deodorizing the fridge which added to our overall loss. The twenty dollars spent on the salmon was not only a total loss to my family but also to the economy at large.

Periods of inflation tend to drive consumers and producers to spend additional time and effort in trying to manage their business or personal affairs as they attempt to factor in an unstable medium of exchange which creates friction in the economy. Friction in this case consumes resources which do not provide utility to consumers or producers. The net effect of any wasted resources is similar to the spoiled salmon as it diminishes the quality of life provided by the economy. Had I, instead of buying the salmon, invested the twenty dollars in my 401K plan it would have flowed into the available capital for the nation's growth.

Controlled inflation, as experienced by the United States economy in the 1990's and early twenty-first century, places little friction on the economy compared to uncontrolled inflation *(also known as runaway inflation)*. Compared to runaway inflation, controlled inflation is a comparatively minor hardship and can be easily managed by our government's control over the money supply.

Earlier we touched upon the effect of monopolistic pricing and how there was little within the natural workings of the free enterprise system to control price increases when a product's supply is controlled by a monopoly. Fortunately, within the United States' economy, most products and services are not subject to monopolistic competition and are therefore priced in a competitive environment. In the next few paragraphs we will explore how competitive situations effectively self-regulate prices thereby avoiding the complications, such as the inadequate money supply, that we saw on Adam's Island.

Let's suppose that the inhabitants of Adam's Island now have access to a second supplier for their wool... with this change in circumstance the Sheppard family will now need to consider more than just how equitable the pricing of wool is on the island compared to the other products and will need to mull over what their customers' and competitor's reactions might be before deciding on any price increases.

Let's assume for example that the Sheppard family raised their wool prices by ten percent and their competitor, who also thought wool was underpriced, matched Sheppard's price increase. If this occurred then the cycle of inflation could start just as described earlier in this text. Alternatively, if Sheppard's competition chose to raise their price by only five percent then Sheppard would lose some of his market share to the competition.

Now granted price is not the only factor customers consider when making purchases… quality, branding, and service are also considerations. However, in our example we will ignore these influences and assume that the wool is of equal quality and the two providers provide equal service which means our island consumers will choose a supplier based solely on price and as a result the Sheppard family will quickly lose all their customers unless they adjust their price increase to match their competitor's new price. This change in strategy will enable them to share the market while still being able to earn a five percent higher price for wool than before.

The preceding example is a fairly crude description of the concept of the money supply compared to what goes on within a sophisticated modern economy. In the United States the money supply is largely the concern of the Federal Reserve, often referred to in the media as the "Fed", and while not all the controls are held by the Fed it is without question the most influential organization when it comes to managing the United States' money supply.[3] The Federal Reserve has been lead in recent years by a number of Chairmen who have become household names like Alan Greenspan and Ben Bernanke.

Most modern countries have institutions similar to the Fed so the concepts used for influencing the money supply are similar in many developed free market economies. For our purposes we will focus on the United States as our example.

---

[3] http://en.wikipedia.org/wiki/Open_market_operation; http://en.wikipedia.org/wiki/Money_supply

The Fed Chairman has a powerful position, one in which he or she can and does influence the money supply. One of the ways the Fed can have an effect on the money supply is by changing the reserve requirements. The Federal Reserve requires banks to keep a certain percentage of funds deposited in "reserve". Regulations require the bank to lend out something less than the full value of the funds it receives in deposits, hence holding some part of the deposit as a cash "reserve".

For example, if you deposited a thousand dollars in your savings account, the bank would only be permitted to lend out a portion of the money while keeping the rest of it in reserve. Let's say the Fed's current requirement is a ten percent reserve. If Sally comes into the bank and requests a loan and all the bank has to work with is your one thousand dollars then the most your bank could lend Sally is nine hundred dollars. By the Chairman varying this reserve requirement the Fed can influence the amount of money available to lend thereby either stimulating the economy by lowering the reserve requirement or slowing it down by increasing required reserve percentage.

You may have heard about the economic concept of banks creating money through their lending operations. It is this effect that the Fed attempts to manage by adjusting the reserve requirement. To illustrate let's continue with the example of your one thousand dollar deposit. The bank used your deposit to loan Sally nine hundred dollars, so at this point you have a thousand dollar deposit and Sally has nine hundred dollars in cash. Generally speaking, borrowers rarely hold on to the borrowed cash instead they almost always use the borrowed funds to buy something. Keeping this simple, let's say Sally takes her borrowed nine hundred dollars to your business and makes a purchase. You now have your thousand dollars deposited in the bank plus the nine hundred dollars Sally just paid to you which gives you a total of nineteen hundred dollars available in cash and banked funds. For the sake of simplicity let's assume you don't need to replace any of the products Sally bought so you take the entire nine hundred dollars to your bank and deposit it into your savings account giving you a nineteen hundred dollar account balance.

The bank now has another nine hundred dollars against which it can lend eight hundred and ten dollars *(remember the Fed's current requirement is a ten percent reserve)*. Shortly after you make your deposit Jim comes into the bank asking for a loan for a purchase for which he coincidently needs exactly eight hundred and ten dollars. Jim also was eyeing something in your store's inventory for that exact amount and buys it. The cycle then repeats itself again and again. It is through this process that the combination of your deposits and the bank's lending that creates new money in your local economy.

Suppose in the days between Sally's purchase and Jim's purchase the Fed announced the reserve requirement was being increased from ten percent to fifty percent in order to dampen the prospects for inflation. You might at first think that when you deposit the nine hundred dollars the bank will be able to lend four hundred and fifty dollars but in reality the new reserve applies to all the loans the bank has outstanding. Given this, the bank now has to hold back a reserve of five hundred dollars on your original deposit and four hundred and fifty dollars on your second deposit for a collective reserve of nine hundred and fifty dollars. So now when Jim comes in to borrow the eight hundred and ten dollars he needs to make the purchase from your store the bank only has fifty dollars it can lend. Jim will need to either delay his purchase or find another bank with available reserves which will be unlikely with the recent Fed reserve requirement change.

Inflation concerns come into play when there is too much demand. As an example, if you made the sale to Sally on one day and a day later made another big sale to Jim you might decide to raise your prices by ten percent because of the high demand for your products or because your supplier can't keep up with the demand and raised their prices. Either way the products you are carrying have become more expensive to consumers and if this effect is going on throughout the country the Fed would see this as a start to potentially disastrous cycle of inflation. The Feds quick action in this example swiftly dampened demand avoiding your price increase and potentially many others throughout the country.

If instead of inflation, the Fed saw signs of a coming recession they may have reduced the reserve percentage from ten percent to five percent. In that case, when Jim came in for a loan, the bank would have had nineteen hundred in deposits and a reserve requirement of only ninety-five dollars giving them loanable funds of eighteen hundred and five dollars. Since the bank had already loaned Sally nine hundred dollars they had nine hundred and five dollars available to loan when Jim came to the bank. In this situation the loan officer may have been able to talk Jim into borrowing nine hundred and five dollars *(instead of eight hundred a ten dollars)* which Jim then uses to buy a more expense product from your store thereby increasing your next deposit and your next order from your supplier. In this way *(this sequence of events multiplied by millions of consumers and loans)* the Fed could hypothetically pull the country out of an approaching recession.

Although this process, in one form or another, has been used in numerous textbooks and online references not every economist agrees that it works as effectively as this example indicates. It is a theory that most agree with and I believe in practice does work although there are numerous other factors that come into play such as consumer confidence and the amount of credit risk lenders are willing to take.

Another tool the Fed uses to influence the money supply is open market operations. There are a few different tools the Fed uses within this area. All of these tools have a goal of adding to or reducing the money supply. One of the tools the Fed uses for this purpose is buying or selling treasury securities. If the Fed sells securities then money is coming out of the money supply and when the Fed buys treasuries it is putting money into the money supply. This process, in my opinion, is a more direct way to impact the money supply and achieve the Fed's objective of either stimulating economic growth or cooling down an overheated economy.

These actions can also have an impact on the interest rates banks charge. In this case the interest rate effect can be the result of buying and selling monetary investment securities or by changing the Fed Funds rate… the rate at which banks borrow from one another or on some occasions from the Fed itself. Interest rates can also impact the money supply by inducing customers to borrow by making the interest cost of loans cheaper thus fueling the lending and deposit cycle described earlier which effectively acts as a stimulus to the economy.

Chapter Nine

(Trader Moves to the Island)

The quality of life in our little island had improved and, although the island was not well known to the outside world, a family from a hectic and industrialized part of the world asked permission to move onto the island. The family was the Trader family. The husband and wife had spent their early careers working on the trading floors of a major stock exchange and reached a point in their lives where the attraction of more money did not outweigh the time their careers were taking away from their young family. They decided it was time to seek out a location where they could move with their family and start a new life, one which would allowed Mr. and Mrs. Trader to have more time with their children.

The three heads of the island families met to discuss the Trader family's request. The first concern was that it was a small island and there was not an excess of quality farming land and none of the families wanted to give up any of their productive land. After some discussion Fisher offered to give up a section of his property that was not suitable for farming but did share his easy access to the ocean. Sheppard and Farmer agreed with that idea but wondered how the new family would make a livelihood for themselves while residing on a part of the island that had little in the way of natural resources.

The Trader family was approached with the offer of Fisher's property. As part of the deal Trader would pay Fisher for the property using goods they had brought along from their soon to be former homeland. Additionally, Trader brokered a deal with the other two families where Trader would provide them goods in exchange for their assistance in building their new home and helping them get started on the island.

The island's original three families asked the Trader family how they planned to make a living on the island. Trader explained that his family was going to set up a store and stock it with goods purchased from other lands and that they would trade these goods for the islands mainstays of wool, wheat, and fish. Trader went on to say that their former life had left them with sufficient wealth that they could afford to trade goods with the original islanders until they found a way to contribute to the island's economy. The other three families could not imagine how this would work but were nonetheless attracted by the prospect of obtaining access to the new products Trader mentioned. The original islanders concluded that, even if one day Trader would have to leave the island, their lives would be enriched by the goods they received as a result of the Trader family's attempt to make a life on Adam's Island.

As time progressed each of the families increased their production to provide for the Trader family's needs. Trader made a point of buying as much as he could from the other families so that he could furnish the store with surplus products from the island *(domestic goods)* as well as goods from the outside world *(imported goods)*. Trader, conscious of his status as a newcomer to the island, kept the markup on domestic goods sold in their store *(wheat, wool, and fish)* to only ten percent above the previous trading price. Each of the original families soon found it was more convenient to go to the Trader shop to pick up all the goods their families needed. Trader's ten percent markup on the domestic goods was something the families were happy to pay for the convenience of buying what they needed from one location and the other families were eager to be able to purchase previously unavailable products that Trader was importing from the outside world.

Why, one might wonder, did Trader's ten percent markup not create the same problem that we saw happen in the island economy when the other families increased their prices? The difference in this situation is that there is an added demand that results in added income for each of the three original families. The additional goods they are selling to Trader more than made up for the ten percent markup on the domestic goods at Trader's store. In fact, the families were actually selling a third more product than before while the cost of the goods they're consuming had only increased by ten percent. Furthermore the added convenience, along with some labor saving products imported and sold by Trader, had allowed the families to produce more goods with only a fraction more effort.

What we saw happen on the island is something we take for granted in our everyday world. We seldom buy what we need directly from the person or company producing that product. In our society, throughout the development of our market driven economy, we have come to depend more and more on distributors and retailers to make shopping easier and more convenient and, for the most part, neither consumers nor producers give much thought to the premium added to the cost of goods being sold by the retailer. In the United States, prior to the 1970's, the process of moving goods from the producer to retail stores often included one to two distributors handling the product. Wholesalers and distributors often serviced retailers by breaking up the larger quantities sold by the manufacturers into the smaller quantities which the small mom and pop retailers wanted to stock in their stores. Each step within the producer-to-retailer process added a cost to the good so by the time a product ended up in the retailer's shop its price included the cost of the good made by the manufacturer, manufacturer profit, the wholesaler's markup, a distributor's markup, and the retailer's profit.

As an example, a set of dishes in a small retailer's shop sells for $30. The manufacturer sells the dishes in bulk to the wholesaler for $12 a set *($10 manufacturing costs plus a $2 profit)*, the wholesalers marks the dishes up $2 per set and sells them to the distributors for $14, the distributors add an additional $2 markup and sells the dishes to the retailer for $16 per set. The retailer typically adds a larger profit margin so in this example let us say retailer added a $14 markup making the consumer price $30 for the set of dishes. In this example nearly two thirds of the $30 paid by the consumer was for the retailer's profit plus the cost to move the product from the manufacturer to the retailer's shelf.

In recent years retailers like Wal-Mart have focused on taking steps out of the distribution process effectively eliminating the need for wholesalers and distributors. The result has been lower costs for consumers but the change has also created significant trauma for the old distribution and retailing process which is, in some part, why Wal-Mart is such a controversial company. Ignoring for the moment any negatives associated with Wal-Mart's tactics, the effect to the economics of moving goods from producer to consumer has changed with the most noticeable part of the change being a lower price to the consumer.

In theory it might be cheaper for consumers to buy products exclusively from producers but in practical application it simply doesn't make sense. Consider a family's typical weekly grocery shopping trip... now imagine if instead of going to one store you had to go to each manufacturer in order to purchase each of the goods you needed... the time and added expense involved to shop that way would create a hardship in the lives of modern families. Clearly paying the markup Wal-Mart or some other retailer adds to the manufacturer's cost is much more efficient than buying directly from the manufacturer. In this respect Wal-Mart and our fictitious Trader family bring the same benefit to their respective societies.

In past generations communication and transportation were more challenging than they are today, populations were more disbursed and, in order to serve consumers, retailers tended to be smaller and geographical spread out. Therefore, in order to meet the challenges of the times and facilitate the movement of goods between producers and consumers, it made sense to add wholesalers and distributors into the supply chain. These intermediaries served an important role… manufacturers produced products in large quantities, the wholesalers and distributors purchased the products directly from the manufacturer, broke them into smaller quantities, and sold them to the small retail stores. But, as time passed, the population in the United States grew and the percentage of the population in rural areas decreased while the population in urban centers increased and became more concentrated. With these demographic changes it became possible to have a few larger retailers versus many widely disbursed "Mom & Pop" stores. Servicing many more consumers, these larger retailers were able to move larger quantities enabling them to purchase directly from the manufacturers thereby negating the need for distributors and wholesalers.

Just as improved transportation aided in the movement of goods between producers and retailers it also made it more convenient for consumers to travel greater distances in order to take advantage of better prices. In the early part of the twentieth century traveling *(even as little as five miles)* was much more difficult since most people didn't own a car which made a small general store, that was within walking distance, much more practical than a super store twenty miles away. Big retailers like Wal-Mart did not put the mom and pop retail stores out of business, instead their demise was due to changes in technology; effectively the mom and pop stores were rendered obsolete. Someday technology may drive Wal-Mart out of business possibly due to some new process that enables goods to flow smoothly and directly between producers and consumers... I only wish I could envision what that new process might be as I am sure there will be large profits for that innovator.

Back on Adam's island the islanders have made progress due to the addition of the Trader family. The Trader family not only brought additional consumption to the island which helped absorb the island's growing productivity but they also, through trade, introduced new products into the lives of the island families. Often we as consumers view a markup on the products we buy *(like what Trader applied to the island's domestic goods)* as a negative however the convenience of buying from a retailer often more than offsets the markup charged. Retailers, like

Trader and Wal-Mart, help their respective economies by acting as a lubricant to the economy. Anything that facilitates the movement of goods between the producers and the consumers is a lubricating function.

The Traders' are providing a service to the island that has improved trade efficiency but, if this service were handled differently, it could instead create friction and have a negative impact the island economy. Let's imagine for a moment that a gang of armed militia took over our island and required the three families to turn all their produce over to them for redistribution. We will assume the leader of the gang is kind and considerate and his intent is to give the families what they need. How might an arrangement such as this affect the island and how would this arrangement compare to what happened when the Trader family joined our small community?

The process applied by the militia and the Trader family are pretty much the same in that the production of the island is consolidated at one location giving the islanders a one-stop place to obtain their needed products. The big difference is that militia accepts whatever output each family generates with no incentive or benefit to anyone who works harder to produce more. Without an incentive for working harder Farmer, for example, would not care if the production of her wheat dropped off because, as long as the family appeared to be working hard, the militia leader would continue to supply Farmer with whatever wool or fish was available to distribute.

You might imagine that over time Farmer, Fisher, and Sheppard might begin to find that there were shortages of goods. The most obvious reason being that the militia was taking what it needed out of the island's production but the bigger problem was the lack of productivity increases which was a direct result of the islanders' loss of motivation. The militia might react to these shortages by demanding higher production and inflicting punishment on the islanders if they did not hit higher levels of output. These actions might in fact work to some degree but long-term the use of punishment would not work as well as a more natural motivation that comes via a free enterprise economic environment.

The militia example is a thinly veiled, good natured version of the communism experiment that occurred during the twentieth century. I say good natured because the concept of communism held by the true believers was that, by having an economic system where the central government distributed production and gave everyone what they needed, the distribution would be fairer than in a purely capitalistic economy. Unfortunately the communist concept failed to consider the role of motivation and how the lack of the direct cause and effect of added effort leading to added reward would and does impact output. This of course ignores the other failures of the communist system we know including the tendency toward totalitarian leadership and the loss of most personal liberties.

Chapter Ten

(Imports, Exports, and the Balance of Payments)

Importing and exporting are not that different from the day-to-day trading we all do… we exchange our labors for the goods and services we want or need. However, in order to be considered an import or export, the good or service must cross a national boundary. Trading is a competitive sport and as such there will be winners and losers. When trading is done domestically the winners and losers are determined by the amount of income tallied up on the company's profit and loss financial statement. However, with international trade, not only are there winners and losers at the company level but also among the trading nations; trading success between nations is determined by the balance of payments between the two respective countries.

In domestic trading wars, some companies grow market share while others lose market share *(sometimes to the point of going out of business)*. In international trading there are numerous artificial elements that go into the winning and losing process which can make it less clear who is "winning" at any given point in time. Governments are often the most common source of artificial factors… these factors may include import duties, tax incentives for exports, and direct influence in the decision whether to buy an import or a domestic product.

When there is availability of both imported and domestic products consumers are the ones who make the decision as to which product to buy. Consumers do not act purely on price considerations but instead take into account a host of influences before making a buying decision. Some decisions are very rational and factor in both quality and price while other decisions are influenced more by less rational factors, for example prejudices about domestic and imported products sometimes greatly influence how some of our buying decisions are made.

Many years ago, before I met and married my wonderful, beautiful and intelligent wife/editor, I had a girlfriend who came from an old money, upper class family. This family had very specific opinions about many things including what constituted an appropriate vehicle for a member of their family *(and me by extension)*. As misfortune would have it I was in the market for a new car and I quickly was introduced to what this family considered acceptable. Me, I just wanted to make a rational buying decision that took into consideration price, quality, and suitability to my transportation needs. However the preferences *(or prejudices)* that, through duress, became factors in my purchasing decision included 1) American made cars were unacceptable *(some of this prejudice was driven by the family's opinion of the UAW and also because they viewed American cars as options for the "middle/lower class").* 2) The Hyundai brand was a cheap vehicle driven by predominantly lower class consumers *(Hyundai, at the time, was establishing itself as a low cost, quality automaker).* 3) A Mercedes was the optimal vehicle of choice for a family of their status.

Regardless of the pressure, I was not about to buy a Mercedes just to satisfy this family's image requirements. My preference *(based on price, quality, and my transportation needs)* was a Hyundai which, one would have thought, would have torn a hole in the fabric of space and time had I actually purchased one. Eventually, so as not to disrupt life as we know it, I purchased a Saturn which was just barely within this family's limits of acceptability *(and only because one of the rebel members of the family owned a Saturn and had a very good experience with it).*

In hindsight my buying decision was not the best. The Saturn was a good car but long-term was evaluated by consumer rating agencies as a problem model *(despite the auto demonstrating many of the favorable attributes of some of the best buy models within the Saturn brand)* whereas the Hyundai *(similar style as the Saturn)* which I had wanted to purchase was later rated as a "Best Buy" by the same consumer rating agencies. The Hyundai was also a couple of thousand dollars less expensive than the Saturn so at a minimum my compromise cost me that amount in cash plus the loss of the added utility that would have come from what appears to have been a better quality vehicle. The Mercedes, on the other hand, sold for about seven thousand dollars more than the Saturn so, if I had kowtowed fully to the pressure, it would have cost me that additional money plus I would have lost even more utility since it would not have been able to do some of the things I wanted my new car to do.

In the end bowing, even somewhat, to the purchasing prejudices of my former girlfriend's family cost me money and utility but my decision also affected the import/export situation for the United States and Korea by whatever the differing amounts of domestic versus imported content was within the car I bought versus the car I should have purchased.

To see the impact of buying decisions based on prejudices let's assume that in the United States two billion dollars in vehicle purchases are influenced by an unjust prejudice against American made cars which, assuming a forty thousand dollar average purchase price, would equate to fifty thousand cars each year. For simplicity's sake let's assume that one hundred percent of the cost of a German auto is German and likewise for the American made car. Based on these assumptions Germany would bring in the equivalent two billion dollars of value annually into its trade account balance with the United States. If the importing of German cars into the United States was the only trading activity between the United States and Germany, then the resulting balance of trade debt between the United States and Germany would grow by two billion dollars each year.

In simple terms, if Americans were sending two billion dollars a year to Germany, the Germans must put a value on the U.S. Dollars received and this value must at least equal what the cars would have sold for in Germany or what they would have been purchased for by other trading partners. If this is the case then the underlying value of the U.S. Dollars in U.S. goods, services, debt or property must have that value to the German people who are ultimately holding those Dollars. The choices for the German holders of the U.S. Dollars making up the trade debt could be used to buy U.S. treasuries which would help to fund the United States' budget deficit *(which is the primary use the*

Chinese, in the early twenty-first century, had chosen to do) or buy U.S. products or services.

The Germans could also invest in the United States' economy by buying stocks, starting up companies or divisions in the United States, or by investing in real estate. When foreign people chose to invest in a country they are assuming at least two things, one is that the nation's government is stable and will honor the foreigner's property rights and two that the economy they are investing within will grow and allow the owners to earn a profit on those investments. There are many schools of thought on the merits and negative aspects of having foreign ownership of American property but we are not going to delve into those arguments in any depth in this chapter.

The alternative to investing in the United States would be for the German's holding U.S. Dollars to purchase American made goods or services. In that event the balance of payments between the two countries settles without any change in the ownership in either country's debt or property. Most people would agree that result, at least from a long-term perspective, is better for both economies. The main reason it's better is that the trading of goods and services is sustainable long-term while the accumulation of debt of the trading partner or buying property of the other country are not sustainable activities. This does not mean that short-term either the buying of the other country's debt or investing in that economy are intrinsically bad just that in the long-term it cannot be sustained because neither the debt or the accumulation of property can have long-term value as at some point the debtor nation is not making goods or providing services other nations desire to purchase. For example if , on our island, Farmer stopped growing wheat at some point his family would run out of Greenbacks and property to trade for the necessities of life.

Either the buying of debt or buying the property of another nation can be a long-term recipe for disaster as it may be masking the problems of the nation accumulating the trade deficit. The nature of a continuing trade deficit is one where the nation accumulating the trade debt is consuming more than it is making. A family financing their lifestyle by taking out additional mortgages and running up credit card debt would be a simplified example of what a nation might be doing when it is allowed to continue to buy more than it is selling to its trading partners. The family, once they can no longer borrow money to fund their lifestyle, will have a day of reckoning when they will either need to drastically curtail their spending and begin to pay down their debt or face bankruptcy.

Smaller countries have faced similar situations like the family described above where foreign nations no longer wanted the currency of that nation nor were willing to buy or hold that country's debt. History does not provide us with an example of a significantly sized economy, such as the American economy, becoming dependent on foreign countries to finance a continuing large trade imbalance so, in the absent of a clear historical picture, I will use the following fictitious set of circumstances to present one possible outcome.

For twenty years the United States had a trade deficit with China. With each passing year this deficit was becoming a larger and larger percentage of the U.S. GNP ultimately reaching fifty percent at which point China held ninety percent of the U.S. debt and owned fifty percent of the companies and investment property in the U.S. As the Chinese were acquiring U.S. debt many U.S. industries closed their factories and the labor flowed into service jobs.

But then, China suddenly changed their trading strategy (focusing their output on domestic consumption) and no longer sought to buy and hold U.S. Dollars. Once the decision to stop financing the U.S. economy had been made the value of the U.S. dollar plummeted to the point that no foreign government or company wanted to hold U.S. dollars. The Chinese dumped their U.S. treasuries on the market and the U.S. had no choice but to print money to redeem the debt which further devalued the U.S. currency. The U.S. could no longer buy manufactured goods as imports U.S. so consumers had to look internally for needed products only to find there was no domestic production capability since the U.S. industries had closed their factories. As consumer confidence plummeted service companies, both domestically owned and foreign owned, began to quickly downsize.

During the build up to the Chinese move, sophisticated investors in the United States' economy moved their funds into fixed value commodities such as gold or invested their capital in countries that had a more sustainable basis to their economies. As a result the retirement funds of the low and middle class Americans, who predominantly invested in U.S. based companies, vanished overnight and any other savings held by those two groups effectively lost its buying power due to the devaluation of the Dollar. The nation shrank into an economic depression much worse than the era known as the Great Depression.

At this point you may be thinking… "Wow, this is an interesting and possibly scary story but what is the basis of this frightening message?" I will admit that my projection of events is, at best, purely speculation but there are some factual elements that support this narrative. China might not be the only candidate for the bad guy in this story; other large economies could play a part as well. I choose China for the black hat in my story since it is not a normal free enterprise economy but instead the sole large planned economy controlled by a totalitarian government. Since free market motivations tend to act as release valves on spending and trading imbalances, only a totalitarian regime could manage its currency values and trade imbalances to set up an unsuspecting or naïve nation, like the United States, to fall into this economic trap.

You might argue the United States is a nation full of very smart people who would never allow a situation to go this far. To this I would offer the S&L crisis of the 1980's and the mortgage and derivatives' disaster of 2008. In both cases very sophisticated investors took advantage of weaknesses within the financial systems for the financial gain of a few at the expense of the United States' economy. Their actions negatively impacted the majority of the United States population and resulted in years of economic weakness. There are many enlightening books on both subjects that provide numerous examples of Americans willing to sell out the greater economy for their own financial gain. More importantly there were prominent "whistleblowers" who have attempted to shine a light on the dangers within the United States' economy but went unheard in the years leading up to both crises. Even as I write this book there are a number of "lunatics" predicting the demise of the United States based upon our predilection of falling into traps just like the ones I described. Could they be right, could my fictional Chinese scenario come true? Let us hope that we as a nation are smarter than that.

In chapter four our fictional island economy encountered a trading situation where trading with Fertile Isle was going to disrupt the island's economy. This situation was averted by self-imposed regulation on the part of the islanders to keep the foreign goods off of Adam's island. However later, in chapter nine, trading was established with Fertile Island in such a way that it was mutually beneficial to both islands. This type of importing and exporting was good because it sought to benefit both of the tiny economies. For purposes of providing an example of sinister trading motives we will return to our island and work through a far different set of circumstances.

The inhabitants of Fertile Isle were ruled by a single family by the name of Illgot, this family for many years had exploited the Fertile Isle people by keeping the bulk of the island's wealth for themselves. As time progressed the Illgots grew to admire the development of the Adam's Island's economy, its resources and the productivity of its people, and so the Illgots formulated a plan where they would gain control of Adam's Island's resources.

The Illgots began by cutting the price of their wheat and regulating the imports it had been receiving from Adam's Island. *(As you will recall Fisher was a much more effective fisherman than anyone on Fertile Isle so the normal trading consequence would have had our islanders buying wheat and selling fish to the Fertile Islanders).* The Fertile Isle people suffered from the changes mandated by the Illgots but, since the island was ruled with an iron hand, there was nothing that could be done to change things on the Fertile Isle side.

Since the Illgots were selling *(versus trading)* their wheat through the Trader store *(which meant the only thing they were importing from Adam's Island were Greenbacks)* and because Trader was still receiving Greenbacks in exchange for products from the families on Adam's Island it took a while for the change in trading practices to be noticed however, over time, the Island families began to run low on Greenbacks. As was their plan, the Illgots quickly stepped in with a remedy for this impending Greenback shortage problem.

One of Sheppard children was a gifted mathematician and the Illgot family hired her to establish a bank for the Islanders explaining that, "due to the sophisticated trading arrangements to which the Island was now a party, the island needed a financial services business to ensure that the economy continued to function effectively in the new economic environment". Ms. Sheppard was given a large salary and assigned the responsibility to keep Adam's Island economy moving by offering loans to the islanders on very friendly terms. An element of those terms required that the Islanders pledge their property to the Illgot's bank as collateral for the loans. Everyone was assured that credit would continue to be offered as needed and the economy would continue to prosper as the value of the island's property would certainly keep pace with the need for borrowed funds. The lending programs offered by Ms. Sheppard began by limiting the debt to only eighty percent of the market value of the property but, over time, this was raised to one hundred and twenty-five percent of the property's value. This process continued until the Illgot's bank held the entire Island's valuable property as fully pledged collateral.

The Illgot clan eventually came to the Island and called in all the loans in the space of one day and in doing so assumed ownership of the island nation of Adam's Island. Each family was now a tenant within the homes and lands they once owned. Illgot specified the amount of cotton, wool, wheat, and fish that must be exported to Fertile Isle on a weekly basis which amounted to the rent each family owed to Illgot. As a result, the Illgot clan grew in wealth and even the other Fertile Isle inhabitants had more to consume than before.

We will not continue this story line for our Island families but will leave this hypothetical outcome as an example of what can happen to a nation when its balance of payments allows a shift in control of the nation's economic resources. In the Adam's Island example control was the ownership of the island, in the case of an economy like that of the United States the result could be ownership of personal property or control over the resources needed to produce. Since the United States is *(and should be)* a net exporter of food, the chances are that the United States will be able to feed itself but... what about other consumer goods? Oil, for example, is needed as an import in order to provide the energy the United States requires to maintain the country's lifestyle. If our currency were to lose its value to the point where we could no longer get credit we would not be able to import oil and our economy would suffer from a lack of affordable energy.

Another aspect of my apprehensive view of potential sinister Chinese motivations, to which I alluded, is the movement of manufacturing capability out of the United States. We have been careful to keep the ability to manufacture weapons in our country but, as we enter the second decade of the twenty-first century, many other products are no longer made in the United States in any quantity. If we do not have the ability to make TVs, computers, and other consumer goods it would be extremely difficult for Americans to maintain their accustomed lifestyle in the event the nation lost its ability to import those products. Virtually no toys are made in the United States so, at a minimum, it would be a very tough Christmas for young children in this projected economic disaster.

Like other topics we touched upon thus far, international trade can be a complex set of processes hence difficult to understand and to manage. Our leaders, in endeavoring to manage our international trade, must make a judgment regarding when *(and when not)* to intervene in the trading process. Nations and their citizens must maintain their awareness of what is going on with their trading partners and, just like a family should monitor its budget, the voting population of a country should watch their nation's balance of payments. Just because things are going well at any one point in time does not preclude the possibility that an economic disaster is in the process of developing in the country. The old adage "if it is too good to be true, then it probably is" is a good adage to keep in mind when evaluating international trade. Citizens of every nation, especially their leaders, need a combination of common sense and knowledge of the financial aspects of international trade.

As we wrap up this chapter, it's important to remember that, on its face, international trade is good since the importing and exporting of goods and services tends to increase the wealth of all nations. Short-term trade surpluses and deficits are normal and both must be monitored and debated within every nation in order to make sure that a short-term imbalance does not become a chronic problem. Alert leaders should be quick to address manipulated trade and anything else that would place their nation at risk from undue foreign influence or the loss of a capability that is critical to the nation's survival. No country wants to be taken over by the Illgot tribe or any other actual nation that would seek to benefit its economy while potentially destroying the other nation's economy.

Chapter Eleven

(New Products for the Island Consumers)

As the Adam's Island inhabitants became more prosperous, the families often had more goods on hand than were required to meet their immediate needs which created the dilemma of how to store the excess for future use. In order to store their excess each family began to make storage containers and then, finding that they needed more room to hold their increased wealth, began expanding their homes creating a need for building materials. Initially the families attempted to make their own storage containers and produce their own building products but soon realized, as they had with the production of wheat, wool and fish, that trying to do it all on their own negatively impacted everyone's quality of life.

The families soon identified what each was able to produce most efficiently and established a trading arrangement for the goods that enabled everyone to meet their needs much more efficiently.

- The Fisher family's land included a forest with an abundance of wood that was easy to work into lumber for building.

- The Sheppard family found that on their part of the island there was a plant that produced strong fibers that could be made into ropes, storage bags, and fishing nets.

- The Farmer family's land had deposits of iron ore that allowed them to make tools such as hammers, shovels, plows, and nails.

Fisher traded lumber for fishing nets and nails. Farmer traded nails and hammers with Sheppard for ropes and storage bags. These new products all tended to be less critical to the three families than their three primary products but, nonetheless, the families found these goods added a great deal to their quality of life.

Using the lumber from the Fisher family and the nails produced by Farmer the families were now able to construct larger, sturdier, and more elaborate homes. However, to produce the new materials would take time away from their core production of fish, wool, and wheat. Fortunately the new products also proved to help the three families become more productive, effectively yielding added available hours of work time to their days.

- Fisher found that the new fishing nets made by Sheppard were vastly superior to the old method of line or spear fishing and, as a result, they could catch the required amount of fish for the entire island's population in half the time as before.

- Sheppard also found ways to enhance their family's wool production. Sheppard's first innovation was to construct fences to keep the sheep together which reduced the amount of time they had previously spent herding.

- Farmer soon found that their family could also benefit from the new products now available to the island. First they found that they could make new iron tools that allowed them to be much more productive raising wheat. The iron plows, hoes, and rakes were much better than the wooden tools they had been using. They also found, that using Fisher's lumber, they could construct a superior threshing device which increased the amount of wheat harvested and decreased the amount of time required in doing so.

All the families found ways to use the new products to create efficiencies in their work processes which gave them the additional time needed to produce the new products and to spend on constructing or renovating their homes.

In the real world we seldom see dramatic changes that are deployed in the space of a few years, however we can see an example of this demonstrated in the changes to the quality of life in the years following the start of the Industrial Revolution. Rapid progress, during this period, has continued largely unabated through to the present day. Wars and depressions are the only periods in between where the benefits of progress have not steadily flowed through to consumers within the developed nations of the world.

One of the most significant changes that clearly demonstrated this type of benefit has been the mechanization of farming. In this case, as a society, we moved from an economic environment where most people were engaged in raising food to one where only a small number of people are farmers. About ninety percent of people were farmers[4] in 1790 but by 2011,

---

[4] http://inventors.about.com/library/inventors/blfarm4.htm

according to the USDA, less than two percent of the United States population was engaged in farming. This change means that eighty-eight percent more of the population can now work on producing other goods and services instead of raising food. Most of the consumption Americans do today is for things other than food, in fact there are more people cooking and serving food to consumers than people who are purely engaged in raising the food we consume.

In 1790 farmers consumed ninety percent of what they raised or conversely the farmers only had ten percent of what they produced to trade for other goods. Clearly the farming population had very little beyond what they produced for their own consumption with which they could use to buy other goods to enhance their lives. Comparing that to today's average consumer, the 1790 farmer was very poor only being able to eke out slightly more than a bare subsistence. Most of the remaining ten percent of the population in 1790, such as blacksmiths, sailors and shopkeepers, only had a small amount of their income available as well to spend on goods outside of the basics needs of food and shelter.

The majority of the population in 1790 spent most of their earnings on basic survival. This contrasts dramatically to the twenty-first century where a much smaller amount of income is devoted to basic survival. You might argue that a low income person is not much better off than their 1790 counterpart as ninety percent of their income also goes toward food and shelter however, that is not really a fair comparison. Chances are today in the United States, even as a low income person, your home is vastly superior to your 1790 counterpart... central heat, indoor plumbing, and others amenities. In terms of food, you are buying better quality food that is less risky to consume and more of it. So, even if you are spending ninety percent of your income for food and shelter, you are still significantly wealthier than your 1790 counterpart.

At the start of the twenty-first century we must be, on average, about eighty-five to ninety percent better off than our forefathers were at the time of the American Revolution. Over the course of time between 1790 and 2011 there were many labor saving devices brought into use as well as changes in the approach to farming. Most of these changes were mechanical in nature however, education and scientific development also contributed to the incredible growth in farming efficiency.

Progress in the technology of transportation and storage were also contributing factors to this growth in efficiency.

One example of how other factors, such as transportation, impacted farming efficiency is the development of the railroads which made the movement of food from one part of the country to another not only practical but also economically feasible. Prior to this technological development you could have a surplus food in one part of the country and a shortage elsewhere yet very little could be done to move one area's surplus to alleviate the other area's shortage. In effect both farmers and consumers suffered or thrived based on their area's farming situation. This lessened productivity because a larger number of farmers were needed in order to mitigate the probability of shortages which resulted in a waste of resources in areas during good years with bumper crops.

Economies benefit from new products and it's important to consider how new products come about. It's innovation that brings about new products and innovation itself is the product of mankind having the resources to devote to the pursuit of innovation. If you examine the past two centuries and consider the rate of innovation as measured in the number of new or improved products or processes that have occurred in contrast to the beginning of recorded history *(which for our purposes we will arbitrarily assign as five hundred B.C., through the dawn of the nineteenth century)* you would find that ninety-nine percent of what we use today was developed in the past two hundred years. This would mean that the rate of innovation in the last two hundred years is more than a thousand times what it was in the prior twenty-three hundred years.

Certainly the larger population accounts for some part of the increased rate of innovation but the greater part, I would propose, comes from another factor... I believe the real reason for the unprecedented growth in the rate of innovation is that during the past two centuries we have had the resources to devote to innovation that were previously not available. Some might disagree and argue that innovations have increased because humans have evolved to be more intelligent or otherwise more capable of innovation however history would indicate that exceptional individuals were likely as prevalent then as they are now, to what degree this is correct would be difficult if not impossible to quantify. One of the best known innovators in the past two centuries is Thomas Edison, do we suppose that there was no one approaching his capability in the many centuries since the genetic equivalent of today's humans arose. It's possible that an even more capable person lived in those centuries but could not devote their life to innovation because the risk of starvation and other life threatening perils kept that person otherwise occupied.

Just as in our Adam's Island example, it was only after life on the island became easier that the islanders had time to develop other products. The same is true in the real world, as man moved from being nearly totally consumed by survival to having an economy and a society that permitted time for innovation. Equally a part of this was the ability of the exceptional individual to rise up from and out of the masses to become an inventor. Many of today's inventions have come out of developed nations initially starting in Europe and the United States then expanding to include other developed nations. The pattern is clear; as countries joined the community of nations where there exists the freedom to demonstrate innovative capability, the right to be rewarded for exceptional ability, and there is the relative prosperity to allow these exceptional individuals to have the time to innovate only then did the monopoly of innovation move into more areas of the world.

Consider for a moment the small percentage that the United States population made up within the world in which Thomas Edison *(1847-1931)* lived. It's quite possible there were many more exceptional individuals who were born in that same time period who were trapped in subsistence lives in China, India, Russia, or Africa who could have advanced mankind in a similar proportion as Edison. It's possible that a serf in Czarist Russia may have been many times the inventor that Edison was but spent his or her life eking out the life of a sometimes starving, near slave in the totalitarian nation of Czarist Russia.

The point of the preceding paragraphs is not to dwell upon the lost opportunities of the past but instead to reinforce the importance of a free society and within that society the need to nurture the environment that allows for innovation. In a free nation, such as the United States, we need to consider what ingredients are necessary within a society in order to promote innovation. As with many things, what was needed for innovation in Edison's time, or in the time of da Vinci, is different than it is today. Certainly there are common factors, such as the freedom to be noticed as exceptional and the economic resources to allow the exceptional individual to innovate, both of which remain part of today's list of ingredients. Additions to the list are constantly coming along as the degree of sophistication of equipment and processes increase.

In the twenty-first century most of the relatively simple innovations, those only requiring a basic education and simple tools, have been developed, at least as a percentage of the total number of innovations being patented. The inventions of the twenty-first century often require an advanced education and expensive laboratories filled with complex equipment. This means as a society advances, innovations are no longer solely the product of the exceptional individual, but increasingly dependent upon support by the larger society. This leads to political arguments as to the role of government, business, and the individual in the process of innovation. As with similar issues, I want to avoid taking the side of either political camp in this argument but I do want leave the reader with the essence of the tough questions that are faced by the voting population as each voter tries to determine what they believe to be the right approach for their nation's position on supporting innovation.

Like many things, what is needed for a culture of innovation is not a fixed list but an ever changing list that requires constant maintenance just like a garden needs constant tending from an expert gardener in order to achieve the standing as the nicest garden in the neighborhood. Just like people in the neighborhood will expend different levels of effort on their gardens, citizens of a free society will put different levels of weight on the value of innovation. Just as some neighbors will have untrimmed bushes and weeds in their lawns while other lawns will be immaculate with perfectly manicured shrubs, so too some voters will have only a passive interest in this element of the economy. The argument being made here is that the informed voter needs to study the society in which they live… consider the role of innovation and how productive the society is in generating new products and other innovations while, at the same time, considering how well aligned the innovations being produced by the nation are to what that voter believes to be in the best interest of their society.

Consider as an example the Soviet Union of the nineteen fifties through the early nineteen eighties. In this time period in the Soviet Union, the communist government mandated that innovation in the nation be devoted largely to the space race and the weapons' industry. The Soviet leadership had the benefit of complete control over the nation's resources and chose to devote a large percentage of those resources to these areas of innovation. The population of the Soviet Union was larger than that of the United States *(not even counting the populations of the then puppet states in Eastern Europe from which the Soviets could extract the best and brightest to devote to the state dictated areas of innovation)*. But despite the clear focus and allocation of resources, the Soviet Union ultimately fell behind the United States and the weight of the Soviet Union's failure in this area would be a significant factor in the fall and eventual breakup of the Soviet Union. A book I found insightful on the factors leading to the Soviet Union's demise is <u>Farewell, The Greatest Spy Story of the Twentieth Century</u> by Sergi Kostin and Eric Raynaud. While the Farewell book is not focused on the economy of Russia, it did discuss the motivations of a Russian KGB agent who began spying for the West. The Soviet Union's society had become one where an individual's success was closely tied to cronyism. The book strongly implies that it was the social and economic barriers, created by the overwhelming influence of nepotism and political connections, this Russian agent found so frustrating and served as a catalyst for his turning against his country. This same culture no doubt had the same effect on potential innovators within the Soviet Union. As it relates to innovation in a modern society the truly exceptional individuals within the Soviet society had to not only have the ability to innovate but also the political connections along with the personal skills to navigate the communist political system. It's quite likely that what makes a great inventor doesn't typically include the political talents needed to get into the position to receive the education and attain a position at a facility devoted to that person's chosen area of innovation.

Like the untended garden mention earlier, the Soviet society was not maintaining the best environment for developing its innovators. The blame for this failure lands on the political system that allowed this dysfunctional culture to develop. The Marxist economic model certainly did not mandate a society where political connections would keep the exceptional citizens in Soviet society from being developed but, as in many societies including democratic nations, the political, legal and economic conditions are a reflection of the leadership of those nations. No nation can hope to fully achieve the ideal of having everyone make the most of their capabilities. This is again where the informed voter must make a choice and vote for the leaders who will best balance the many needs of society and provide laws that best balances the needs for a free society where innovation is maximized while still protecting individual freedoms such as property rights.

Implied by the concept of equal rights one could argue that everyone should start from birth with exactly the same opportunities. To do this would require, among other things, a one hundred percent estate tax and gift taxes to ensure no individual receives an unfair advantage on the road to success. Clearly this type of environment would not be acceptable for a number of reasons. It is somewhere between this untenable ideal and the crony state found in the Soviet example that represents the state in which the developed economies of the world exist today. My point is that it's society's responsibility to continuously consider the innovation environment and make sure this environment is regularly tended to so that society can continue to innovate and progress is made at a sufficient rate to bring each succeeding generation into a better state of being.

Chapter Twelve

(Corporate Governance)

You might be wondering how a chapter about Corporate Governance fits into an economics book. It's because business is economic theory in action and corporate governance, in an all-encompassing sense, is how economic theory is deployed in those larger business entities that make up the greater part of the overall economy. Just like government regulation impacts economics, the methods by which businesses are operated impact how economic theory is used in practice. Pure free enterprise is, in theory, motivated by pure success of the business entity as it serves its customers who have the freedom to buy or not buy. Regulations in general seek to modify the actions of businesses to remove, theoretically, those elements of unrestricted capitalism which are harmful to society as a whole. In the same way, those who manage businesses may strive to make the business successful or to seek some other objective including, among the worst case situations, to unduly enrich an individual or group at the expense of what may be best for the business. It is on this foundation that the means of managing businesses *(corporate governance)* is as relevant an economic topic as government regulation. While I'm not sure of the presence of any statistics on the subject, it is certain in my mind that as many *(possibly more)* businesses fail due to ineffective corporate governance as through oppressive governmental regulation. This chapter's goal is to shed light on the economic impacts of this seldom examined aspect of economics.

It seems everyone has a strong opinion on how corporations are run and what is wrong or right with their operation. Largely most Americans seem to be content with the assessment that the problem is either greedy CEOs or too much government regulation. Without any question both assessments are true to some degree but the more important question is why both of these conditions exist. If you are looking for someone to blame I would propose that all you need to do is find a mirror. After all corporations are made up of people, people own stock in most of the larger corporations, and we elect the officials who attempt to regulate the business environment within which our corporations do business.

The actions of corporations are guided by the leaders appointed to manage those companies. Every corporation answers to two primary sets of directing mandates, the first coming from its Board of Directors and the second are the laws of the nation or nations within the corporation operates. In our society the laws applying to corporations are often referred to as regulations and there are many regulations, most referring to the operation of the business with relatively few that relate to the corporation's responsibilities to its stake holders. The focus of this chapter will be on the role of the corporation as it serves and interacts with those stakeholders.

Corporations serve the interests of four groups of people... the company's stockholders, employees, management, and customers. From an economic standpoint each of these groups has an economic stake in the operation of the corporation. The company's stockholders have freely chosen to invest in the company and collectively they own the corporation with their interests represented by the Board of Directors. Employees work for the company and this work represents an effective investment of the employees' time and energies for which they receive compensation. Management is, in theory, appointed by the Board of Directors and is guided by the periodic meetings held with the Board. Customers are those people and businesses who pay the corporation for the products of the corporation's work.

Elsewhere in this book we have discussed the interplay between the other stakeholders so here we will focus on the relationship between ownership and management. In small companies, which are usually closely held by a handful of investors, the connection between ownership and the actions of management is very clear. In the smaller company setting, if ownership wishes to focus on driving maximum cash flow to ownership or increasing the company's market share, the conveyance of those goals usually flows easily between ownership and management. Ideally the goals of management and the needs of the society within which company operates would be aligned so that effective operation of the business would yield both maximum benefits to ownership and to the community where the business operates.

Throughout history there have been numerous examples where the needs of society and the business are at odds. Society has, in a number of ways, tried to place boundaries around business in the forms of laws or regulations that define what are and are not acceptable business practices. The adoption market is an extreme example… the legal adoption market is closely regulated but since the demand dramatically outweighs the supply there is an opportunity for immoral and corrupt people to exploit the imbalance by illegally procuring and selling children. Anyone who has had occasion to watch legal dramas on television has certainly seen a fictitious example of this crime depicted on the small screen and can no doubt appreciate that in the real world there exists an illegal underground market where unscrupulous people seek to sell children for large profits. Society has determined that the procurement and sale of children is morally wrong and, on that premise, is illegal and those involved face prosecution.

It is an acceptable objective, in most of the population's mind, for companies to earn a profit. Given that, it is generally accepted that management has strong motivation to improve the profitability of their company. Profitability is, in my opinion, a concept that is not as well defined as it needs to be. This is not only true as a general concept for the public but is equally true in the guidance provided by the company's ownership to management. Particularly the differences in long-term profitability, short-term profitability, and questionable profitability are all shades of what might be the profitability of a business. Most individuals view profitability in terms of *black and white* or *light and the absence of light* but, as a measure of success, profitability is proving to be a much more complex measure of business success. In some cases, stockholders may have seen the company they invested in as having a record year but what followed in subsequent years was a steady pattern of lost market share and profitability hence, what initially appeared to be good, was ultimately a false indicator of the success of the investor's money. To help put this into perspective, in the remainder of this chapter, we will explore some examples where corporate governance went awry.

Investors are not looking to be misled but instead expect indicators, like sales growth and/or increases in profitability, to be indicators of the health of the business and they expect that their goals and management's goals are in sync. Naturally not all investors have the same goals so, one would expect investors, with a desire for steady returns and long-term stability, to invest in stable companies and investors who are seeking higher and quicker returns, at the expense of taking on more risk, would choose to invest in companies who have that risk and reward profile. Anyone who looks at the literature which accompanies their 401K or mutual fund is presented with investment pools that reflect different variations of those two types of investment profiles. It's important for investors to bear in mind that within these variously labeled investment pools are individual companies who are managed by people and people don't always manage in predictable ways. Anyone who reads the literature regarding the 401K funds available to them or the prospectus for a particular company's stock will find descriptions in those documents as to risk and return profile for those investments. Sometimes a company's management can deviate from its expressed corporate strategy, as stated in its prospectus, which misleads investors, as in you bought what you thought was a low risk stock but the stock ended up being high risk investment. In those instances where the management of a company changed the business's strategy in a way not made clear to investors this result makes the investment process less efficient. Inefficient because the investor's expectation is not aligned with what the company's prospectus indicated. Being inefficient creates friction within the investing process that not only leads to investor surprises but subsequently leads to less future investment which then decreases economic growth. A simply analogy to this inefficiency in the investment process would be in the case of consumer going to the store to buy a peanut butter and chocolate candy bar and then finding when they unwrapped the candy bar that it was instead a toffee bar. Just as the investor might get lucky when their investment in the low risk stock *(that was actually high risk)* paid big returns so too the candy bar consumer might find, in their unintended purchase, their new favorite candy bar. It is however more likely that the investor and candy bar consumer will be unpleasantly surprised with the miss-represented purchase which will then lesson their likelihood to repeat those choices.

Late in the twentieth century and early in the twenty-first century there were a number of examples where the actions of a company's management were without question not aligned with the goals of the company's stockholders. A discussion on this point would not be complete without some reference to Enron, a failed American energy, commodities, and services company that's success and ultimate demise was attributed to "… institutionalized, systematic, and creatively planned accounting fraud"[5] In the Enron case let us first discuss one element of the fallout from this debacle… the dissolution of the company's former accounting firm, Arthur Anderson. For the younger reader, Arthur Andersen was at one time one, and possibly the best known, of the Big Five accounting firms. As are virtually all big accounting firms, Arthur Anderson was owned by thousands of partners who were either past or present

---

[5] http://en.wikipedia.org/wiki/Enron

employees and who, as a result of their success, had risen through the ranks and were awarded a partnership in the firm.

In a professional partnership organization such as Arthur Andersen, a major success measure accruing to any partner includes bringing in and retaining clients. It is within this element of the motivations of Arthur Andersen that ultimately allowed the partnership to be brought down. The Arthur Andersen partners involved with Enron, although knowledgeable with Enron's business practices, choose to continue to do business with Enron and, by doing so, become complicit in the Enron management's deception that brought down the company.

Maximizing revenues and acquisition/retention of large business clients were at least two high priorities that drove the actions of the partners at Arthur Andersen *(and other public accounting firms as well)*. Partners, at firms like Andersen, should be motivated to look at the long-term effect of their decisions since much of their retirement income is tied to the enduring value of the firm. As a collective group the Andersen partners should have been resistant to taking on business which would put their current and future incomes at risk. This should be especially true for retired partners or partners nearing retirement. Despite this clear alignment between the needs of the collective partners and the right thing to do for society, Arthur Andersen failed to act properly in its handling of the Enron situation.

What should have happened was, once any partner at Andersen came to understand the nature and extent of the fraud within Enron, that partner should have escalated the concern to the lead partner at the Houston, Texas office. Then, given the size of the revenue at risk and the potential for disaster, the matter should have quickly gone to the firm's headquarters for a decision which would have led to an earlier public disclosure by Andersen of the fraud present at Enron. This did not happen and, as a result, Andersen was disgraced and by order of the government of the United States was effectively put out of business. Beyond the survival of Arthur Andersen, why this is important? It's important because earlier notice would have meant less investor losses and, even more important, those investments could have been redirected to companies that would have produced real profits for the investors and delivered real value to the economy as a whole... a result that would have lessened economic friction and made the investor to investee process more efficient.

Returning to Enron itself, its Board of Directors did not protect the interest of the many people who owned or who were buying stock in Enron including the Enron employees. Many individuals who owned stock in Enron *(directly or through investment funds)* intended to have the stock provide long-term income. The concept that governs investment in business within the Western world, particularly the United States, is that investors are risk takers and that the companies, in which they invest, will provide them with information that accurately describes the business, including both the potential for profitability and enough information that will allow them to understand the nature of risk associated with that business. What made the Enron calamity financial fraud was the intentionally misleading information coming from Enron's management. Much of this financial information was audited by Arthur Andersen, who certified the accuracy of the information, and then this faulty information went to investors leading them to continue to invest in Enron. If accurate information had been presented by Enron's management to existing and potential investors it's likely that new investments in Enron would have stopped much sooner.

The Enron situation was clearly a case where the interests of management were not in alignment with those of ownership, more specifically those who held Enron stock as an investment. Most of Enron's management, the ones who knew what was going on within the company, did own stock but not as investment. By this I mean the stock was not intended to be held long-term for the Enron management but instead as a means of gaining quick cash compensation for those members of management. On the contrary, the rank and file employees were buying and holding Enron stock as a major component of their Enron retirement program.[6] Our goal in using this example is not to further highlight the Enron case but to better understand why it's important that, through corporate governance, the goals of ownership and management are aligned.

---

[6] http://articles.cnn.com/2002-01-14/justice/enron.employees_1_enron-shares-enron-employees-enron-executives?_s=PM:LAW

It's possible the early ownership of Enron liked the high returns they were getting on their Enron stock and supported management's actions solely based upon this performance. However, as the ownership of Enron stock broadened, it's likely that the average Enron stockholder would have liked to have had a balance between share value growth and the amount of risk being taken by management. At some point in the process, between the creation of the business known as Enron in the 1980's to its bankruptcy in 2001, the alignment between the desires of the majority of stockholders and Enron management were no longer in anyway aligned.

The role of corporate governance is to align the interests of management with the desires of the investor. Consider how well that role is being performed in our economy as a whole... this alignment is what keeps investors interested in investing in businesses within the nation they live. As voters, when we consider the politicians running for office, one of our obligations is to consider if the candidate's views on corporate governance supports our individual view of what we believe is needed in society. On a more personal basis we as individual, when investing in a business, should demand that any investment we hold be in companies that we are confident are being managed in a way that is in sync with our investment goals.

There are many factors that go into judging why the desires of ownership, society, and corporate management differ, one of which is time windows. As an investor, whose 401K includes stock in a corporation, your goal might be a long steady return on your investment in that company. As an employee you may either share that same time window for success or not.

Many years ago I worked for a company that acquired a manufacturing plant in small city in Kentucky. The plant had several hundred workers who had a much longer tenure than you would normally see in similar sized plants located in larger cities. This group of workers clearly had a long-term time window as they looked at their company. While this plant worked in a business line that was cyclical, often resulting in periods of layoffs and shortened work weeks followed by heavy forced overtime, these employees remained with the company.

The owners, of this one time closely held plant, made the decision to sell the business to a larger company. This new parent company *(which was where I worked)* was considered a fine long-term investment type of company, one that was quite popular with retirees because it provided steady income from both stock appreciation and regular dividend payments. In this case, the time horizon and approach to business for investor, employee, and management appeared to be in near perfect sync.

However, after a number of years, the parent company brought in a new Chief Executive Officer who wanted to grow the business rapidly. *(We can't pretend to know the CEO's motivations but later we will examine some of the possibilities)*. This change in focus altered how success was measured as it related to this business. The employees at the small Kentucky plant, along with the employees of the parent company, were now working for a business with a short-term success window instead of the previous long-term success window. As a result what employees and investors once counted on from this corporation had changed. Clearly management makes decisions of this type, not the rank and file employees, but one wonders if the owners of the corporation were aware of the impact this shift in strategy would have on their investment?

The many pensioners who owned stock in this company didn't know the company was making a radical change in direction.

While the annual report talked to the changes coming as a result of a change in management strategy, there was nothing in the report that would have alerted even the savviest of investors that, as a result of the new CEO's strategy, they, as investors, were getting off of a commuter train and onto a roller coaster. In this way the actions of this CEO were much like that of the Arthur Anderson partner(s) who put retaining a lucrative but risky client ahead of the associated global risk to the company's ownership without notifying the rest of the Andersen partners whose livelihoods were being put at great risk.

The parent company of the Kentucky plant was now embarking on a risky path that could potentially grow this sleepy pensioner owned company into a rapidly growing and vastly more profitable company. If it worked the pensioners would be seeing great increases in their stock appreciation and dividends but if it failed what they had been counting on as fixed annuity could now become very uncertain.

The CEO, after consulting with the Board of Directors, decided to pursue a billion dollar series of acquisitions that were largely focused on the same market that the aforementioned Kentucky plant served. A former boss of mine, who at the time was working at a leading competitor, was also bidding to acquire the same companies but he was consistently out bid by this CEO. And while he did not know at first who the other bidder was, he shared with me that the price being paid was significantly higher than he would consider paying for those businesses.

When we say management, or a CEO, consults with the Board of Directors or gains approval on an action from the Board of Directors what does that really mean? Boards can be very different from company to company. For example, if I wanted to play golf on a certain Sunday *(as opposed to visiting my aging parents or spending the time with my wife and children)* I might check with my Board of Directors before making this decision. If the Board was composed of my three golfing buddies I might get a different answer than I would if the Board was composed of members from my household. The same is true with corporate Boards of Directors; the Boards of smaller companies that are made up by senior employees with long-term ties to the business and hold large stakes in the business might provide different guidance than a Board of Directors that was hand-picked by the CEO.

Another example, suppose your company hires a new manager and not long after, this new manager brings in many of their former subordinates to work for him/her. As you might expect, this group of former employees is much more likely to support any changes that the new manager proposes. An executive I once worked with bragged to me that within six months of his being hired he had replaced his entire staff with people he had brought over from his previous employer. It's a strategy that worked for him but not one that I agree with for a number of reasons, primarily the same reason I made in my Board of Directors' analogy where my golf buddies would likely support my decision to golf whereas my household members might view things differently. My experience has been that, by working with an inherited staff, I received more honest and certainly more dissenting feedback on plans or changes that I proposed. These longer term employees also tended to share their historic knowledge of what worked and what didn't work at that company. In several cases, this candid and straightforward employee feedback, kept me from making decisions that would have not been good for the business and, by extension, for me professionally.

Prior to electing new Board members, Stockholders *(in addition to analyzing candidates' résumés)* should consider how well those candidates will represent the stockholders' interests. Board members are compensated for serving on boards in a number of ways and those compensation plans may not always encourage behavior that is aligned with the investors' expectations. If investors prefer a stable investment with steady returns, as opposed to having and holding a riskier investment, then the Board members should be selected to reflect that preference and compensated in a way that is aligned with those objectives.

If the stockholders prefer a high growth and high risk investment then the Board should be compensated based on delivering that type of high return and not penalized heavily in the event some of the risks taken result in losses or leads to the failure of that business. If, on the other hand, the stockholders of the company have a preference for stability and have a long-term investment window then the compensation of the Board should reflect that goal. In the case of a steady return and safer investment preference the stockholders should insist upon a Board of Directors' compensation plan that rewards profitability, not only in the current year but possibly ten or more years into the future, and avoid a compensation plan that provides stock options that could be cashed in quickly at the first sign of trouble. Obviously there are insider trading rules that prevent some of this but, rather than counting on generic national regulation to instill an alignment of Board and investor goals, Board compensation should be designed at the individual company level to reflect investors' goals. Regulation in this area would be ineffective and too restrictive on Boards of Directors as it would result in a one-size-fits-all situation whereas the economy and investors need companies that follow different risk level approaches.

Senior management, like the members of the Board of Directors, is also compensated with incentives such as stock options and bonuses. Today's media might lead many to believe bonuses and stock options are bad and represent excesses that should be unilaterally eliminated. Quite the contrary... incentives are effective motivators. Rather than throw the baby out with the bath water we need to dig into the details of incentives. Investors want Boards and management to be motivated to improve the business. The best way to motivate is to provide incentives. Like many things in life the devil is in the details, and that is particularly true when it comes to incentives.

For example, as a parent you may want your child to graduate at the top of their high school class. Putting aside the fact that the child should want to do well for their own sake, let's consider what might be the appropriate incentive for your child. Would it be effective to develop a single incentive that, if your child makes the honor roll you will immediately buy them the sports car of their choice? It's possible using this incentive tactic that, after you have already shelled out the money for a shiny red sports car, your child, having already received their incentive, has a change in attitude and ends up dropping out of school two years later... clearly this incentive, while effective short-term, is wildly ineffective at achieving the long-term goal of your child graduating at the top of their class. A better aligned goal would be to provide your child with the use of the shiny red sports car as long as they remained on the honor roll every grading period.

Back to the story of the Kentucky manufacturing plant and their parent company... as an incentive the parent company provided stock options to management *(including the CEO)* that provided lucrative payouts if the stock price hit a certain level. This was an attractive incentive for management as it provided a very handsome short-term reward that allowed the holder to quickly cash out the stock and bank the compensation. But, similar to buying your child the sports car after getting on the honor roll the first time, there was no downside for the CEO or management if the high stock price was followed by cataclysmic results in a future period.

The structure of the aforementioned stock option program is not wrong for every company situation but, I would argue, it was clearly wrong for this company. Without proof that the investor profile had changed, to one where the average investor was looking for a quick hit, the stock option program should have been structured differently in order to reward management for longer term success. One possibility would have been to not allow the stock options to be cashed out immediately but instead required them to be held for a longer period of time. For example, the CEO's incentive might have required that the stock be held for at least five years and then allowing no more than ten percent of the stock to be sold in any one year. The same could be true for bonuses. A bonus program could be set up to reward everything based upon achieving a high profit in a single year or based upon maintaining steady profitability where that bonus from year one is paid out in installments provided that profitability is maintained in the following years. Again, as with stock options, there is nothing inherently wrong with paying out large bonuses based upon short-term results if that result aligns with the goals of the company's investors.

So you might ask where does this leave employees when it comes to the alignment of goals or desired time frames as it relates to either long-term or short-term business success? Employees must recognize that their desire for stability versus short-term success may not align with that of ownership. In some cases government regulation seeks to protect employees from shifting management and investor risk profiles however, it is much more difficult and most likely economically inefficient to hope to align employee desires with that of ownership through specific government regulation. Mitigating this risk is probably best left to the employees; employees should periodically evaluate how well their employer's goals align with what their expectations. When the employer's goals diverge from the employee's then the employee should either attempt to negotiate a correction to their compensation package to offset the effect or choose to find an employer whose goals are a better match.

Chapter Thirteen

(Deficit Spending)

Deficit spending is a both a hotly debated and an often misunderstood economic topic. Many of us, even those of us who consider ourselves well informed, find the subject difficult to comprehend. Thus my task for this chapter is more than a little daunting.

Let's start by trying to frame up the concept in more personal terms. For this exercise we will consider the situation of a family household consisting of a wife, husband, two children, and one of the husbands aging parents. This family is made up by a husband and wife who are both working and each earning thirty-five thousand dollars a year. The family lives in a house they purchased ten years ago on an FHA mortgage with only a three percent down payment. The family at this point has good credit with only a small credit card balance of five hundred dollars and two car loans, one with a balance of five thousand and the other with fifteen thousand.

Both husband and wife have been in the workforce for fifteen years and have been contributing to their respective 401K plans at the rate of three percent of their salaries, the wife for fifteen years and the husband for ten years. The family also has a one thousand dollar savings account which they periodically take up or down based upon the family's needs.

Now that we have set the stage for our story's family let's consider how a nation's finances relate to this family's finances. The couple's combined income of seventy thousand dollars per year would serve the same role as a nation's tax receipts. In both roles the incoming cash, to the family as income and to the nation via taxes, is in fact very similar and as an example fairly easy to follow. The family has a number of items where they owe money to others... their home mortgage, the two auto loans and the credit card debt, similarly the United States government owes money to its citizens, bondholders, etc. The family also has their 401K retirement savings plan which in some ways correlates to the Social Security Trust Fund of the United States. You might wonder about this analogy but it makes sense when you consider that throughout the Social Security Trust Fund's history it has usually held significant surpluses of social security receipts over the actual social security payments being made.

Nations and families are similar in that each enjoys some periods of financial progress while at times also suffer financial setbacks. In the case of a country, like the United States, periods of financial growth is similar to periods when a family's wage earners are able to work overtime, earn high sales commissions, and/or receive bonuses. On the flip side, periods of recession or depression for a nation are similar to when a family suffers through a layoff, downsizing, reduction in hours, etc.

Families, like nations, must manage through their financial good times and bad times in a way that keeps the most important aspects of the family or nation safeguarded during bad times and good times. If our fictitious family was saving a portion of their incomes in a savings account during the good times then, when they are faced with a short-term crisis such as a two month layoff from one of their employers, they would have more options. Decisions families are faced with during personal financial crisis are not always easy, the family could force their aging parent to move out in order to cut their day-to-day living expenses, if one of the children was in college or in a private school the family could pull the child out to make up for the current shortfall in income, or the family could tap into the savings account. Every day in our society families have to make tough choices like these and their choice will depend on their individual family's resources and value system.

A country's government, the United States for example, also has to make financial choices but in a more structured and, unfortunately, a more politically charged atmosphere. In the event of a severe recession a nation might choose deficit spending as a tool to counter the recession's effects… that is, to spend more money than it has coming in for a period of time in an effort to prop up the society's economy. The time period, or what we might call planning horizon, for a nation tends to be longer than it is for a family. In the case of a family, the heads of the household have a discrete period of time where they can work and earn an income. This means a family has to make a plan so that, by the time the income earners reach retirement age, they have sufficient savings to afford the retirement they desire. This planning horizon forces the family to make difficult decisions at different times throughout their earning years. If, in the case of our example family, both wage earners are on a highly advancing income path the family may choose to go into debt to fund the best preparatory education for their children or to take that great family vacation to Disney when the children are at the best ages to appreciate it. Alternatively the family may choose to be more conservative with their spending in which case they might make less expensive educational or vacation choices. When a family is young neither choice is innately wrong, it's just a reflection of the value system of that particular family.

Nations too are faced with similar choices. If a nation is running a budget surplus, that nation can choose to bank the budget surplus, to save for difficult times, lower taxes, or increase spending on education, defense, park systems, etc. Those of you who are already parents know how difficult it can be to achieve family consensus on things like savings and where to spend the family's discretionary income. Logically then, obtaining consensus on anything within a nation, where there are millions of differing opinions, puts into perspective why economic and social policies tend to be such lightning rod issues within our national political environment.

In the case of a budget surplus, the government could choose to increase spending on educational programs or benefits for senior citizens such as social security. Fortunately national spending in these two areas are viewed by most of the population as a positive thing just as, on a family level, most individuals are proud of their ability to aid their older family members and help their children to get a good education. There are other examples of spending that also make it easy to see the similarity between managing a family budget and managing a national budget… investing in a good alarm system or, if you are so inclined, a gun and some target practice, is similar to national defense spending, maintaining *(repairing & improving)* your home is similar to the nation's spending on infrastructure *(roads, bridges and parks)*.

We, as a voting population, tend to approach political debates *(and our subsequent voting decisions)* about choices *(like those in the previous paragraph)* one of two ways… both of which are misguided. The first is that many voters, because the issues are complex, defer to experts they like and will, to a degree, blindly follow their advice. The second misguided approach is to focus on only one issue or a few issues and vote based on a candidate's position on that or those issues. The first approach is flawed because not all "experts" are created equal and the "experts" that are provided with a media platform are selected by people who have their own agendas and priorities which may or may not include the quality of the expert's opinion. The second and equally flawed approach, selecting a candidate based on their position on a single issue such as education, abortion rights, lower or higher taxes, is akin to using only a hammer for every home improvement project. Just imagine how well you would paint your bed room wall using your hammer instead of a paint roller.

Flawed experts have been prevalent throughout our history examples are so numerous it's a challenge to choose just a few as representative examples.

- Rasputin in the court of Czar Alexander of Russia, Herman Goring in Nazi Germany are but two of the worst examples of expert advisors who could have easily been improved upon.

- In terms of elected officials consider Andrew Johnson who proved to be the worst President of the United States. Andrew Johnson, the elected Vice President, was sworn in as President following the assassination of Abe Lincoln who was seen as one of our best Presidents. Given the proven capability of Lincoln it's hard to imagine, yet quite telling as a reflection of compromises made in national politics, why he would have selected someone like Andrew Johnson as his Vice Presidential candidate thus putting the nation at risk of being led by someone with such undersized capabilities.

- A more recent example, but one which has not yet proved to be a success or failure, is the financial experts chosen, by the Bush and Obama administrations, to lead us out of and to fix the failures in the nation's key financial institutions that resulted in the 2008 financial catastrophe.

In the book "The Big Short: Inside the Doomsday Machine" by Michael Lewis, Mr. Lewis explains that it may not have been wise to place so many Wall Street insiders like Timothy Geithner, Secretary of Treasury and Ben Bernanke, The Federal Reserve Chairman, in key positions for the design and implementation of the correcting regulations intended to fix the flaws in the financial systems which lead to the 2008 crisis. In "The Big Short" Michael Lewis takes the position that using experts who were so connected to the bad system was likely not the right choice for making a wholesale system makeover. Time will tell if Michael Lewis was correct in that position but for our purposes the example is one that's worth reviewing. Presidents George W. Bush and Barrack Obama may have taken the easy way out by choosing well known experts in the field rather than seeking out non-Wall Street insiders who would have been the more difficult or possibly the more controversial choice. The point is that voters and public officials need to be willing to expend the extra effort required to find the right experts, experts whose skills and experience match the task at hand. Much like the hammer analogy used earlier, if you want to fix a leaking pipe then a pipe wrench would be a more appropriate tool as opposed to continuing to use the hammer which may have made lead to the leak in the first place; therefore using financial industry insiders like Bernanke and Geithner might not be the bravest or best choice to complete a major remake of the financial systems.

Returning to the focus of this chapter, governments can choose to run deficits and accumulate surpluses just like a family can save for retirement or the proverbial rainy day as embodied by a period of unemployment. If a nation is in an economic boom period it should allow its tax and government spending structure to accumulate surpluses just like the United States was doing from 1998 to 2001. Economic booms for nations don't last forever so it's likely that the temporary surplus will be used during an economic downturn to pay for the higher cost of safety net programs like unemployment, food stamps, and Medicaid. The real test of a nation's ability to manage its economic house is in dealing with both the good times and the bad times.

The following graph shows how the United States Federal Government has performed in terms of managing its finances over the past one hundred plus years. This graph shows the annual deficit as a percentage of gross domestic product or GDP. Keep in mind as you look at this graph it's not shown in comparative dollar volume but instead the percentage the deficit represents in proportion to the GDP. This means that it represents relative over/under taxation or over/under spending or the more apt description as the mismatching of revenues to spending. Note particularly the periods of the two world wars *(1917-1920 and 1941-1945)* both of which were periods of massive deficits and both of which were followed by periods of surpluses where a good portion of those accumulated deficits were repaid.

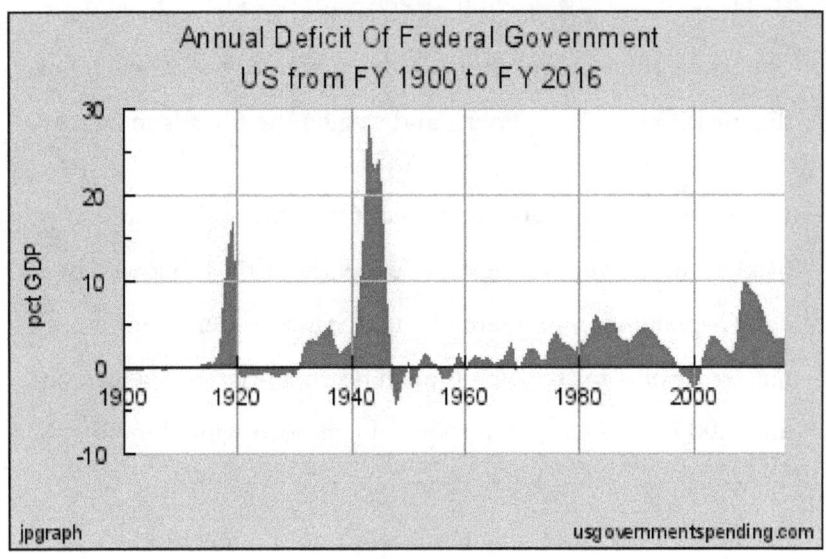

Most adults have personally experienced or have observed where individuals and families have not managed their finances in a responsible way. As an example a couple might receive a large tax refund in March and splurge on any number of luxuries then by September they are out of cash, behind on their rent, and are seeking help from relatives. In these cases those on the outside observing this irresponsible behavior wag their heads in dismay. When this happens to a nation, the United States for example, there is not someone the nation can ask for help but instead the nation must borrow money from either the taxpayers or from other nations *(both of which are usually handled in*

the United States by the sale of U.S. Treasuries) and it's usually the opposite political party of the one in power or the members of the media who are observing and waging their heads in dismay.

In the case of the United States government, we have a somewhat recent example of a budgetary surplus followed by deficit spending. In 1998 the United States Government ran a budget surplus for the first time in nearly thirty years which, up until 2003, was being used to pay down borrowing done for the many prior years of deficit spending. This might be the equivalent to our example family who, after a few months of unemployment by one of the parents, are now close to maxing out their credit cards. Once the period of unemployment is over one would expect this family, who now has ten thousand dollars outstanding on their MasterCard, to devote a good portion of their discretionary income to paying down the credit card balance so that their finances will be prepared for another potential financial reversal. However, the family might choose to defer paying down the credit card balance and instead use the remaining credit line available to them to take a celebratory vacation. Most people would suggest that paying down the credit card balance would be the more prudent and certainly the more conservative approach to addressing the family's financial situation.

Families make the choice regularly to celebrate the return to good times and, in a similar fashion, the United States reacted the same way to the 1998 surplus by passing a large tax reduction following the 2000 election when they could have chosen to retain the existing tax structure and spending levels in order to pay down the accumulated deficit from the prior quarter century. Admittedly it's oversimplifying the situation to purely equate what has come to be called the Bush tax cuts to a hypothetical family taking a celebratory vacation. While some believed the nation's political leaders were simply taking a politically popular action there were in fact a number of economists who believed that the 2001 tax cuts would bring about economic improvements.

Tax cuts unfortunately will always be the easy and consistently well received addition to many candidates' platforms and certainly no one likes to hear that anyone's taxes will go up, especially not when the potential tax increase hits their own pocketbook. Parents can identify with the situation facing a candidate running for election as it is similar to a parent saying "yes" to their child's request for a candy bar when deep down the parents know that saying "no" is really the better answer. The lofty goal I have for this chapter is for you, as a voter, to not always go for the candy bar but to be willing to rationalize what is the better answer for the country in the long-term when it comes to things that impact our pocketbooks. Unfortunately tax cuts will continue to be dangled by political candidates just like stores will continue to strategically place candy bars near the checkout lines.

Like the parent at the checkout, we *(the voter or elected official)* need to be able to say "no" to unnecessary spending or an ill-timed tax cut when the economy is at a place where the more austere approach would be better for the country. A parent may be thinking about the short-term expense of the candy bar cutting into the family's savings budget or adding to the net monthly credit card debt *(it's an expensive candy bar)* or the parent's reason for the "no" may be more long-term in that the effect of the unnecessary candy bar purchase would cut into the savings for college or retirement *(it's a really expensive candy bar)*. As a voter or public officeholder, the decision might be short-term in trying to balance the current year's budget or long-term with the goal being to manage the deficit so that it doesn't unduly burden future generations.

There is another aspect of deficit spending that is of critical importance to a nation dancing on the edge of too much debt. If a nation carries an accumulated deficit of a trillion dollars and the current average interest rate on outstanding treasury bonds is two percent then that nations interest cost for the year is a mere twenty billion dollars. Suppose the nation passed the point where investors were willing to buy the bonds either because the market interest rates were higher or the risk of default was higher. This happens to nations all over the world on a frequent basis. The fortuitous position of the United States has been one where U.S. Treasury Bonds have been, for many years, considered a safe haven investment and by that I mean they are largely considered to be a risk free investment. At some point in time, if the United States maintains the large deficits that we have had for a good part of the twenty-first century, there will be a point when United States and international investors will decide that U.S. Treasuries are no longer the safest place to park their money. In fact, in 2011 Moody's did down grade the debt rating of the United States but fortunately that move did not increase the country's interest cost.

If the market did change, for either the market rate of interest or the credit quality of the United States, the country's interest cost could change radically. The following graph shows the average interest rate on Treasury Bonds over the past one hundred years. In the example above we determined that a two percent interest rate would cost twenty billion dollars on a trillion dollar accumulated deficit. Suppose how the country's budgetary concerns would change if the interest rate on U.S. debt jumped to ten or fifteen percent?

At ten percent interest the cost of a trillion dollars of debt
would cost the United States a hundred billion dollars. The rate
of interest on U.S. treasuries in 2011 was at near record lows for
the United States but a quick glance at the preceding chart tells
us we can't always rely on rates staying that low so the deficits
of the early years of the twenty-first century could prove much
more difficult to manage if the trend changes to one in which
higher interest rates returns. Similarly a family with a hundred
thousand dollar mortgage at four percent, who can easily
manage their four hundred and seventy-eight dollar monthly
mortgage payment, can easily find, if the mortgage rate suddenly
increased to ten percent, they are unable to afford the increased
monthly payment of eight hundred and seventy-eight dollars.
What was an affordable home with an affordable mortgage can
quickly become too much for the family to handle. Fortunately
many families have learned to get a fixed rate mortgage to shield
the family's finances from the risk of a sudden change in the
cost of servicing the family's mortgage debt but many families
are still at risk for credit card payments that have rates that can
change rapidly. It's more this type of risk that a nation faces as
the country's debt obligations are constantly cycling with a
portion having terms as short as a few days and other parts of

the country's debt are on a thirty year maturity. As a point of perspective in 2008 through 2011 the average maturity of U.S. treasury debt ranged between forty-nine and sixty months. [7]

Given the relatively short time frame within which the U.S. debt has to be repaid or refinanced it is easy to comprehend how quickly the situation could change for the United States. Most voters recognize the risk of continuing deficits and the possible escalating costs in future years for programs like social security but less people recognize the risk element that exists for the interest cost of debt. Many individuals have experienced a situation where they borrowed at a low rate of interest only to find, at some point in the future, that they are paying much higher rates. For individuals these situations most often involve variable rate mortgages or credit card programs with low teaser rates followed by a change to very high interest rates.

An element of what happened in the United States in the 2008 financial crisis involved families securing low variable rate mortgages in the earlier years of the twenty-first century. These loans allowed families to buy more house, at the low

---

[7] http://www.zerohedge.com/article/maturity-average-outstanding-treasury-jumps-8-year-high

introductory rates, than the family could afford at the higher fixed rate mortgages. Unfortunately when the rates adjusted on these mortgages the rate moved to one that was higher than the fixed rate mortgage the family could have originally secured. With the higher variable rate many families could no longer make their payments and were forced to either refinance with another variable rate mortgage or lose their home to foreclosure.

Obviously this would be a pretty dangerous game for the both lender and homeowner but, during the early part of the century, home values were increasing at such a rapid rate that, even if the family paid little principle on their mortgage prior to the interest rate adjustment, the family may well have built some equity from the appreciation of the home's value. The following chart shows what was going on with home values during this period which shows why lenders felt so confident that there would be enough equity to allow the lender to recover their principle despite the increasing debt the homeowner had. At the same time lenders were earning record profits due to the fees the lender earned each time a home was remortgaged. The variable rate mortgage customers and lenders were both banking on a continuation of record increases in home values. The average person may not have taken the time to consider the fallacy of this approach, on the parts of both lender and borrower, but I would argue that it should not have been asking much for the appointed heads of our financial systems, senior leadership of the lending institutions, and the Boards of Directors of those same institutions to have had the foresight to see what was coming.

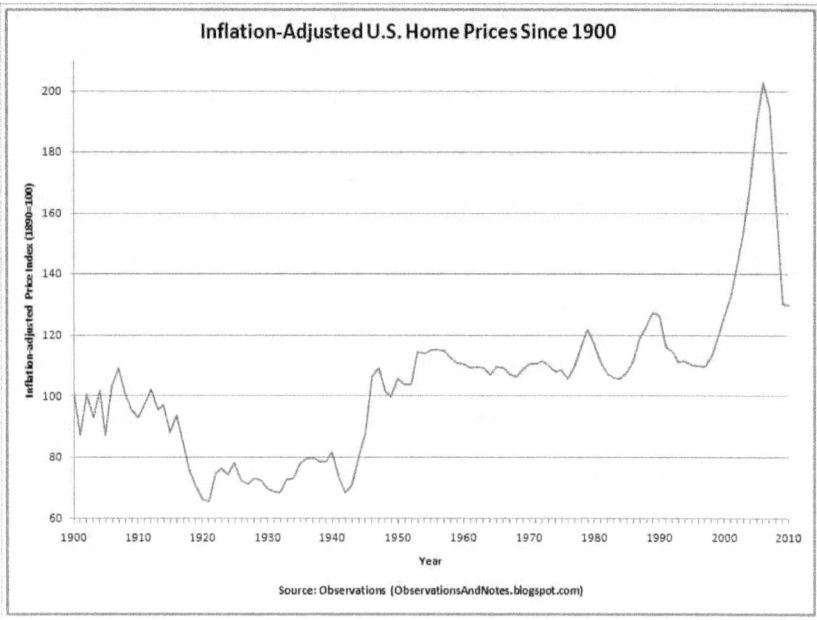

If this is the quality of oversight we can expect from the experts who oversee our financial systems then the concern of properly managing the interest rate risk for financing our federal deficit should be of great concern to every U.S. citizen.

Unfortunately, in the management of economics, individuals tend to look at things as they currently are or, at best, as they were in the recent past. In late 2008 I had the opportunity to attend a presentation put on by a large bank that was intended to educate those in attendance on what was happening in the world of finance with a focus on the developing housing crisis. The key slide of the banker's presentation superimposed a lifetime average over the period showing an average cost of a home, using the slide the banker predicted that there would be a serious price correction in the housing market. Obviously I too am playing Monday morning quarterback well after the game is in the books, but still I wondered, where this banker was with his prediction in late 2007. His foresight was not enough to protect his bank as it too suffered through its own large chunk of bad mortgages.

You may be wondering what this has to do with the deficit spending. The answer is that our government, in fact any government, has to deal with financial situations that arise. The financial crisis of 2008 was one of the more significant crises to occur in modern times and its effect is still being felt years later. Some would argue that the government did not have to, or need to, intervene in the manner it did which created enormous levels of deficit spending in the years to follow. Almost everyone would agree that the marketplace, if left on its own, would have suffered larger setbacks, setbacks that would have impacted tax revenue that in turn would have had its own impact in driving deficit spending. Following the crisis, the government would have lost tax revenue without the bailouts. AIG for example, would have been unable to pay the many speculators who held the infamous "credit default swaps". *(These derivatives were a form of investments made during the 2006-2008 period where investors/speculators were betting on the failure of the housing and mortgage markets)*. These "swaps" investments were paying off so big that AIG could not cover them. Without the government bailout funds, these investors would have not earned their huge payouts on the credit default swaps they had purchased and the United States government would not have received the hefty capital gains tax receipts from these investors.

A crisis like the one in 2008 again has its parallels to personal finances. For example, if at some point our fictional family had lost their home in foreclosure they would not waited to see what would happen next but would have instead look to manage the immediate situation by using the resources at their disposal to minimize the long-term effect to the family. They might have rented a motel room for a few weeks while they found a new place to live, traded in one of their cars for something less expensive, and looked for a cheaper home or apartment to rent while the family saved up to buy their next home. None of the actions are particularly positive or likely to lead to a quick fix but nonetheless are better than having the family sleeping in their cars until they could afford to buy another house.

The point I'm attempting to make is that deficits are likely to continue to present their bath of red ink as we continue to make economic mistakes *(hopefully not the same ones)* and the deficits, on balance, are not themselves the problem but our failure to balance out deficits with surpluses. Reiterating the point, just as families spend money obtained on credit then pay down that debt by using a portion of their current incomes to apply against the principle, governments and their tax paying citizens should be proud of running surpluses and having the strength to say no to increasing spending or cutting taxes until earlier accumulated deficits are paid down.

Chapter Fourteen

("Feudal" to Futile)

Within our recorded history, economic systems have changed
and by that I mean they have changed through a series of
choices. In economic theory, similar to the evolutionary process
where the fittest plants and animals survive, the better economic
processes survive while the less effective economic systems die
off. The system that was developed and sustained the longest
was the "feudal" system. This system came into being following
the fall of the Roman Empire and was in use to some extent
through the early twentieth century. The last vestige of the
"feudal" system was eliminated with the Communist Revolution
in Russia at the end of World War I.

The "feudal" system was developed and maintained based on
the use of force and a hereditary right to property. The
dominance of the "feudal" economic system, in Europe, also
coincided with the period known as the dark ages, a period
where the collective knowledge of mankind remained largely
unchanged. Most anthropologists would agree that man, in the
dark ages, was very much the same creature as today in terms of
capability and mental capacity. Given this, why did the western
society of mankind languish for around five hundred years in
the dark ages failing to move society's collective knowledge
forward? In this chapter we explore possible causes and parallels

to aspects of today's society, and in particular the role in which economics played, in keeping the dark ages so dark. Throughout this chapter and beyond we need to keep in mind that understanding mankind's history may well be our best means for determining what aspects we should seek to repeat and what aspects we should attempt to avoid.

In "feudal" times there was typically minimal, if any, central or national government and where there was it was usually in the form of some sort of king. Holding the most power over their subjects' lives in "feudal" times was the regional power of the lord. The "feudal" lord derived his power from the land which he owned. Those who lived upon the land within the lord's domain were his vassals. The lord made the laws as he saw fit and the people in the lord's domain filled their stations in life based upon the lord's direction. Certainly an able lord was more likely to prosper if he ruled effectively nonetheless not all lords were good rulers and bad rulers were very difficult to unseat. If you compare the situation in "feudal" Europe to eighteenth century America, a remarkable child born into the early American society was many more times likely to attain wealth and a leadership role than an equally remarkable child born to a lowly station in "feudal" Europe. Another way of considering this is a lord's heir, with little in the way of capabilities, was very likely to assume his father's role at some point, much more likely than the most capable of the serfs working his father's lands.

Since our emergence from the dark ages the ability of talented individuals to use their talents to improve their circumstances has been a cornerstone to the development of mankind. Most of what we hold today as knowledge in our society has come about in the past two hundred years. The centers for this development have tended to be in those parts of the world where the society was the most free and where self-determination of individual success within society was the most open.

During the dark ages there were no doubt exceptional people born in the dwellings of the "feudal" vassals and serfs, some with possibly as great a mind as Einstein, Edison, or Newton. So why then did no one rise up and make a noticeable impact during these five centuries? One reason might be that this society was rigid, in terms of religion, education, and political structure. You might say that this society was entirely focused upon the maintenance of the status quo. The truth is, there was so little recorded during the dark ages concerning the lives of the common people, that we can only guess at what opportunities even the most capable individual might have had and what change they could make on their status in society.

If we put ourselves into "feudal" times how do you suppose we would we feel? Let's suppose that a talented writer was born in the hut of a poor serf family in the south of France in 900 AD what chance would this child have to become any sort of writer. During that period education was only available to those in religious orders and a child from a low station in life would have found it difficult to join such an order. If this exceptional child did by some chance overcome the odds and become part of a religious order he would still have little choice in the type of education he would receive. Most likely his education would have focused on the bible and possibly have included some of the works from Greek and Roman classical writings. How could this exceptional author succeed in writing anything which would help brighten the dark ages? First and foremost the writer would need to seek a sponsor, as earning a living was an all consuming activity for anyone other than the lord's family. As a result the opportunity to devote time to enlightened study and writing existed only as a favorite in the most successful lord's courts or within the medieval Catholic Church and neither of these places afforded a fertile spot for the growth of knowledge.

In defense of the "feudal" lord and church officials, the dark ages was a difficult period where maintaining mere sustenance was a difficult challenge, one that quite often eluded many of those persons of lower stations in society. We can't blame our distant forefathers for placing more value on maintaining the status quo than on exploring the possibilities of furthering human knowledge. Success in "feudal" times was usually the result of a well-placed family and absolute military strength. As such, the requirement for having a great mind was well down the list of the needs of the "feudal" lord or church official. We can safely say that, unlike today where most exceptional individuals can become successful, in "feudal" times most of these exceptional people simply found their desires for bettering their position in life to be the most futile of endeavors.

In the twenty-first century there are thousands, possibly millions, of potential Einstein's being born every year and the degree to which our society is successful is dependent on these individuals being able to rise up to deliver the product of their gifts to society. The percentage of these gifted individuals afforded the opportunity to use their talents to our best advantage will determine if at the dawn of the twenty-second century we will be plying the universe in starships or mired in an energy deprived and polluted society well on our way into a new dark age.

Maintaining perspective is a critical part of our journey in learning how economics drives forward human progress. Within this perspective is our understanding of the element of degrees of success. Consider for example Russia under Stalin... here was a country who modernized itself during Stalin's rule *(1922 and 1953)*[8]. Does this mean that, as a system, communism was particularly great or that the authoritative leadership of Stalin was supremely successful? Without question the answer to both is "no". The Communist system, and the comparative openness to advancement within Stalin's leadership, was just dramatically better than the "feudal" society lead by the Russian Czars. The rigid society of the Czar kept anyone outside of the upper class from being able to be productive at advancing society or themselves. Once this impediment was removed the people in the Soviet Union responded by making rapid advancement.

---

[8] http://en.wikipedia.org/wiki/Joseph_Stalin

Whereas in Czarist Russia the status quo was held to the highest of regard and the concept of educating Russian serfs, to allow potential great individuals from that multitude to rise up, was not considered. The fact that Communism opened up, by a degree, Russian society allowing more exceptional people to contribute was successful in making dramatic improvements to the Russian society. Communism however, found that it ran out of momentum by the 1990s when the system could no longer deliver a better economy year-after-year. The Soviet society could no longer keep up with the free market economies because the Soviet version of Communism was no longer able to make effective use of their exceptional individuals… at least not as well as the free market economies were able to. Here again the Russians are not an inferior people they just suffered from living within an inferior economic and political system. Ideally every society would always open its doors to the best and brightest from within their nation as well as to those from other nations *(which has been the thing American society has done best in the country's comparatively short history).*

Has America made the absolute best use of its talent throughout its history? Obviously not, but America has done comparatively better than most other nations. As a truth this is evidenced, most unquestionably, by our higher standard of living. The million dollar question is… are we still doing the best at utilizing the talent we are blessed with or are we living off of past laurels? Only time will give us that answer. The critical concept we must keep in mind is that it's crucial for the United States to maintain a society where the best can rise up and make a difference. The greatest risk we have to our future success is not properly recognizing how our past success was achieved.

Returning to our island let's explore a possible example of how societies have, in the past, lost opportunities to have greater success.

After a couple generations our three families have settled into their new found prosperity which had been brought about by the advent of trade. (*In this scenario we assume the second generation of islanders decided that they had achieved the greatest possible success and needed to establish a means of maintaining this success.*)

The three heads of the families met to discuss how they might cement their achievements for generations to come. The greatest challenge was in assigning leadership for each family. The three considered what would be best for the future generations and thought it best to provide a clear path to determine who would lead each family as one generation passed on and another took its place. The three family heads agreed that the oldest male child from each family would, forever forward, become the new family head when the current head of the family died. Each agreed they would spend time and resources in teaching the eldest son the ins and outs of being the family leader, thinking that this would ensure good leadership for every subsequent generation. The female children would be free to marry anyone on the island and the junior male siblings would be subordinate to the eldest son of each family and would be required to work the family business for their entire life.

In the succeeding generation each of the families succeeded in having a male heir born to their family leader making the path to leadership very clear. The family of Fisher and Sheppard had eldest sons of good sense and with adequate intelligence however Farmer's eldest son appeared to be afflicted with a mental disorder which caused him to be erratic in his decision making and somewhat paranoid about his position of leadership. The parents of Farmer's heir apparent did their best to prepare their son for his role as leader and spent little time or resources on the other children in their family.

When the elder Farmer died, the eldest son took over the role of family head. Soon the output of the Farmer family began to suffer. The first year there was a shortage of wheat despite the fact that growing conditions were good. The next year Fisher and Sheppard began to work together to grow some of their own wheat. That same year there was a mild drought which minimized the effect of the additional wheat Fisher and Sheppard were able to produce and the continuing bad management by the Farmer family head resulted in even lower output from the Farmer farm. This all lead to an acute shortage of wheat on the island. Many of our islanders went hungry over the subsequent months. In the space of three years the island went from a place of plenty to one of scarcity and rising discontent.

As the next growing season approached the Fisher and Sheppard families met to discuss the loss in prosperity. They quickly came to the conclusion that their hardship was rooted in the new head of the Farmer clan. Their island rules of succession did not cover what to do when one of the families could no longer perform their part of the triangle of trade which was critical to the island's continued prosperity. The two families therefore decided on a two prong strategy to find a way out of their dilemma. The first action item was to augment their own wheat growing strategy which would result in both families working more hours per week then in the past. The second part of the strategy was to engage the other members of the Farmer family to find out what was going wrong.

One of the junior members of the Sheppard family had a good relationship with the second oldest son of the Farmer family and agreed to use his relationship to obtain information on the recent downfall of the Farmer family's output. What young Sheppard discovered was that, as hard as it was for the Fisher and Sheppard families, it was much harder for the Farmer families. They were very hungry all of the time and since they could not trade enough wheat for fish and wool they were in short supply of both food and clothing. The elder Farmer brother was not a good planner or manager, one year he waited too long to plant that season's wheat and the next year he did not save enough seed back for the following season's planting. Additionally, as head of the family *(which he believed also made him the sole owner of the clans land);* he felt that he, his wife, and his children should not have to work in the fields. The field work instead should be performed by the other members of his clan, his extended family, while he and his immediate family reaped the benefits.

The junior Farmer was a bright and hardworking man and was frustrated by the hardships his older brother had brought upon the land. It was with great distress that he suggested to his friend Sheppard that the island should consider removing his brother as the family head. Young Sheppard too was aghast by the thought of violating the succession law and was unsure how the family heads would react to the suggestion that the law of succession be violated.

The heads of both the Sheppard and Fisher clans were wise men who knew the heavy responsibilities that came with leadership and both leaders had already been questioning the law agreed to by their parents. Young Sheppard was relieved when the elders of the two families did not show revulsion when he relayed the younger Farmer's suggestion. This did however create a dilemma for the two family heads… by going against the law they would effectively nullify the law of leadership succession which meant that a new succession law would need to be developed and ratified.

The two elders, the younger Sheppard, and younger Farmer agreed to meet clandestinely to discuss what the new rule of succession should be. The two elders realized that the new rule would not only apply to Farmer's clan but to their clans as well. Fortunately the four were inspired towards a selection approach that would involve more members of each family. As was the practice with ancient Greeks[9], the clandestine group agreed that an election from all the members of the respective clans would determine each clan's new leader and that this election would be held every four years. Anyone over 18 years of age could vote and anyone over 30 years of age was eligible to serve as leader.

With clear concern as to how Farmer would react to the new leadership plan, the Fisher and Shepherd elders arranged a meeting to discuss the changes in law. Not surprisingly, the head of the Farmer family was furious with the suggested change but the other two leaders held firm and demanded that Farmer offer a free election within his clan too. Fortunately the

---

[9] http://en.wikipedia.org/wiki/History_of_democracy

elder Farmer's wife was a reasonable person and, especially after Fisher and Sheppard offered them an all-expense paid vacation to a nearby country, implored her husband to accept the demands and agree to the new law. Farmer's wife used the vacation as an opportunity to get medical care for her husband, which helped him better cope with the election results that put one of the other Farmer clan members in charge.

After a couple of harvest seasons with the new leadership the three families were once again in sync with production and trade and surprisingly they were finding new ways to grow the productivity of their island faster than ever before.

As we reflect on what happened to our island families, let's consider what might happen to our country if at some future time there were increased impediments that prevented exceptional individuals within our country from moving into positions of leadership or other positions that drive progress? We consider ourselves the land of opportunity but what if that opportunity for success was less equal than it is today?

Consider for example the accounting profession… within accounting there is a considerable emphasis placed on an individual having a CPA designation *(Certified Public Accountant)*. Now let's suppose the AICPA, which in the United States is the national organization of CPAs, decided that fewer CPAs would allow the remaining CPAs to demand higher wages. In this fictitious example, the AICPA decided to increase the educational requirements, reduce the number of schools whose degrees were an acceptable prerequisite, and dramatically *(by ten-fold)* increase the cost of taking the certification exam. The CPA association publicized that the new regulations for becoming a CPA were solely to improve the quality of service that members of the association would provide to the public.

These new regulations would certainly have an effect but not necessarily the one the CPA Association was hoping to achieve. By creating a steep financial barrier to becoming a CPA it's likely that many individuals from low income families may decide to enter other careers, careers without a steep financial barrier. This might mean that some potentially high quality accountants might be lost to other career fields such as marketing… good for marketing but not so good for those businesses needing CPAs. What affect will fewer CPAs have on businesses? The cost of hiring a CPA will most likely increase since there will be less availability but, even as the cost for hiring a CPA goes up, the quality overall of those services will be lessened since many exceptional individuals will avoid entering into the accounting field due to this new financial barrier.

Individuals in any society generally want to succeed, however the individual level of motivation varies greatly amongst the population. I think most people would agree that an individual's propensity to have the drive to succeed is equally distributed among the people of the world so why then do some societies produce more successful people than others? I would argue it is the conditions within that society that cause the different frequency rate of producing successful people. Individuals may have a great ability to succeed based on their intelligence and their drive but are limited to the level of success that they might achieve based on the opportunities that exist where they live or where they have access to live.

Suppose there existed a society that provided the ultimate level of opportunity for success… how many out of one hundred people chosen from a cross section of that society would succeed? There is obviously no way to get this exact number but it would be higher than any society currently in existence because all societies today have some impediments to allowing people to succeed. Just like walking up a gravel path versus a paved road, you can get where you are going on either one but one is going to be easier than the other. Using this analogy some societies would be more closely compared to the paved road while others would be the equivalent of climbing up the most difficult side of Mount Everest while blindfolded.

In a society where success is the most difficult to attain, achieving success may often prove to be allusive to the point where more and more of the society's individuals simply stop trying and accept whatever comes easier. Anytime a productive individual stops trying to produce society loses out and not just that society but potentially the entire worldwide economy. For example, if someone in Iran had an idea that would allow for the development of cold fusion but, due to the closed nature of the society, gave up on pursuing the research and development of that concept then that advance would be lost to the world, at least until another equally gifted person was born into the right type of society. Biographies of great people often show that they came close to falling through the cracks on their path to greatness and this certainly makes me wonder just how many great advances have been lost over the ages because the society in which these highly capable individuals lived frustrated them to the point where they lost interest in trying.

The title of this chapter, "feudal" to futile, is an attempt to bring to light how important a nurturing environment is to economic growth. Consider where you work, how well does your company perform in giving opportunities to the individuals who have the best idea? How often has an otherwise great idea been dropped because it runs into conflict with someone up the chain of command's personal values or ideas of what will work in their business? Fortunately in a free society there is an ability to move from company-to-company or from state-to-state so someone who is really committed to an idea can choose to leave their job for a place more receptive to their idea. In the United States society there are significantly fewer barriers to bringing into the light a new product or idea than in many other places in today's world.

Maintaining a society that enables exceptional individuals to deliver the benefits of their capabilities to society is critical if we are to maximize our economic potential. Avoiding the creation of a futility barrier ensures a more optimal rate of progress. Many things go into developing a climate that provides optimal economic growth. Among these are enabling exceptional individuals to take the risks necessary to bring their ideas forward. Throughout our history some of our greatest innovations have been met with various forms of resistance. Today, in most developed countries, there is some form of safety net that allows people to quit their jobs and try to start their own business and, while a person might threaten their quality of life by doing so, their family will not be at risk of starving or going without healthcare because they took that chance.

As an example, a person can start a business as a corporation thereby limiting their potential losses in the event that their business fails. Laws, such as the bankruptcy code, allow companies to take risks that owners and managers might not take if they had to put their entire personal wealth on the line. Looking back in history there used to be laws where the owners of failed business ventures could not only lose all their wealth and belongings but also end up in debtor's prisons. Societies in today's world all seek to strike the right balance between protecting those who hold wealth and debtors. Debtors obviously are not just people starting businesses but are also people who manage businesses as well as others who fall upon hard times.

This balance between the protection of existing wealth and debtors of all types must truly be an exercise of maintaining balance, for example, without police protection of property and money those who hold wealth could not keep it from those who would attempt to take it from their rightful owners. The other extreme on this subject would be the circumstances found in "feudal" times where there was virtually no possibility of wealth moving from those born into it to someone born as a serf. In "feudal" times it was futile for the gifted serf to attempt to gain wealth or seek to become the lord of the castle.

In the twenty-first century the opportunities exist for a gifted person born into the middle class to get an education at the best universities in the United States such as Harvard. A current example is Barrack Obama… born into a middle class family Mr. Obama was accepted into Harvard which created the opportunities that led to Mr. Obama being elected as the President of the United States in 2008. The opportunity to get into Harvard is open to the best minds in the nation however there is some level of preference given to the holders of wealth and in particular those children of former Harvard graduates. Keeping with the Barrack Obama example his two daughters will not need to be nearly as exceptional as their father in order to gain admittance into Harvard. Some might argue that opportunity to the best education should be based purely on the merit of the individual student and that wealth and family status should be ignored. Let's again consider a young Barrack Obama, possibly part of why he worked so hard to get into Harvard was to give his children a better opportunity. No one knows the right balance between the rights afforded to the wealthy and those people who are born with less, but it is important to recognize that there is a need to actively seek to find the right balance, and then attempt to move society towards that better state.

One of the most controversial topics in today's American society is the estate tax. I think most people agree that it wouldn't be economically healthy to establish barriers that didn't allow for parents to pass on some portion of their wealth to their children. Some argue that there should be a one hundred percent estate tax resulting in zero dollars of inherited wealth while others argue that there should be no "death" or estate tax. But how healthy would a society remain if it allowed wealth to be concentrated amongst a relative few individuals and maintained amongst that select few indefinitely? Wealth like any other resource needs to be economically optimized or, in other words, kept productive. By having the potential for new individuals to achieve wealth, while competing on a somewhat level playing field, serves to keep a society dynamic. A dynamic society makes for a dynamic economy and from the dynamism comes the best ideas and inventions thereby progress for that society.

Chapter Fifteen

(Free Markets and the Real Price)

As a person interested in the power of free markets, specifically in how the price of products are determined by the markets, I have wondered why some products have comparatively high prices when compared to others. Basic economic theory tells us that additional suppliers will enter a market whenever there is a better than average profit opportunity. Given this fact, one would assume that in a free market, competitors would be actively entering into a high profit market until such a time the price for that product or service fell to where the market price only provided a normal profit. That is in fact the widely accepted economic theory but in practice we need to keep in mind that suppliers are doing everything they can to maintain as high a price as possible, which to varying degrees stymies the natural workings of the market.

Often, in an otherwise unregulated marketplace, there exists ways that allow the producers or suppliers of a product or service the ability to maintain a price that provides more than this basic level of profitability. In this chapter we will delve into what is in the prices we all pay and examine some of the ways in which producers are able to extract a higher price from consumers.

Once again, using our Island community as an example, we will see how the method of marketing a product to a consumer can result in confusion and allow the true price of a product to increase or be maintained at a higher price than the normal supply and demand conditions would otherwise yield.

The Trader family has regularly been purchasing large quantities of wheat from the Farmer family for two Greenbacks per bushel and then reselling it for 2.20 Greenbacks per bushel. The islanders found that being able to purchase most of the items they needed, including wheat, at a single location was very convenient and for that convenience they were willing to pay the additional ten percent.

Over time the Trader family found that Farmer could produce more wheat than the island needed for consumptions so Trader began selling some of the wheat surplus to ships that visited the island. Eventually the reputation of the quality of the island's wheat spread to other islands and, as a result, Trader could easily sell Farmer's entire harvest of wheat. Trader soon discovered that the ships visiting the island were willing to pay a higher price for the wheat than Trader charged the islanders. Trader knew that the Fisher and Sheppard families would not tolerate an increase in the price they were charged for Farmer's wheat so Trader kept the island price for wheat at 2.20 Greenbacks but began charging a higher price for the visiting ships.

As the competition amongst the visiting ships increased, Trader was soon able to charge more than twice what the islanders were paying for wheat. Since the visiting ships didn't have the island's Greenbacks they would either trade goods or use foreign currency to purchase the wheat from Trader. The Trader family's success soon led to supply problems… often the Trader family didn't have any wheat surplus to sell to the visiting ships and Trader feared that these shortages would cause them to lose customers but, on the other hand, when Trader would get too aggressive selling to outsiders they would then not have enough wheat for their island customers.

The Trader family met to discuss their dilemma. One member of the family suggested they try to get Farmer to increase the wheat production by offering to pay a premium for any bushels they could produce above the current production level. Everyone agreed this would be a good idea and they promptly arranged a meeting with the Farmer family. At the meeting

Farmer agreed to increase production but, at their best, Farmer could only increase production by about fifty extra bushels per year. For these extra fifty bushels Farmer would receive three Greenbacks per bushel instead of the two paid for the normal production.

Following this successful meeting with Farmer, the Trader family returned to their store to evaluate their wheat inventory. They counted how much wheat they had on hand, calculated the number of weeks until the next harvest, and then estimated the amount of wheat the other two families would buy during that timeframe. Historically the Trader family would generally run out of wheat shortly before the next harvest but this time their calculations showed that they were going to run out of wheat several weeks before the next harvest. Trader knew that the islanders would consider this a major failure on the part of the Trader family and would no doubt lose faith in Trader's store. The Trader family considered their options and then the head of the Trader family met with the head of the Fisher family to ask their advice. Fisher suggested that Trader consider buying wheat from the Fertile Isle people as Fisher had once contemplated doing but, he cautioned Trader to first discuss the problem with Farmer and Sheppard given the resistance Fisher had met with when their family had previously proposed importing wheat from Fertile Isle.

Trader arranged a meeting with Farmer and Sheppard and honestly told them that he had sold too much wheat to outsiders and would like permission to buy some wheat from Fertile Isle to ensure that the island's store would have wheat available for sale until the next harvest was ready. Farmer and Sheppard agreed to allow Trader to import wheat from Fertile Isle on three conditions.

1) Trader must buy all the wheat produced by Farmer every year before buying any wheat from Fertile Isle.

2) The price paid to Farmer must stay as agreed… base number of bushels for two Greenbacks then three Greenbacks for the extra fifty bushels.

3) The price charged to the islanders must not increase regardless of the cost of the wheat from Fertile Isle.

Trader quickly agreed to all the requirements proposed by the Adam's Island families and soon made a trip to Fertile Isle to arrange for the purchase of wheat. Upon meeting with the heads of Fertile Isle he found that they had an excess of wheat but were in want of many other things. Trader offered to supply Fertile Isle with items from their store's surplus… some wool, dried fish, and other assorted goods that had been accumulating since they began selling wheat to outsiders. Trader and the Fertile Isle leaders quickly consummated their deal and the first shipment of wheat arrived at Trader's store the next day.

Since Fertile Isle always had an excess supply of wheat the price that they negotiated with Trader was equivalent to 1.50 Greenbacks. The Fertile Isle people thought they were getting a great deal and Trader knew that the family had turned potential disaster into a great increase in profit. They would sell the wheat for 2.20 Greenbacks but instead of making a profit of 0.20 Greenbacks per bushel they would now be making 0.70 Greenbacks per bushel.

The Fertile Isle people stored their wheat in special covered baskets constructed from the sturdy waterproof leaves of a plant that grew only on their island. The baskets were easy for the Fertile Isle people to make and, as such, they gave little thought to including the baskets as part of the sale of wheat. These baskets were not only sturdy and waterproof but quite beautiful.

When the Sheppard family next came into Trader's store to buy wheat they were quite impressed by the Fertile Isle basket. Sheppard inquired if the 2.20 Greenbacks included the basket itself. Trader being a wily business person said that to keep the basket would cost an extra Greenback. Trader kept a straight face until Sheppard left but then allowed his true emotions out as he immediately announced to the family that they were now making 1.70 Greenbacks on each of the Fertile Isle bushels of wheat they sold. The family was very happy with the turn of events that would now greatly enrich the family. They also anticipated that, because of the baskets, the islanders would prefer to buy the wheat imported from Fertile Isle which would then allow Trader to sell more of the Adam's Island's wheat to the visiting ships.

Given what we have learned thus far about how economics works in a free market it's difficult to believe that a retailer, like Trader, could maintain such a high profit margin. To understand how this can happen let's examine the marketplace Trader is working within.

[Trader has the only store on the island but the islanders can trade amongst themselves if they choose to do so. The islanders have agreed not to trade directly with Fertile Isle but have agreed to let the Trader family do so as long as Trader adheres to very strict parameters that have been set and agreed to by the other families on Adam's Island.

Unknowingly, in their desire to protect their island market from competition, the islanders have given the Trader family a monopoly on the wheat trade both import and export and, as a result, are paying much more for wheat than the market would dictate. Trader has full control, a monopoly, over the price of wheat being sold to visitors to the island.

By not opening up the opportunity to sell island wheat directly between Farmer and the visiting ships Trader has been given full control over pricing and is only limited by what the visitors to the island are willing to pay.]

In the real world there are many examples, in varying degrees, of monopolistic pricing controls. A recent example is the De Beers diamond cartel who for many years, up until the year 2000, had effectively maintained a monopoly on diamonds[10]. This cartel had controlled much of the world's distribution of

---

[10] http://en.wikipedia.org/wiki/De_Beers

diamonds and actively managed the supply of diamonds to keep prices high. Like Trader's control over access to the island's wheat, DeBeers controlled the flow of diamonds into the world's jewelry markets. What would have happened to the diamond market if the world's diamond mines had sold their production of diamonds to multiple distribution companies? Prices would certainly have gone down but, that would not have been the full extent of what would have happened within the diamond marketplace.

We consumers tend to be rather fickle in our purchasing decisions and if the diamond distribution market was suddenly hit with a flood of diamonds it's very possible that diamonds might have lost part of their allure as premium jewelry. Rubies, for example, might become more valuable and possibly replaced diamonds as the jewel of choice in engagement rings. Between the glut in the supply chain and the loss of the engagement ring market the price of diamonds could have dropped radically, something the De Beers cartel had successfully prevented for decades.

In fairness one of the reasons the diamond has maintained its appeal has been that diamonds are scarce and mining diamonds in quantity is difficult and expensive. On that basis alone diamonds have remained and are likely to remain expensive but, even so, the market price was undoubtedly higher during the period the De Beers cartel held a monopoly on distribution. The De Beers control of diamonds in the real world economy was very similar to the control Trader had with the wheat in our island economy.

The influence that De Beers and Trader had on their respective markets acted as friction on the economy specifically as it relates to the trading and production of the commodities they held control over. It's easy to see how a party, with monopolistic pricing control, can affect pricing but how do they affect supply? In the case of the De Beers they would buy the production of the world's diamond mines and strategically release price optimizing quantities into the market in order to maintain the price De Beers wanted. If De Beers had not bought the bulk of the worldwide production of diamonds then one of at least two possible changes would have occurred... 1) the diamond mine would have run out of cash and gone out of business or 2) the mine would have found another avenue to market. If the diamond mine were to go out of business production would go down but the De Beers' monopoly on supply would have been maintained. However, if the mine sought out another distributor or sought to sell the mine's diamonds directly into the diamond market there would suddenly be two places diamond cutters and sellers could go to for diamonds and what had been a simple monopolistic marketplace would now be one where there was competition… this is exactly what happened after the year 2000 when the De Beers' monopoly was broken.

Once competition is brought to a previously monopolized market the price of the product will usually decrease. The current diamond marketplace has more competition than it did prior to 2000 but it is still a large market with a small number of distributors and it would be more accurate to refer to the diamond market as monopolistic competition. If the diamond marketplace had been fully opened up with numerous distribution companies vying for the retailers and diamond cutter's business then possibly we would have seen a greater drop in the retail price of diamonds. If this type of change would someday occur what would the likely effect be to the diamond marketplace?

Starting at the end of the process, the supply of diamonds in the retail market would initially increase and consumers would be able to buy diamonds at a lower price.

- Retailers would most likely continue to make a reasonable profit since their pricing and profit margins would stay the same. Why, one might ask, wouldn't the retailers just keep the prices to the consumers the same and keep the difference as added profit? The answer is simple, the business of diamond retailers is very competitive and as a result retailers must compete for consumers' business and competition drives prices down.

- Distributors would now pay a market driven price to producers *(the mines)* and must sell at a competitive price to the retailers and cutters so the cost of a diamond staying in the hands of the distributors would go down drastically.

- Mines would now be paid a price determined by a more pure supply and demand relationship, the new price may be lower than before since the price is now set by the market rather than by De Beers and the handful of other distributors.

Of the three steps in the pre-2000 diamond supply chain, the price paid to producers is likely to be the most subjective *(it's possible that the role of DeBeers monopoly might have been to hold down supply by paying a lower price to producers and then holding down consumer demand by artificially keeping prices high)*. If, in a free market, the demand for diamonds increased then prices would increase and that increase might flow quickly to the mines which could lead to increased exploration for new mines or additional investment in existing mines.

In short, wherever a monopoly is held in any one step of the supply chain an inordinate and artificial level of profitability will be maintained at that step in the process which works to the detriment of consumers and possibly to those parties elsewhere in the supply chain. In a free working market, prices will go down to where there is only a normal level of profit at each step in the distribution chain... in the case of the diamond market this might mean that a much larger share of the final price to a consumer would flow to the mines. Does this mean the mines will now make the higher profit once going to DeBeers?

Probably not, the larger piece of the end price will temporarily drive higher profits which will be followed by new producers entering the market and/or increased production by the current mines. Ultimately the market would settle into equilibrium where all steps in the supply chain would earn a normal profit.

In the real world, during the DeBeers monopoly, the supply of diamonds was always available to consumers but the price was also steadily increasing. Within this set of circumstances DeBeers, up until 2000 and now with the few additional distributors, are protecting the diamond market from production fluctuations. In a marketplace that is not restricted by a monopoly, changes in supply can and do quickly flow through to the end consumers in the form of new prices. If you consider the crude oil market where every change, be it political instability in a producing country or the tapping of a newly found oil field, will quickly affect the price paid by consumers. If there were the equivalent of a De Beers in the oil marketplace, crude oil would be maintained at a higher price, one that restricts demand more so than a freely flowing marketplace, but the price consumers pay would be more predictable. One result would be changes in oil and gas prices would seldom be in the news.

You may ask if De Beers had been doing something which is rare in the marketplace. The answer to this question is "no", all companies operating in all markets are trying to find ways to develop and maintain a higher price for their step in the process. Again using the crude oil marketplace as an example, there was a point in time when the oil producing countries were more in control of supply than they are today. These countries agreed amongst themselves on a level of supply by putting production quotas on what each nation would sell to the consuming nations. Political pressures on the oil producing nations has kept this consortium of oil producing nations from being as effective as De Beers had been but to some extent these nations are still influencing supply and thereby the price paid by consumers.

Other means of controlling pricing are used by companies to avoid the effect of a purely market driven price for their products. Breakfast cereals are a good example of this. This market is largely controlled by a handful of large food companies with very recognized brands and only a small part of the market is held by lower priced store brands and generic brand cereals. These lower priced alternatives have been in stores for many years yet, based upon the amount shelve space devoted to each cereal, the lion's share of the market remains with the well-known national brands. How do the major brands convince consumers to pay more for what is largely the same products?

The major brands use advertising to differentiate their name brand cereal from the generic equivalent. If you are a fan of an o-shaped cereal with a honey bee as its spokesperson you may well buy the name brand cereal despite the availability of the lower priced generic or store brand alternative. Your reason for spending the extra cash on the name brand may be for a variety of reasons. One of the reasons might be that you as a consumer believe the quality of a name brand product is higher, the higher price and higher profile of the name brand infers higher quality although more than a few store brands have advertised to the contrary. Another reason is peer pressure, as an adult shopping you may be embarrassed by having a shopping cart with generic or store brands in your cart or as a kid with a friend spending the night you might be mortified by bringing out a bag of generic O's.

Another factor in the buying decision you make may be the packaging of the product. Often the packing used by store brands and generics is to varying degrees less significant than the major brands. Admittedly I, as a consumer, am very price conscious and buy my favorite cereal as a generic in a bag on the other hand, my wife being a fan of the O cereal with the honeybee mascot insists on the name brand for her consumption. When I was putting up the groceries my wife's box of O's fit neatly into the cabinet while my bagged generic slumped over interfering with the access to my wife's O's. Inconvenient result yes, agreement on the inconvenience being worth the savings is clearly a matter of opinion and since this is my book not my wife's the definitive answer is the savings far exceeds the benefits lost due to the lack of neat placement in the cabinet. *(Sounds like time for a kitchen remodel, clearly someone forgot who their editor is).*

Circling back to our island we saw the first sign of packaging consciousness when Sheppard choose to buy the Fertile Isle wheat because of the basket in which it was packaged. You might argue that there is difference here between the wheat basket and cereal packaging in that the basket might have future utility to Sheppard where my wife's O's box will quickly end up in our recycling bin once it is empty. There is some element of similarity in both situations. Let's say my book flops, I lose my day job, and my wife's business is unable to support us in the manner to which we have become accustomed. This may cause my family to buy more generics than we currently do since we will no longer have a margin of excess income over what it costs to meet our basic needs.

Sheppard too, at one time, struggled to meet the family's basic needs and having a pretty basket was not part of what they would have been willing to work harder to procure. Later Sheppard, because they have excess income, may choose to spend the extra Greenback to buy the wheat in the pretty basket just like my wife chooses to spend the extra money to buy the nice rectangular box with all the clever marketing materials printed on its six sides. The wealthier an economy is, the more opportunity there is to steer consumers to a higher cost alternative like the pretty basket or a well-designed cereal box.

These are but a couple of the examples of how producers keep prices higher allowing the producing company to retain a higher level of profitability. Marketing methods, including advertising and packaging, allows the party in control of product access to demand and receive a higher price than if that product was priced solely upon the commodity it is. Arguing the benefit of branding products and developing a preferred place in the mind of consumers is outside of the scope of this book. Let's suffice to say that every company's motivation is to make a higher profit, sometimes that is accomplished by providing product or production innovations that provide the consumer higher value and in other cases the higher price is largely for the perception the company has been able to create amongst consumers even though the extra value is less tangible.

What are the impacts on the economy if a producer or retailer is able to earn higher profits than the normal profit for a product or service? The answer to this question is more than a little complicated. Let's use a drug company as an example. If the drug company earns a fifty percent profit on a new drug, whereas the normal profit is ten percent, then you could infer that the extra forty percent in profit represents unneeded friction on the economy. But that answer is almost certainly not true. In the worst case, let's say the profit is retained by the company and put into a savings account. *(There are a number of impacts here to the supply of money from the effect of funds being available for lending and etcetera but that is outside the scope of our text so we will keep it simple and suppose that forty percent goes into the bank and is held out of the lending and spending processes).* Given this you would suppose that this profit does nothing to further benefit the greater economy which is way too pessimistic of a view.

We can generally accept that what we described above is the worst case result of the higher profit going to the drug company. If instead, this added profit is distributed to ownership then this profit is now in the hands of potential consumers who could then use it to make purchases in the marketplace which would largely serve to allow the added forty percent premium to flow through the economy driving growth elsewhere. If the investors are wealthy it might drive the purchase of a seven hundred series BMW instead of the five hundred series, a mid-income investor may choose to upgrade their home, take a vacation, or add to their 401K investments. You can argue the merits of any of these benefits flowing through to investors as not being as valuable as keeping the price of the new drug low but that takes us down a more political path than the I want to explore in this book.

As a third alternative we could imagine the drug company's primary motivation is to develop new drugs and grow revenues instead of retaining profits or distributing the profits back to investors. If the company is successful in developing new drugs and thereby improving the health of the world, is that better for the world than having sold the original new drug for at the normal ten percent profit level? There is not an absolute answer to this question as it depends on the drugs being developed and the utility of those drugs to the world's population. In this context utility is an abstract concept of value. For example, if you live in the United States and one of the drugs developed through the investment of the higher profit is for malaria then as an American your utility or benefit would be largely as an intangible since malaria is a third world disease. In the case of Americans their direct utility would come from knowing that people in other parts of the world would be spared this disease in the future. Indirectly, if people in the third world are not battling malaria, they may be in a better position to be more productive, better educated, and better consumers of American goods and services.

The price of prescription medicines, especially since the pharmaceutical company holds exclusive manufacturing rights during the twenty year following the awarding of a patent[11], is set on largely monopolistic terms. Like other patents, the

---

[11] http://en.wikipedia.org/wiki/Generic_drug

concept is to protect the company or individual who developed the product or concept. In the case of drug companies, they invest huge sums of money to develop a drug and are compensated for taking on the expense and risk of development for the opportunity to enjoy the potential higher prices during the period of the patent's protection.

The higher price of new drugs is a controversial topic and the arguments on both sides are quite valid. Let's say a fictional drug was developed that was fifty percent more effective in the treatment of cancer than any other drug available. What price for this drug would generate the optimal profit for the company that developed it? Absent other factors the price the market would be willing to pay would be very high. But let's look at the human cost... let's say that the optimal price would leave one hundred thousand cancer patients unable to afford the medicine. If the other alternative medicines would be effective in treating sixty percent of these patients, whereas the new drug would have saved ninety percent, then the price that allowed for optimal profit would cost society as a whole thirty thousand lives.

If you stop our examination after the last paragraph then you would castigate the drug company executives for their callous drive for the extra profits, however let's take this a step further. Suppose the success of this cancer drug drove the company to fund and successfully develop a drug to treat heart disease which saved a million lives. In this course of events the self-serving executives would now be credited with being wise stewards of the company they were charged with managing and on a net basis saved nearly a million lives from the development of these two new drugs.

Given that either of these results could have driven the unusually high profit for this fictional pharmaceutical company, it's easy to see why people on either side of the argument for regulation and pricing controls on drugs can become so passionate. As voters and consumers all we can do is realize there is risk of both great good and great greed and all we can hope to do is to promote an economic environment that optimizes the value the pharmaceutical firms deliver to our society.

Obviously, just considering these few examples, most would agree that what is fair and what could or should be regulated is a complicated set of circumstances. It is this fact I would like you, the reader, to take away from this chapter. Simple answers are more comfortable in this part of the economic debate but unfortunately just employing any one of the simple answers will do more harm than a more studied response. Efficient pricing can be defined as the pricing that yields the most utility to society whatever the market. The market often can deliver the best price but, particularly when we attempt to regulate the free market to meet social objectives, it becomes a more complicated and risky affair.

As you consider the benefits of an efficient economy at a macro level, which ultimately leads to driving prices down to eliminate excessive profits, there are merits in some cases to having higher profitability that allows businesses to invest in research and development, like what we examined in the case of the drug company. In a later chapter we will dig deeper into the financial impacts of how high profitability may cause excessive friction on the economy and prevent the free flow of financial funds to places where it can be put to the best use in the economy.

Chapter Sixteen

(The Economics of Branding)

Depending on your perspective, or your line of work, the concept of questioning the economic effects of great marketing may generate a defensive response. If it feels as though I'm treading on hallowed ground I would ask that you, at least temporarily, try and look at this subject in a neutral manner. Honest consideration of both the good and bad effects of effective marketing is important in the understanding of pricing and the absolute efficiency of the economy.

Shoppers, whether an individual shopping for their family's groceries or a purchasing manager of a major corporation who is preparing to conclude a multi-billion dollar contract, all go into the buying decision process with some element of baggage. Euphemistically when I say baggage I mean personal knowledge or experience that may get in the way of our ability to make an effective decision. This baggage can consist of things beyond branding, things that can cross the very faint gray line where we leave the effective marketing of a brand and move into something that might be considered illegal or immoral.

Advertising, in almost any form, is paid by the maker or developer of a product and is an expense used to build a brand. Gray line items could include everything from the promotional pen given to the buyer or their employees, dinner for the purchasing manager, free samples to consumers, up to outright bribes to people making purchasing decisions. It should go without saying that at some point between promoting a product with a magazine advertisement and bribing the purchasing agent is that line where the effort of product marketing and promotion goes too far.

There are many sides to building a brand some of which are not overtly obvious to the majority of the population. Let me add a personal experience that will hopefully bring some context to the discussion or at least a little color.

Early in my career, in my first job as a financial controller, I came to be responsible for my company's logistics which included the selection of freight carriers to transport the company's products. This responsibility came to me after a downsizing that eliminated the warehouse manager's position, the position that had previously held sole responsibility for choosing the company's freight carriers.

I quickly learned that we were paying too much for our trucking costs and decided to investigate other options. Never having been knowledgeable on the subject of freight or the trucking industry I approached this task much like buying groceries for my family. I checked with a couple of different trucking companies, asked for pricing quotes, spoke to our operation's people about on-time delivery reputations, and identified what the acceptable parameters *(i.e. delivery time between locations, types of equipment, etc.)* were in terms of working with various trucking companies. After analyzing all the information I selected two carriers, one for our small load or LTL *(less than truckload)* and the second for full truckload shipments, which reduced our total freight costs by about thirty percent.

A few months later another salesperson from a different LTL trucking company came into our office to meet with me in order to try and obtain our business. Here is where the story becomes a bit colorful, this salesperson was a young lady dressed as if she was ready to hit the local clubs on a Saturday night. She was without question one of the most motivating women I had seen in quite some time. A few minutes into our meeting, I noticed through my office glass, that the hallway traffic had picked up dramatically with every guy in my office, several times during my twenty minute meeting, suddenly needing something on the other side of the office.

Throughout the meeting the salesperson was very professional in presenting her company, assuring me that her company could do a better job handling our trucking business than the LTL Company I had already selected. I was very clear in this discussion that we had achieved substantial savings when moving to our new trucking arrangement. This fact did not dissuade her as she was certain that her company could do even better. After some discussion I agreed to try a shipment with her company. The question I have for this past me is… would I have been willing to give this company a try if the sales representative had been a man instead of an attractive young lady? Marketing strategies like these, that are intended to distract buyers from the product, are also intended to attract a broader audience in order to garner support. For example, within minutes of this salesperson's departure the company's number two executive, who also happened to be our company "wolf", stopped by my office to ask all the vital questions including "who is she" and "when will she be back". Clearly he was letting me know how he would like me to make that particular buying decision.

True to my word I arranged two identical shipments, one with our current freight company and another with this young lady's company. Within a few days both freight bills came. Being a numbers' person I was not surprised, but also a guy I was disappointed, when I compared the two invoices and found that the trucking company with the really hot sales representative was about twenty percent more expensive than the company I had already selected. A few days later I received a phone call from the perspective freight company representative and she asked if we would be moving our business to them. I told her that unfortunately their rates were twenty percent higher than the other company and unless they could beat our current LTL's price we would not be changing freight carriers.

As I learned more and more about the trucking business I came to understand that trucking companies marketed their companies in different ways, while some competed with a focus on service and price others tried to lure new business with invitations to lunch or golf outings or, like in the previous example, by having young attractive sales ladies represent their companies.

How did my decision to go with the more economic LTL Company impact my two main customers, the ownership of the company and the end customer *(those who bought our product)*? The ownership of the company clearly benefited from the savings on shipping costs which translated into pure bottom line savings and since our costs were lower the pressure to raise our prices or find a cheaper but less effective carrier was avoided. In pure economic terms the low cost, quality freight carrier was best for ownership and the company's customers.

What happens when a decision is made for reasons other than factors that impact the price, quality, and delivery of a company's product? Suppose I made a freight carrier decision based on which company would provide the most side benefits to me and the company's staff. In this case we might have selected a company that provided doughnuts to the staff every week, baseball tickets a few times a year, and or "eye candy" for the office wolf. If I had gone this route it's possible the staff would have been more motivated, maybe even delivered more sales as a result, but most likely it would have resulted in lower profits and less value delivered to our customers.

Let's examine another scenario. You're grocery shopping and one of the items on your list is "cereal for the kids". Now just before you left home, you saw your children watching a named brand cereal commercial advertising that they were now putting a toy from your children's newest favorite movie into every box. As you approach the cereal aisle you see the brand from the commercial and right next to it is the cereal's generic equivalent. Which do you buy? If your family was down economically, to your proverbial last dollar, and the package of generic cereal was half the cost of the name brand you would probably buy the generic. However, if you were independently wealthy, the value you would get from pleasing your children with the cereal that comes with the toy would probably be more valuable to you than the savings received from buying the generic.

The retail cost of the cereal brand promoted by the commercial includes the cost of the advertising as well some percentage of royalty that is going to the company who owns the intellectual property rights to the movie used in the cereal's marketing. In pure economic sense what is your purchasing decision telling the cereal market? Well, if most people buy the brand name cereal, it's telling the store that it should devote less shelve space to generics and it's telling cereal manufacturers that customers value marketing efforts over lower prices. I can certainly tell you that from the perspective of my children and grandchildren *(ages of three and twenty-three)* there is no rational basis for buying any generic cereal… only bad people would bring generics home for children's consumption.

Let's put aside the extenuating circumstances brought into the decision making process by branding and focus solely on the product and, for arguments sake, let's assume that the quality of both the generic and the name brand cereal are the same. On that basis which product would you consider most efficiently serves the marketplace? If the whole world was made up by cereal makers and cereal eaters which product would deliver the most value to consumers? Let's assume that it takes 100 people to make the generic cereal and 100 people to make the name brand cereal however, with the brand cereal there are an additional ten people who market the product. If we base efficiency on what the consumer is giving up in order to acquire the same benefit, it would seem clear that the most efficient producer was the generic manufacturer.

In the real world branding and the marketing resources required to build and maintain brands are an essential to most, if not all, successful companies. Consumers remain motivated by branding to purchase brands they recognize and with which the can identify. For example, all five of my daughters would be embarrassed to be seen shopping with me if I had generics in the cart. This was true even when it was something they didn't use themselves such as my shaving cream. For my daughters, and many others in society, buying generics is a sign of being poor or of at least not having good taste. The fact that I researched the available products, completed a cost/benefit analysis, and determined the best buy was the generic didn't matter. The upshot being, effective advertising can mute the effects of good pre-purchasing analysis on the part of the shopper.

On the other side of this argument is the fact that sometimes brands do provide to the consumer more than prestige. Most dads I know and more than a few moms, when receiving tools as a gift, appreciate the proven value provided by one of a number of well-known brands. As someone who has been hurt more than once by the failure of a cheap wrench, screwdriver, or drill bit, I now think twice before buying a no name product that may be of dubious quality, and tend to buy a trusted name brand instead. There is no one right answer when it comes to purchasing generic versus name brand it all depends on the real value delivered by the product. In the case of consumers, value is most often calculated as the overall utility provided by the product which can mean something more than just price and quality.

In a perfect economic situation consumers would buy the product which combines the best combination of quality and price. Branding can infer quality is present but it does not ensure that the quality is at the level the brand name would imply. Let's say that all cereal makers were required to submit their product to a battery of tests that would then neatly be reported on the package. In this scenario if you saw that the generic product scored higher in quality and in the purity of the contents *(fewer rat droppings per thousand pounds, yuck)* you might be less likely to buy the poorer quality product with the brand name and the toy from the high profile movie.

Absent definitive testing and clear meaningful comparisons, consumers are most often left relying on what they know about a brand instead of having an easy to understand scorecard to help them make the best buying decision. Clearly consumers might like it to be easier to identify the best value but producers know that if competition is based purely on price and quality that the laws of supply and demand will ultimately lead to a price that provides only a minimum profit. For this reason there remains a permanent disconnect between the types of information consumers would want to have available and what the producers, when left on their own, choose to provide.

Producers want to maintain as high a difference between the selling price and the production cost of their products as possible. If there is competition in their product's marketplace then the producer must find ways to convince the consumer to buy their product even though the relationship between price and quality might not provide the best value to the consumer. This is where building a brand can effectively maintain a higher profit for the producer. If the producer can spend ten dollars convincing the customers that their brand warrants a price that delivers twenty dollars more in profit then, for the producer, the ten dollars in promotion expense is money well spent. However, the consumer might be swayed into spending more than they needed to for the product which means that they have less money to spend on other things.

The higher cost paid for the more expensive product, versus what the consumer would have paid for the equivalent but less expensive product, effectively reduces the quality of life for that consumer. In my case buying a name brand kid's cereal with marshmallow shapes versus the generic might add up, over a years' time, to the equivalent of one golf outing. Assuming there are not any other factors, effective branding delivered extra profit to the cereal maker and that higher profit cost me the opportunity and added consumer utility of a round of golf. If success for me is measured by the number of times I can afford to play golf then my success as a consumer is diminished by the value I place in playing eighteen holes of golf for that year.

If in our consumer marketplace we spend an extra few thousand dollars a year paying an unwarranted premium for certain products then effectively our quality of life is diminished by whatever you could have used those dollars to buy. The entertainment industry would have us believe, and it may in fact be true, that in some cities businesses must pay protection money to the mob. I would hope most people would agree that having a "mob" industry in a city doesn't really add value to the consumer's experience in that city. The higher price paid for "mob protection" would not deliver any real value to the consumer at least by comparison to shopping or dining in a city where that extra cost isn't included in the price.

Equating marketing people to the Mafioso is more than a bit harsh but outrageous analogies tend to make the point better than the more bland ones! In economics understanding what contributes to raising the quality of life and what contributes to building a company's profitability are valuable pieces of information. As a consumer we are always going to be motivated by advertising, brands, and other extraneous influences. This motivation is not inherently good or bad but, and this is important understand, there are factors that make companies successful which do impact the quality of life for consumers. Understanding these factors will allow a consumer or business person to assess what is really important to them or their company. A business person needs to understand that their key to success is not solely about being the low cost producer but instead success can be achieved by being the more effective advertiser. Just as there are risks to being the no name generic, there are also risks associated with being the brand bought on the basis of branding. Many of us work for, or own in some part, businesses that place differing levels of value on their brand; knowing the underlying value proposition of a company and its brands or the lack thereof is a valuable piece of information to both employees and investors.

Elsewhere we have discussed the concept of friction within an economic process and have learned that any factor that causes a consumer to use a larger amount of their resources to obtain a product or a service constitutes friction within the chain of processes that delivers that product or service to the marketplace.

Let's say John Doe consumer can afford one week of vacation each year but, if he ignored the negative effects of branding and eliminated all purchases that were not made at the optimal price, he would be able to afford two weeks of vacation each year. The friction for John Doe consumer caused by branding is therefore equal to one vacation week per year. This example works in a microeconomic setting but, as in most economic situations, it's not as simple when applied to the broader economy.

In the broader economy the extra money spent by consumers for the higher priced brands goes to the manufacturing companies in the form of higher profits some of which are then used to develop and buy more advertising. If however, John Doe consumers across the country collectively elected to ignore advertising and took that added week of vacation, the money that had been going to the product manufacturers *(resulting in higher profits and more marketing)* would instead flow into the vacation industry. The money, that was previously spent on marketing, should then theoretically flow smoothly into the products and services the consumers are buying with those dollars... plane tickets, hotel rooms, amusement park admissions, etc.

Unfortunately just because economic theory says it should happen that way doesn't mean it will. The more efficient buying process, the one without the effect of branding, could lead to the unemployment of marketing professionals and, because of lower profits, could also result in investment capital fleeing to other marketplaces in the world where consumers are, depending on your perspective, either less price conscious or more easily swayed by effective marketing.

So what is the answer? Is branding a good thing or a bad thing?" The answer is that marketing is neither good nor bad and both good and bad. Just as the day's weather may be either good or bad, weather is not something we can change but instead a condition that we need to be aware of and then intelligently adjust our behavior. If it's cold outside you use that information to make the decision to wear a coat. In the case of branding it's a condition of the marketplace and it's not likely to go away so, as a consumer or a business person, you need to be aware that effects of branding exist and then shrewdly navigate the marketplace aware of the effect that advertising and branding has on all of us.

Chapter Seventeen

(The Lottery Mentality (a Portrait of Economic Inefficiency))

Based on the title one might think this will be a chapter devoted to the effect that gambling has on the economy and society as a whole. Instead, this section is an illustration of how a certain type of approach to earning a living can be a drag on the economy.

In the United States, during the latter part of the twentieth and early years of the twenty-first century, it seemed like a new record for the largest lottery jackpot was being set every year or so. Our society has grown very interested in news about the latest overnight multi-millionaires and most of us have dreamt of winning the jackpot ourselves. Pretty harmless stuff, dreaming that is, hitting it big, provided an individual or a family doesn't make winning the lottery their only plan for retirement or the family's sole means for sending the kids to college.

We could take the lottery discussion further and chat about the inefficiency of lotteries as a way to create wealth or why the average lottery player would be better off putting their dollar bet into their savings or 401K and while that would be a meaningful dialogue there is a bigger point to be made using this illustration. Individuals are prone to think and do what achieves their objectives rather than direct their energies to doing what is best for society. The latter, individuals working hard and efficiently for the collective good, is one of the aspects that the economic concept of communism was built upon. Earlier in this book we dug into why that did not and does not work. Just as the communist concept proved ineffective so does the lottery mentality where an individual seeks to hit it big and then lives the rest of their life off the proceeds.

Much has been written and broadcast in recent years about the greed of Wall Street and how harmful this greed has been on society and the impact it has had on the economy. In economics, as in many parts of life, there can be too much of a good thing. Most parents have witnessed one of their children overdoing it on the Halloween candy or some other treat to the point where the child became ill. It is this analogy I apply here to some of the runaway incentives and bonus programs that have been used in recent years.

As an example let's take a look at the 2008 financial crisis and examine one of its many aspects. Most adults who lived through the 2008 crisis heard the term "credit default swap" but few truly understood what these financial derivative instruments were, what they insured, what was covered, or who held them.

Like many reasonably financially aware individuals, I thought I knew enough about these financial tools to understand the nature of what went wrong but it was not until three years later, after happening upon an eBook on the subject, that I decided to learn more.

The book, The Big Short: Inside the Doomsday Machine, by Michael Lewis, one of a number on the subject, contains a number of alarming facts around what caused the collapse of the housing market and brought down AIG to its knees. If you are like me you may have assumed the problem was that AIG either underpriced their credit default swaps or sold too many of these to mortgage lenders in the years leading up to 2008... if so, you would be incorrect. The normal assumption was that some, or possibly many, of the mortgage holders had the good sense to insure the risks they were taking on some of the poorer quality mortgages that they were holding. If this had been the case it would have been one part of the financial marketplace losing and another being protected. Unfortunately this was not the case... the big mortgage lenders were for the most part unprotected on their bad mortgages by the credit default swaps sold by AIG and other financial services companies.

As I thought back to the months following the crisis, which was a couple years prior to my reading Michael Lewis's book, I remembered hearing some financial experts talking about speculation versus investing although I did not appreciate the significance of the difference between the two terms at the time. As it is, the concept of speculation is what embodies the lottery mentality which is more about getting rich quickly instead of growing wealthy by creating something of enduring value. In the small town where I spent my early years in business there was an individual whose road to wealth was truly about investing. This individual had worked hard to get a McDonalds franchise which was the first real fast food place in this rural town of about five thousand people. This new McDonalds' franchisee was truly a great store and the owner's efforts were obvious throughout the restaurant. The owner was well rewarded by the community and after a few years I was surprised to hear the restaurant was changing hands. As it turned out the owner's next goal was to own three restaurants, not just one, and to do so the owner had to sell the current store and move to the location where he was buying three McDonald's stores. This entrepreneur was taking his time and profits and investing them into a bigger and potentially more profitable venture.

In contrast to investing, speculation is more like gambling in that the speculator is attempting to take advantage of conditions which might allow for a quick profit but really does nothing to build anything of lasting value within that process. The ultimate speculator would be someone trading on a hunch or using insider information. The result of speculation is a clear winner and a loser. On the contrary, investing often ends with the investor making money but at the same time delivering something of lasting value to others or the society at large. In the case of the McDonalds entrepreneur, his hard work in building his franchise from one restaurant in one community into three restaurants in another benefited not only himself but also the community in which he operated since that community would now have three restaurants that would be well run and servicing the community's needs more effectively.

In my opinion the credit default swap *(part of the 2008 financial crisis)* was an example of speculation. In the years leading up to the 2008 financial crisis many of the credit default swaps were not sold to mortgage lenders seeking to insure their companies against potential mass defaults but were instead sold to people betting that mortgages would not be repaid. In this scenario someone, not connected to the mortgage in anyway, would be paid by insurers like AIG when the mortgages hit a certain level of default. If, for example, AIG was providing insurance at a premium price of two percent per year of the face value of a block of mortgages and would pay off when the failure rate hit fifty percent then, for a two percent bet, the speculator would earn a profit of ninety-eight percent on the value of the defaulted mortgages if they held the insurance for one year, ninety-six if they had to hold the insurance for two years and so on.

You might wonder what the harm was of AIG selling this type of insurance … well there was no harm until it produced an unfair transfer of wealth. The speculators, who were buying the credit default swaps, were betting that the financial system was making a huge error in how mortgages were being vetted and were driving up home prices beyond their real value. In this respect, the credit defaults swaps were not solely to blame but were part of a broader system failure. Credit default swaps were priced based on the theory that mortgages were safe investments. However, by 2008 conditions changed. The process for obtaining a mortgage deteriorated to the point where they were being issued without the lender taking sufficient care to ensure that they were low risk and, as a result, mortgages became risky investments. The speculators buying the swaps knew this and realized there were windfall profits to be made but at the expense of making the eventual financial collapse worse. In this way, as a product of the bursting of the real estate bubble, there was a double cost to the average American.

- The first cost is the reasonably expected risk of losing value in one's home once the housing market corrects itself. In this scenario the home builders, real estate agents, and homeowners who took advantage of the bubble and cashed out at the right time earned above average return on either their inventory of homes sold at the above normal price or as a homeowner who sold at the market peak and banked their profits.

- The second cost, the new or unnatural loss that exacerbated the impact of the bubble bursting, was the payout to those speculators who gambled on the widespread financial mistakes made in the years preceding the 2008 financial crisis. In this case we had a financial product in the credit default derivatives that did not really serve a purpose but created a financial system risk. As you may recall, the United States' government had to bail out AIG because AIG was not able to cover the bets placed by the speculators. Since the crisis itself, much has been said either suggesting these derivatives should have been regulated or maintaining the government should not regulate these types of business transactions thereby simply allowing businesses to buy/sell what they wish in a free environment. Ignoring that part of the issue let's instead focus on who gained and who paid out in this situation.

Up to the date of the crisis, the marketplace for credit default swaps was largely working on the mistaken premise that mortgage loans were nearly risk free. In the earlier years of the twentieth century conservative lending practices had been effective in keeping mortgage values well under the value of the properties being held as collateral and, as a result, when a foreclosure was necessary the losses incurred by the mortgage holder were small, if any. In the past, the normal lending approach was for the mortgagee to put down ten to twenty percent of the home's value when they made a home purchase. This practice provided the lender with some cushion if a homeowner suffered a financial setback like the loss of a job. As an example, if a homeowner purchased a one hundred thousand dollar home with twenty percent down *(twenty thousand dollars)*, the mortgage would be eighty thousand dollars. If the homeowner then lost their job and the bank had to foreclose the bank could sell the house for the one hundred thousand value and use the money to cover the eighty thousand dollar principle, accumulated interest, realtor commissions, and any other costs related to selling the home. In this example if the various costs of selling the house plus accumulated interest were less than twenty thousand dollars then the lender would come out of the bad mortgage without a loss.

The mortgage situation in 2008 was much different from the preceding years in that many mortgages were issued without any significant down payment and, during the same period, there was an unprecedented decline in home values. The crisis came about when homeowners began to rapidly default on their mortgages and this, combined with the rapid decline in home values, resulted in a high level of mortgage defaults which is what the buyers of the credit default swaps had been betting would happen. As this day of reckoning came about, much like the roulette ball falling into their number, the credit default swap holders hit their big payday. The only question left for these gamblers was, "Would the house be able to pay off their bets?" Fortunately for those speculators the United States' Government stepped in with U.S. taxpayer money to make good on the bets.

Most of us were not aware that, in order for these gamblers to receive their payout, our country's deficit would grow by nearly innumerable billions of dollars. Hopefully by this point you would agree that having provided an environment where credit default swaps could be used in this manner provides no offsetting benefit to our society as a whole. So, as a society we need to ask ourselves why we would allow this to happen. Although you might find some people who will argue the merits of helping AIG make good on these bets at taxpayer expense, the financial hardship borne by millions of taxpayers who have to cover these bets stands as pretty good argument against it. I would agree that the "too big to fail" theory might apply in AIG's case but there could have been a discussion, once we knew all the circumstances involved, about if an arrangement should have been made where the payoff was less than 100%. My point being that, we live in a free enterprise system and speculators, such as those in the 2008 swaps debacle, should know that this type of speculation also comes with the risk. A risk that society, as a whole, may not feel obligated to mortgage itself to enrich speculators who engage in harmful transactions that are not being used for their intended purpose, like credit defaults swaps.

In the months and years that followed the 2008 crisis we heard much about the bonuses being paid within various firms including AIG and these were held up as the poster child for the cause of the crisis however the real root cause was speculating by investors and the absence of effective regulation on the financial markets. Investments in financial instruments should be tied to producing something that benefits society. Common sense, to use an overused term once again, would tell us that buying insurance on something you do not own is speculation and most people would agree that speculation is gambling.

The point here is that gambling has no place in the critical financial marketplaces of the world and it should have been obvious to the management of companies like AIG that they were selling products to speculators not investors. The people involved in this process at AIG and the other companies were busy selling products in order to earn commissions and bonuses. Obviously you could not expect the sellers of these products to stop selling or the buyers to stop buying when the opportunity to earn huge profits was available. As a believer in free enterprise, try as I might, I cannot see a natural way in which this problem could be averted absent either government regulation or eliminating the expectation of government guarantees for the financial institutions involved in these type of transactions. You might offer the argument that responsible management would or should have done the responsible thing and stopped the practice on their own accord. As a counter to this argument I would ask, "What would be management's motivation for stepping out of a lucrative market"? *(More discussion on this specific topic can be found in the chapter on corporate governance).*

Had the United States government proactively and concretely put a policy in place that it would not support companies like AIG when they engaged in transactions that could be deemed as speculation then, possibly, the gamblers on credit defaults swaps would not have placed so many bets on the premise the mortgage market would collapse sometime around 2008. *(Keep in mind my comment here is Monday morning quarterbacking and any regulation or law can be bypassed by a crafty speculator when there is the potential available for winning big).* The complete answer to how to prevent a future crisis, like the 2008 crisis or the savings and loan crisis of the 1980's, will not be found here nor did I find it in Michael Lewis's book. The answer is complicated but one of the aspects is that, as a society, we must be aware of the human tendency to try to make the big win, bank the winnings, and retire to a life of leisure. For every one person or investor who profited in the credit default swaps there are tens of thousands of taxpayers and homeowners who are suffering as the product of having to pay off the gamblers' winning bet. Those of us who did not win on this bet may want to grab our gun or ball bat to take back our money but our energies would be better spent on trying to prevent the next occurrence. Prevention protection will require a change in mentality on the population's part and in how our government manages the financial sector. Instead of "too big to fail" possibly we could simply replace that term by "too big to gamble".

Chapter Eighteen

(Financial System Friction)

During the period of time known as the Dark Ages, an economic system developed in parts of Europe and Asia that some believe *(me included)* served to hold back a large part of humanity from making normal progress in developing the human civilization. In my discussion around the Dark Ages, my base assumption is that the people who lived during that time had the same capabilities as those living in subsequent generations and therefore what stymied human development during that period in history was not the lack of capabilities amongst the population but the economic system used by the society within which they lived.

The primary social and economic systems during the Dark Ages were made up by a society where only a few people held virtually all the economic capital within a specific geographic area. Inheritance and the capacity to wage war *(thereby taking capital from others)* were the two factors that determined who held the capital and controlled the population during the Dark Ages. In today's world we generally don't wage war on our neighbors and take their stuff but, as in the Dark Ages, inheritance still plays a role in our economy and does allow for wealth, capital, and influence to remain with some families for generations. Rulers during the Dark Ages were successful, either through lineage or force, while people today can become successful in a variety of other ways utilizing a variety of other traits. Unlike the Dark Ages, success and the right to own capital is no longer limited to a select few, today success is enjoyed, and capital is held, by people from all walks of life. When we think about it, most of today's successful people would not have been successful had they been born in the Dark Ages.

Let's take a moment to gain a better understanding the Dark Age's economic systems. At the top of the feudal system were large landholders who historically carried a number of titles but the most recognized is "feudal" lords. The lords owned the land and in most cases ruled the land in an autocratic way. At the bottom of this system were the serfs who were effectively slaves to the lord and worked the land the lord owned.

The lord of the land would dictate that the serfs provide him and his family with the fruits of their labor in whatever amount he desired. This would, in many cases, leave the serf families with barely enough to survive from harvest to harvest. The lord considered the goods taken from his subjects to be a tax, a tax that was levied not only on the serfs but on anyone who worked for the lord's family including blacksmiths, bakers, soldiers, and anyone else the lord chose to keep in his employ. During the Dark Ages movement between classes did not occur frequently and there was little accomplished in the way of innovation or in the building of capital. Two major contributors to the lack of development were the absence of education and the "feudal" economy itself. Education was not "wasted" on the serfs and without access to education individuals could not hope to achieve to their potential. Therefore gifted individuals, who had the misfortune of being born into the Serf population, could not develop their exceptional minds and help advance the economy at large. The "feudal" economy, the second hindrance, was structured to maintain the status quo. The lord did not want residents of his lands to develop any skills or learning that could potentially lead to his reign being challenged. Any exceptional individual would have been viewed as a threat to the lord and his family and it was therefore in the lord's best interest to suppress these exceptional individuals along with their special talents.

The effect of the "feudal" system described here is probably among the most severe examples of economic friction… in fact it was so severe that economic growth was stagnant for hundreds of years. What's important to recognize however is that this system was maintained by choice… those in power during the Dark Ages fiercely guarded their places within their world even though their actions were detrimental to the world as a whole. The rulers believed that what they were doing was important and, in their view, the lord's role was crucial to the maintenance of social order. During that time it would have been impossible to win an argument to the contrary but today almost everyone would agree the "feudal" system was a bad system and one that stayed around for much too long.

By now you are no doubt wondering why I have taken you down this path of history and what significance it has to economics in the twenty-first century. It's important to learn from the lessons of the past. The access that we have to education today and knowing what has and has not worked throughout history are two reasons that our motivations and mental capabilities today are different than they were in the Dark Ages. Centuries from now our descendants will look back on our society and wonder why we didn't utilize our abilities more efficiently to deliver a better economy to our society. Today neither you nor I have the answer to what could dramatically improve our economy and possibly lower unemployment, generate a higher standard of living, increase

productivity, and build a more stable economic environment.
Just as the "feudal" lord thought what he was doing was in the
best interest of his domain so do we today and just like we judge
the "feudal" lord our future descendants will judge our society.

In today's world there are functions being performed and
resources being consumed that are, in my opinion, not
providing benefit to society at large. Among these functions are
some elements of the financial systems. Within this broad range
of systems are steps, processes, and businesses that range from
marginally effective to completely useless. One example of a
useless structure is the trading system which is used by some
companies to trade and re-trade stocks in order to make a small
profit on millions of stock trades. Companies are investing
incredible sums in sophisticated computer equipment and
complex programming to skim small profits out of purchases
from buyers and sellers of securities. The companies using these
systems do not intend to buy and hold any stock but are in
effect performing what amounts to day trading on steroids.

The goal of these companies is to make money on transactions
being processed rather than building a system to smoothly link
companies that are seeking capital to investors looking for

companies in which to invest. Since these companies are consuming large amounts of resources and do nothing to aid the primary functions of these markets, the profits taken by these companies add cost therefore friction to the investing process. In fact, these services have forced in new regulations and have caused stock market disruptions that have made it more difficult to match investees to investors.

Any aspect of stock trading that is not useful in helping to match available capital to business opportunities should be questioned. Most seasoned business people and investors would agree that investments in stock should be thought of as a long-term marriage as opposed to a one night stand. Investing that is done to turn a short-term profit, such as day trading, is very much the same as gambling. Nothing happens in days, weeks, or even months that makes the nature of an investment change. With that said, some might argue that the firing or hiring of a golden child CEO or Chairman would prove that statement wrong and, in these situations, I would agree... but only marginally. Changes like these may radically alter a company's stock prices but they don't change the fundamentals of what makes a company a good investment. Even the best executives need time to improve a business so investing on the basis of hiring a great executive is logical but expecting the business to grow in real value quickly is not realistic.

Regardless of the flaws you might see in, or exceptions taken to, my last set of statements, companies generally bring the right resources to bear upon an opportunity in the economy *(such as the next miracle drug, a more efficient electric motor or some yet to be thought of marvelous widget)* and as a result are properly positioned to return better profits to the benefit of their investors. It is for this reason that an investor should invest. Anyone or any company that siphons off funds in between the investor and investee is adding unnecessary friction to the process of investing.

Throughout my career I have heard many accounts about the colossal fortunes being earned on Wall Street and I have observed a few of those transactions personally that, on the efforts of a relatively small number of Wall Street workers, delivered huge fees to a financial firm. Investment bankers are among Wall Street's elite and are reputed to make large sums of money during their careers. The data I will share here is in its specifics fictitious but in proportional terms representative of the relationship between fees and funding provided.

A company was purchased for five hundred million dollars, four hundred million of which was being financed as part of the purchase. The new owners paid an investment banker six million dollars in upfront fees to secure this financing. After a few months the new owners discovered that what they paid for the new business was excessive and as a result the business could not generate the cash flow necessary to make the payments on the four hundred million dollar loan.

The new owners needed to inject another hundred million into the business so that they could redo the financing for three hundred million which the business cash flow could support. In order to proceed with the refinance it was necessary for the owners to once again utilize the services of an investment bank as well as other consultants which, after a few months of work, resulted in another four million in fees paid to the investment banking firm.

The people involved in the investment banker process were only a handful of individuals *(to be generous let us say it was six people)* working full time on this financing and refinancing initiative. The second financing process *(and again being generous)* took four months. Four month's work, six days a week would be about one hundred days and at an average of twelve hours per day that would calculate to twelve hundred hours per person of work or a total of seventy-two hundred hours. This would equate to about five hundred and fifty-five dollars per hour.

If we assume that the investment bank keeps half of this money the investment bankers would be making two hundred and twenty-five dollars per hour so, in the four months of effort, the investment bankers would average gross wages of two hundred and seventy thousand dollars. The more financially astute of the readers might be saying "Yes, that is a lot of money but what about the risk of lending several hundred million dollars?" The truth is that the bank orchestrating the loan arrangement usually does keep a piece of the debt offered but not always. In financial terms the packaging of a debt arrangement for a company such as this is a separate service and, once it is concluded, the various lenders who make up a consortium of lenders can buy and sell their parts of the deal in the open market. In other words the upfront fees are just that and have no connection to the lending arrangement once concluded. To add insult to injury the financing deals that I have seen done are not like your home mortgage where you have a loan arrangement for twenty to thirty years but these lending arrangements usually only last for three to seven years after which the whole expensive process must be repeated.

The fact that it cost this fictitious company ten million dollars to secure what ended up being the three hundred million in loans not only seems expensive but most top level executives I have talked to have complained about the extreme fees investment banks charge. We can probably safely assume that there is a connection with the fee structure and the fact that many of the most profitable companies are banks involved in investment banking. We also know from the financial crises of recent years that these high profits are made after paying out premium salaries to the investment bankers doing the work. From this set of facts I have developed the opinion that the business of financing businesses might not be as efficient as it could be.

In this context, efficiency is defined as… "Does the price paid and the value given work effectively for the market?" In fairness, being an investment banker comes with a lot of stress and requires, to be effective, someone who is pretty adept with numbers and business strategies. Nonetheless the situation begs the question, "How much is too much?" Until there are less expensive alternatives available to businesses in need of financing the present method will remain in place. It is beyond the scope of this book to fully evaluate this market or propose an alternative instead I will simply maintain that excessive profits and wages paid within any segment of the economy are harmful to the economy as a whole. The harm is the friction that the current process creates. If a business needed to refinance its hundred million dollar debt and it cost two million dollars to do so, whereas in a more efficient process it might cost fifty thousand, imagine the opportunities that are lost for those businesses and the economy at large due to the unnecessary friction.

To provide an example of the concept we will briefly return to our friends on Adam's Island. In our island community the Trader family was making a large profit on the sale of wheat between Fertile Isle and Trader's fellow islanders who now wanted wheat in pretty baskets. Over time the Trader family accumulated a large share of the Greenbacks in circulation and, as a result, everyone in the Trader family felt wealthier. Since Trader had more money than they needed, they developed a desire for more leisure time and toward that end the Traders began to eliminate some of the low profit services they had previously performed such as home delivery of purchased product.

The Fisher, Farmer, and Sheppard families now all had to separately come to the store with their wagons to pick up their purchases where in the past Trader had made a quick loop in the Trader family's wagon to deliver all the goods. Trader, now having more money in hand, could not be bothered with the time it took to deliver the goods to their customers. As a result higher profits to Trader resulted in a less efficient set of services to Trader's customers. The point being made here is that sometimes too much profit to certain members of a society can be a bad thing for an economy. More specifically if the distribution of income creates a situation where some individuals no longer have to contribute to the economy the result may be better for them but at the direct detriment of others.

Just like the conclusion that the socialism model tends to cause an economy to run ineffectively so too can inefficient market conditions which yields a disproportionate amount of profits to a comparative few. Too much of anything has the potential to be bad for an economy. Ideally the financial marketplace should run as lean as a manufacturing plant or the corner grocery *(two examples of businesses that tend to operate in a more optimal way in terms of how they deliver their products to the economy)*. The reason grocery stores and manufacturing plants tend to operate in a lean manner is not because of regulation, but because the "natural" processes of the free enterprise system are working well.

The reference to "natural" is largely the effect of real competition. Competition is not just a matter of the participants working hard but also necessitates the consumer has the ability to seek out a good deal. The investment banking sector is working hard but there is a lack of efficient price competition in this sector. Too much profit causes the cost of investment banking services to be expensive to the point of inhibiting business growth. As a result of the high cost of financing, businesses who want to grow but need financing to do so, may delay or defer acting on a growth opportunity. Some services coming out of the financial marketplace are efficiently priced for example, individual or family banking is quite competitive, mortgage lending is also very competitive as are numerous other services. You do not see local bankers retiring in their twenties or thirties but instead they work every day until normal retirement age. The fact that bond traders, investment bankers, and others on Wall Street have found a way to force incredible pay and bonuses out of the economy is not something we should deny them or be jealous of but is instead something we should be aware of as an indication of an inefficient sector of the overall economy. Once aware, then we should look for free enterprise tools to fix the problem if possible and if not then seek regulatory actions to force these processes into becoming a more efficient.

Chapter Nineteen

(Right Tool, Right Time)

"Right Tool, Right Time". This chapter title brings to mind so many analogies... a cook using a mixing spoon instead of a whisk to whip up some egg whites, a mechanic using a wrench to take out a screw, a craftsman using a hammer to tighten a nut. Hopefully these examples create the visual connections that are analogous to the concept I want to convey. In economic terms political commentators often cite economic tools like tax cuts, adjusting interest rates, and regulations in terms of absolutes... eliminating or using more of one or the other. Seldom do we hear experts speak of using the right amount of any one of these tools thereby tweaking the economy like a mechanic might tweak the carburetor of a classic car. In this chapter we will explore the position that these concepts are tools in a society's economic tool box not absolute solutions or follies as politicians and media pundits often described them to be.

Time is really the only real way to know if we have applied the right tools to an economic situation and sometimes we may not know for many years. The most frequently used example of an economic dilemma is the Great Depression. But what actually worked to bring the United States' economy out of this depression is still a matter of much debate. Many argue that it was the New Deal legislation which allowed the country to pull out of the depression while others maintain that it was only the ramp up of production for World War II (WWII) that finally brought the country out of the depression. Rather than add yet another opinion to this conflict of thought we will instead look at results and what tool or tools may have driven what effects.

Much like a powerful car stuck in traffic, the United States' economy sat idling during much of the Great Depression. During this period of time we had a free market economy that was largely absent of regulation. The workforce was the best educated in the world yet, from 1929 through 1940, there was widespread poverty and extremely high unemployment. Quickly, in a matter of months with the entry into WWII, the United States went from idling along with underutilized resources to full employment. What happened with the entry into the war? There was definitely a huge increase in government spending but how was the war spending different from the public works spending (programs like the WPA) that the Roosevelt administration had tried in the preceding years?

Let's take a closer look at both types of spending. Both the public works spending and the government war spending involved the government using money that it not only didn't have but was also not budgeted to be covered with incoming tax revenues. Deficit spending funded both the public works projects of the latter half of the 1930s and then, starting in 1941, WWII. In both cases the funds were used to hire out of work individuals and buy materials from suppliers. The public works projects were mostly devoted to infrastructure projects like roads, dams, parks, and recreation areas. The war effort dwarfed the public works projects and the influx of war spending touched almost every part of society including additional infrastructure projects similar to the stimulus projects from the years leading up to WWII.

It's likely that the popularity of the deficit spending activity, related specifically to the WWII projects, had something to do with its success in stimulating the economy. It's quite possible that, in some way, moving the economy is like some sort of tug of war where, to be successful, it not only takes sufficient numbers of participants and relative strength but also motivation on the part of the participants to achieve success. This might also explain why the simplest of concepts most often produce the most reliable results… the more of the population that understands the tool being used the better the public can get behind the idea.

Simplicity and ease of understanding may be why it's easier to get people behind the idea of a tax cut than it is to sell them on stimulus spending. With a tax cut, cause and effect is easy to see and understand because the effect shows up in a person's first paycheck following the implementation of the rate change. The same is true with the concept of too much regulation, it's easy to comprehend therefore proves popular at the polls. Stimulus spending however is only relevant to you if you are directly impacted by the first item funded by the spending.

Some on the left would argue that lowering taxes on the wealthy or reducing regulations are almost always wrong just as some individuals on the right consistently advocate for lowering the capital gains tax. Neither is always the right or wrong answer, there is a point where the tax rate can be too low, or more correctly where the tax rates are not progressive enough, and, as we saw prior to the Regan tax cuts, the rates can also be too high or too focused upon the upper income group. The truth is we have to consider changes in tax rates and regulations, like a mechanic considers both tightening and loosening tension on the fan belt, as viable adjustment options.

The following chart, <u>Historical Tax Rates for the Lowest and Highest Income Earners</u>[12], may help to frame up the concept of tax rates as an economic tool. The chart depicts United States' tax rates and makes it easy to see that both the low earners and top earners were paying among the highest tax rates during the WWII years and throughout the boom times that followed the war.

Historical Tax Rates for the Lowest and Highest Income Earners

---

[12] http://en.wikipedia.org/wiki/US_Tax_Rates

Despite the very high tax rates in 1941 and 1942, the country still ended up spending money it didn't have and, during a time when the majority of taxpayers could ill afford to be giving added money to the government, it raised more money from taxpayers through taxes and war bonds. So why did this end up stimulating the economy and ultimately taking the United States' economy to levels never before achieved putting us on a path that continued to result in a steadily improving economy for many years to follow? The Roosevelt economic programs from the 1930's were still in place in 1946 *(in fact many continue to this day)* so, to the degree that these programs didn't work in the 1930's, they didn't seem to impede the good economic times that followed. Thus, we remain with the question of what triggered the economic boom, was it that the deficit spending just needed more time to work or was it something else. The complete answer is not something on which there is a consensus of thought but I would argue that motivation is in some part the answer. Once Japan attacked Pearl Harbor the political discourse ended on what was needed to get the economy moving and the vast majority of people's focus was on winning the war not on arguing about economic approaches that were espoused by Democrats, Republicans, or independents. Since we stopped arguing about the approach and set our sights on a common goal I put forward that we accidently hit upon a formula that not only won the war but also solved our nation's economic woes.

When placed in the hands of poorly motivated employees, tools are often pointed to as the culprit when things don't run smoothly however the problem is often not with the tool but is more the degree of effort being applied by the employee. It's the same with economic actions taken by our political leaders… if we as a society lose faith in a leader's methods then it's quite possible that even applying the right tools might not be effective. At the start of the Reagan administration most people would agree our tax structure did not promote economic growth, specifically the tax program did not motivate investors to take risks. The tax rates were cut, deficits increased and yet unemployment continued to be a sticky problem for a number of years. The fact that the Reagan era tax cuts did not work quickly didn't mean that cutting tax rates was the wrong action it just took some time for the tool to do its work.

During the 1990's and early part of the twenty-first century the Regan tax cuts were paid homage as being the exact right action.

In the following years, during the George H. W. Bush administration, there were some modest tax increases and these increases may have been a factor in Bush losing the 1992 election to Bill Clinton. During the Clinton administration the United States saw some of the best economic times in the twentieth century which were, to a large extent, due to the tools employed by Bill Clinton's two predecessors.

In the year 2000 Americans had an economy with effective full employment and a federal government budget surplus. The 2000 Presidential election however proved just how split the country was in what brought about our economic success with the two major candidates, Gore and Bush, coming close to equally splitting the popular vote. Positions on both the right and left were as entrenched as ever. Since the 2000 election the United States' economy has once again fallen on hard times. Unfortunately economists, politicians, and voters continue to remain very split on what should be done to prod the economy back to a state similar to what we enjoyed during the Clinton administration. Strangely no one has yet suggested that we return to the tax code structure that existed when things were working so well. Obviously (tongue in cheek) that could not possibly work. Even though I'm a man I will admit that while driving I have gotten myself lost on a number of occasions and, as a result, not only wasted time and fuel but became quite annoyed, all of this could have been avoided had I simply admitted my mistake *(checked a map or maybe asked someone for directions)* and returned to a route that had gotten me to my destination on previous trips.

The economic, political, and social circumstances we had in the second decade of the twenty-first century was much like two mechanics working on the same car each convinced the other's solution to the problem was wrong. Each mechanic can only stay employed by proving the other mechanic wrong which, unfortunately, keeps the car in the shop and off the road. Clearly, just like the car needs the mechanics to work together to find the right solution, our economy also needs cooperation amongst our executive and legislative branches of government as well as between the two major political parties.

Cooperation on a national level could be achieved by entering into a third World War. A major conflict would likely get the country to pull together as it has done in the past however, it might be better, if we simply agreed that there are economic tools that, when applied correctly, could accomplish the same thing. Just like agreeing that sometimes a job calls for a screwdriver and other times it calls for a wrench, we need to be able to get politicians and the population at large to agree that different circumstances require different tools. Equally important is to develop a state of affairs where both parties and their sub-groups are working to ensure economic success. Rhetoric tends to inflame and discourage many members of our society and eliminates any chance of the collective nation supporting an economic program and as result we lack the cohesion that the nation had in late 1941.

Tax cuts, tax increases, and stimulus spending are all economic tools and are no more intrinsically good or bad than a screwdriver, wrench, or drill that are sitting idly in a mechanics tool box. Many of our political leaders would lead you to believe that the solution to our problems is to either lower taxes or increase government involvement. The truth is, just like a car runs best on the right mixture of fuel and air; it takes the right mixture of taxes, government spending, and regulations for an economy to work efficiently.

As an example of an economic tool, consider the CAFÉ standards that were adopted in 1975[13], these standards mandated improved fuel economy and became a set of regulations that were largely ineffective. Beginning in the late 1980s, the preference of American drivers changed from driving cars to driving less fuel efficient vans and SUVs. Exploiting a loophole in the standards that allowed vans and trucks to be sold with poorer fuel economy, automakers promoted these vehicles and effectively changed the two car family into a two van/SUV/truck family. This loophole in the CAFÉ standards pretty much made the goal of the overall increased fuel efficiency unachievable. In the absence of effective regulations progress on developing a more fuel efficient car slowed and, instead of being managed by regulation, it was left it up to the free market to decide what type of fuel economy we should have. The result was declining fuel economy and increased pollution. The lower fuel economy lead to higher dependence on imported oil and virtually no innovation in terms of developing high MPG vehicles until we reached a crucial point where our economy and way of life were significantly threatened.

---

[13] http://en.wikipedia.org/wiki/CAFE_standards

Given the benefit of hindsight, most reasonable people would agree that the CAFÉ standards were the right tool and agree that better gas mileage would have been better for society and the economy. Given this why did we as a society allow the goal of better fuel economy to fall by the wayside? While in some cases allowing the market to decide the best path is the right tool for the job other times, such as in this case, solely allowing the marketplace to do as it wishes is not the best tool. We should consider the likely motivation of the affected members of society when judging if a certain tool will work as desired.

In the case of bigger versus smaller cars Charles Wheelan, the author of the Naked Economist: Undressing the Dismal Science, explained that, even though he would have preferred to drive a smaller vehicle, he purchased a large SUV because there were so many big vehicles on the road and he didn't want to risk the safety of his family. Mr. Wheelan's insight was a bit of an "Aha!" moment for me as it made clear that in this case the economic result was the product of basic human nature. Any normal person would first choose to protect his/her family so purchasing a larger less economic vehicle would be a logical choice. I would argue that in this type of situation regulation is needed in order to encourage development of smaller vehicles with better MPG in order to create a better and more rational choice for consumers in our society. More to the point Mr. Wheelan would feel safe putting his family in a smaller car if the other cars on the road were of similar size.

Motivation is the critical factor for a getting a job done well… there are many examples among our successful industries that are proof of how achieving rewards, based on efforts, can drive the most efficient delivery of a product or service. Amazon, FedEx, and many others are products of the alignment of businesses desire to improve profits and the needs of the society. Although there is abundant evidence that links the success of an organization to the success of the individual we still setup so many government services that are largely without the tool of motivation.

Take as an example, the United States' Internal Revenue Service (IRS). As a taxpayer I have twice had the experience to work with the IRS staff who are assigned to work with individual taxpayers, both times I was treated fairly and politely by two very junior employees within the IRS. These individuals were helpful, intelligent, and showed every sign of having the highest of integrity. On the flipside, as a finance professional working in the private sector, I have worked with several senior IRS employees and found some to be the embodiment of the oft criticized career government employee. My experiences have led me to believe that promotion within the IRS must be tied to longevity within the organization not performance or capability. Those who can avoid getting fired for the longest time make it the furthest up the organizational ladder. With that said, there were former IRS professionals working in the private sector who did demonstrate the capabilities I respect but, in my limited sample, it did not seem that the IRS was as effective as private industry is at putting the right people in the right positions.

Successful businesses find ways to hire the right people, promote the right people, reward success, and as a result deliver ever more efficient results to their customers. It's not a perfect system, there are certainly numerous examples of where it has gone wrong; but, just like free enterprise, it is to date the best system that society has found of aligning resources to needs.

Many would argue that there are some functions you can't outsource, functions where the free market alone will not result in the right answer, such as in the case of CAFÉ standards. That very possibly might be the case for the IRS but that does not mean you can't use a more market based methods of hiring, firing, and promoting IRS employees. Just like it was a mistake to think that taking the teeth out of the CAFÉ standards was the right answer, so is the idea that you can run an organization like the IRS without having an effective means of motivation… one that is akin to what is used in businesses throughout the world. In other words run the IRS more like IBM. Reward IRS employees with bonuses if they are able to improve revenue recovery and customer service ratings. Fire ineffective IRS staffers who are just hanging around long enough to earn a lucrative government pension so that they can retire in their fifties and then go to work in the private sector armed with the knowledge of how to beat the IRS at their own game. Businesses are very effective at keeping this type of thing from happening and common sense would tell us that the IRS should have in place similar motivation to keep its best talent at work. We should promote and reward career IRS employees who want to do an outstanding job for their agency, who have pride in efficiently enforcing the tax code, and who provide professional and courteous customer service.

Continuing to do the same thing and expecting different results is a definition of insanity that is often cited. With that said, I contend that the way we attempt to manage public entities like the IRS is absolutely insane. The IRS gives us what we should expect to get based on the tools we apply to the organization. If we want different results it's up to our government to use a different approach. Keeping the IRS as is *(always deserving to be the butt of jokes)* does little for the morale of the IRS employees and certainly is not going to improve the IRS's success. As much as we personally don't want the IRS to be successful when it comes to our individual taxes, in terms of enforcement we absolutely need the IRS to be successful. What many fail to realize is that, if the IRS was perfect in enforcing the tax code then, honest taxpayers would need to pay less tax.

If the IRS was managed using the right tools it's possible that the head of the agency might earn ten times what they earn today and might even be hired from outside the service itself. I suspect that taking this approach would not only reduce the overall cost of running the IRS but would also result in better outcomes. A more efficient IRS would allow for a more efficient economy... if we were able to catch more of the tax cheats and at the same time lessen the burden businesses and individuals experience when working with poorly motivated agents just think of the boost that would provide to the private sector and the economy as a whole. We need to stop doing the same things and hoping for different results, we need to stop using the hammer on government agencies and apply the right tools at the right time to achieve better results.

Chapter Twenty

(The Great Pyramid of Giza)

The title of this chapter, The Great Pyramid of Giza, may have you thinking "Where the hell are you going?" "Why are you taking me there?" and "How does a monarchy in ancient Egypt have anything to do with free market economics?" Please allow me to explain, this chapter is devoted to a discussion of how resources are allocated in a free market economy, such as the United States, and in economies that to varying degrees are less free.

In truth, an absolutely free market economy is one in which those with the resources and products can do as they wish with them. Admittedly ancient Egypt's labor force could not choose who they worked for and had little to say in what they did. It is therefore correct to say many of the requirements for what we consider a free enterprise society were clearly missing from Pharaoh's Egypt but for our purposes this time period and society will work. Our interest is in the pharaoh's life-long project of pyramid building. In concept the building of the pyramids can be applied to free markets and the distribution of wealth and power. My objective is to use the building of the pyramids to demonstrate how resources can be allocated by a society.

The Pharaoh Tutankhamen (King Tut) is among the most well-known Pharaohs of Egypt yet he only ruled Egypt for about ten years and, while his tomb is among the best preserved, it was also among the most modest.[14] During his short reign, King Tut made a series of decisions that lead to expending a great deal of Egypt's resources on his tomb as well as other state projects. It's not clear why King Tut's tomb was modest instead of elaborate like the tombs built by some of the earlier pharaohs. Past precedent and religious beliefs would have been factors, it may also be that King Tut had planned to build a more elaborate tomb later in life but with his death at nineteen those plans were derailed. It's certainly unlikely however, that during his reign he directed any significant resources to more philanthropic endeavors such as building homes for his less fortunate subjects. It's unfair to measure King Tut's choices using our twenty-first century standards or for us to attempt to understand the needs of those who inhabited the nation of Egypt several thousand years ago. The intent here is to consider the broader effects of the decision made by the ancient Egyptian rulers to use much of the nation's economic output to build their tombs. Throughout history nations, individuals, and

---

[14] http://en.wikipedia.org/wiki/Tutankhamun

communities have chosen to build incredible structures that we still enjoy today and our understanding of the ancient world is better as a result. Our appreciation might be somewhat tempered however, as it is possible that the greatest among the ancient wonders of the world might be more a testament to the selfishness of the rulers rather than symbols of an ancient people's achievements.

The largest of Egypt's pyramids was built for the tomb of Khufu. It reportedly required the labor of over one hundred thousand slaves to build.[15] It is probable that the size of the pyramid may be measured in terms of how hated a particular Pharaoh was by his people nonetheless the size of these incredible structures are what has had such a lasting impression on the many generations of mankind since the pyramid's building. If the Pharaoh Khufu had chosen to build schools throughout the nation of Egypt, and then staffed the schools with thousands of teachers, would that have been a better use of economic resources? Hypothetically it's possible that one of Khufu's lesser known predecessors (or successors) could have done something more politically correct (based on today's

---

[15] http://en.wikipedia.org/wiki/Great_Pyramid_of_Giza

sensibilities) but the benefits (of what we would now consider the more enlightened choice) may not have had as a lasting effect, certainly not one that was memorialized in a gigantic stone structure.

Returning to our island community we will work through a small scale example of resource allocation and how those choices could impact an economy. We will join our island economy at a hypothetical time when the Sheppard clan came to rule the entire island. King Sheppard ruled the island with an iron hand, and King Sheppard's decisions alone determined how life would be lived on the island especially when it came to choosing where the island would dedicate its excess resources. As with many a king over the ages, King Sheppard also desired to leave a lasting legacy of his reign upon the island.

King Sheppard decided that he wanted a stone castle of grand proportions constructed, one built to last for centuries that would not only house his family but also house many subsequent generations of the Sheppard clan. He ordered each of the Adam's Isle families to provide one son of working age to work on the castle until it was complete. Sheppard's eldest son would be the engineer in charge of building the castle and he estimated it would take ten years of labor to build the structure he designed. Both the Fisher and Farmer clans were now each made up of four families and each of those families had four to five children of working age. Therefore the effect of the King's order would decrease the available workers by about twenty-five percent in both the Fisher and Farmer clans.

Prior to the beginning of the castle's construction the islanders had been able to provide for the island's needs by working only five days each week; but both the Farmer and Fisher clans knew that things would be more difficult during the next ten years while their kinsmen were off working on the castle. King Sheppard suspected his subjects would struggle to keep up with their output of wheat and fish so, in anticipation of this, he ordered that all subjects must work six days a week and must provide the King's family with enough wheat and fish to not only fulfill Sheppard's needs but those of the conscripted workers as well. In fact the King mandated that the needs of the Sheppard's and of the castle workers must be met before any wheat or fish was kept for the needs of the Farmer and Fisher families.

Despite the extra day of work the two families found that there was less wheat and fish available for their own consumption. They soon found themselves hungry and were spending extra hours trying to supplement their production. As with any society there were limited resources so the families began to reexamine how they utilized the resources available to them including time spent on nonproduction activities. The families found that they could no longer afford to spend time teaching their children or maintaining their homes to the standards of the past… that time now needed to be spent working the fields and catching fish. The cost for devoting so much of their resources to building a castle for the Sheppard family was significant to the island economy and those living within that society.

Living in poorly maintained homes, with their children in want of an education, would not be a popular change in circumstances for the islanders but the despotic Sheppard's would not be any more likely to notice the shift in the population's level of satisfaction than would the Pharaoh have been regarding his subjects in ancient Egypt. In a democratic regime, a leader such as Sheppard, may have been voted out of his leadership position as a result of his spending choices but, like many ancient rulers, the Adam's Island King's decision was law and must be complied with or bear the punishment of not doing so.

You may consider King Sheppard's decision to be a bad one but let's consider a different scenario… let's assume that the island's needs could be met by the Farmers and Fishers only having to work three days each week, in this scenario many of the islanders would spend much of the week idle. In this situation, if the islanders worked more closely to their capacity and there was no fall off in the quality of life for the two clans, it might be a wise decision to build up the infrastructure of the island. Theoretically a castle for Sheppard might be a good choice and when the castle was completed the work effort could be redirected to improving roads, homes for the other families, and possibly an improved harbor. You might argue with the weighting of the priorities established by King Sheppard, particularly making his castle as the first priority, but the end results would ultimately be better for the island for generations to come.

Every society establishes priorities for the application of their resources. In modern times there have been projects that have been selected by the nations through their political leaders. In the 1950s the United States decided to build the interstate system, a project in its scope that was not unlike the building of one of the pharaoh's pyramids, although the amount of hardship upon the average person in the United States would be much less than it was upon the pharaoh's subjects. The decision to build the interstate system was made in a democratic setting and was the brainchild of President Eisenhower. Early in Eisenhower's military career he and a military team made a transcontinental road trip across the United States which took 62 days to complete.[16] While making the arduous journey Eisenhower, as a military man, saw the need for improved transportation and in later years when he became President, Eisenhower framed up the project for the nation and secured funding for the endeavor through congress.

If Eisenhower had instead proposed building a more lavish presidential estate or a gigantic monument to his presidency it's likely his proposal would not have been as easily passed by congress and would not have had the same high approval rating as the interstate project. These other alternatives would have

---

[16]

http://www.fhwa.dot.gov/interstate/brainiacs/eisenhowerinterstate.htm

been judged as less than the optimal use for the country's tax dollars. What if Eisenhower, instead of funding an interstate system, had proposed to finish paying off the country's debts that were left over from WWII and the Korean War? I suspect there would have been, and probably were, many who would have said that objective trumped the potential improvement that would come from an interstate system. Alternatively Eisenhower could have proposed a tax cut lessoning the tax burden throughout the nation by an amount equivalent to the cost of building the interstate system. This too would have had more than its share of supporters and one would suppose the tax cut alternative would have done a lot to increase Eisenhower's chances for reelection.

Fortunately for the United States, President Eisenhower chose to promote the building of a needed infrastructure that has served the country well since its construction. Just like any major public works decision there were results from the building of the interstate system that were not beneficial. Some would argue the interstate system supplanted the nation's rail system and kept the country from developing a more effective rail system similar to that in Europe. Nonetheless the decision to build the interstate system was a decision that fixed a glaring weakness within the infrastructure of the United States. Eisenhower's motivation was from a military perspective but the effect to the American society has been more economic in nature, fortunately how well the interstate system would meet the military needs has not yet been put to any real test.

While the effects of the United States' interstate project may not have been all positive, and the primary need as seen in its developer's mind has thankfully never been put to use, the project is still a great example of how a society chooses to allocate its resources with the result being the betterment of the society's future. Every generation is faced with similar choices in regards to how best to use their resources and based on the decisions made they will leave a lasting mark for future generations to measure them against. In the twenty-first century the United States is facing a similar decision regarding what our legacy will be for future generations... it could be massive debt, a broken economy, a failing infrastructure, or it could be the laying of a foundation from which some great improvement to life in this country or the world in total will spring forth.

Chapter Twenty-one

(Survival of the Fittest)

In its purest form, the free enterprise system is very similar to Darwin's theory of evolution. In order to see the comparison, let's look a couple of examples,

- Darwin's theory: On the Serengeti plain the slowest zebra will become the lion pride's dinner and when two hikers happen upon a hungry grizzly bear, the faster and more agile of the two will most likely to survive.

- Free enterprise: If a town has three gas stations but only enough demand to support two we would expect the two best gas stations to ultimately survive and the third to fail.

It seems harsh when you think of economic theory in this context but it is very much the reality and we are better off for it.

Consider for a moment if, a few generations in the past, our ancestors had become overly concerned with the fate of the blacksmiths and sought to hold course in a manner that would have protected that noble profession but would have stunted the progress that led us to automobiles. From our perspective, it seems ridiculous that anyone would have ever considered that as a real alternative but every day we see stories in the news about industries being hurt by progress and what needs to be done to prevent it. As observers of change we need to understand that it is change that leads our society to have things like cars and computers. Keeping this in mind will help us make better decisions now and in the future so that our fear of change doesn't stunt our progress. We certainly wouldn't want to be responsible for banning the testing and development of motor cars or the first practical warp drive.

As with many concepts we have discussed in this book, recognizing and rewarding the right change can be difficult. The process of evolution in nature is said to take thousands of years to cause even minor changes in the DNA of a species, so the progress is slow. Whether you believe evolution is guided by an intelligent hand or is purely a function of better genes winning the battle to live and reproduce, it's still a process that has proven to take a very long time. The free enterprise system, in its rewarding of success and punishing of failure, tends to proceed at a much more rapid pace than does evolution in nature. However, free enterprise is hampered from pure progress by the intelligent beings who try to influence the outcome of the race for success by attempting to effect the selection of winners and losers.

At one point in time a tourist, visiting Adam Smith's island from a far off land called Kansas, gave the Farmer family a new variety of wheat to try. The head of the Farmer family had heard legends about the vast productive fields of wheat in faraway Kansas and how successful these Kansas farming families were. So Farmer, at the next growing season, planted a small plot of ground with the Kansas wheat and soon had a bumper crop coming to ripen. Farmer carefully guarded the wheat from this plot and saved every seed so that they might use that wheat to seed an even larger planting in the next season. This process continued another growing cycle until, by the third growing season, all the wheat being grown on the island originated from the wheat grains brought to Farmer from the distant Kansas.

The result of the Farmer family's efforts was a much improved harvest and by the third season the new wheat variety was generating a yield ten percent better than any harvest the Farmer family had ever had. This increase in production brought the prospect of greater wealth to the Farmer family and to the island as a whole as there was more wheat available with no added effort required to obtain the greater output.

Progress is not always purely good and what might seem like a ten percent gain is not always exactly that. This proved to be the case for Farmer when the crop came in and the family baked their first loaves of bread made from the Kansas wheat. They found the taste of the bread was different from bread made from the variety of wheat the family had always grown on the island in the past. With the new crop being all that was available for sale to the Sheppard and Fisher clans they too soon noticed the difference. After a few weeks of eating the odd tasting bread the heads of the other two families met with Farmer to question what had gone wrong with the wheat from this crop.

Farmer's family had also been complaining that they didn't like the new wheat so, by the time Farmer met with Sheppard and Fisher, she had come to accept that she had made a mistake. Farmer explained to the others that she had heard so many good things about the Kansas wheat that she did not bother to check the other attributes of the wheat beyond the high yields. The three families resigned themselves to the fact that they would have to make the best of the new wheat until the next crop came to harvest.

This example is a case where the island society initially backed the new superior product only to find out that what they had before had been better. Farmer had unknowingly shortchanged the process that would have naturally and efficiently allowed the island marketplace to select the better wheat. In our economy we often see where bad products, processes, or businesses sometimes win out over a superior one. In the 1980's, video cassette recorders (VCRs) were the latest new product rage and there were two formats VHS and Betamax. In terms of virtually every aspect the Betamax system was superior to the VHS but society choose the VHS format and Betamax died a quick death. Society suffered as a result of choosing the lesser product by paying higher costs related to the larger VHS machines, larger video cassettes and that both were less durable than the Betamax version.

Humans are susceptible to looking at things in less than objective terms. A Chevy buyer who needs a new half ton pickup will buy the Chevy model even if Ford or Toyota has a better rated product. What usually makes a product successful is the more non-partisan buyer, the one who does their homework and then buys the best product available. By being objective and doing this personal pre-purchase homework you help society as much as your help yourself. If you buy the more fuel efficient, less polluting, more reliable half-ton pickup you will be benefiting society, not only while you own the vehicle but, throughout the lifetime of that vehicle. If the vehicle is easier to maintain then there is less cost involved to keep the truck running which will allow you to spend your money on other things, again good for you and good for the economy. More precisely said the better product (the one that meets mankind's needs while consuming fewer resources) will result in making our society a more productive place. The resources saved by purchasing the better product will be available to fuel progress or improve the livelihood of others within the society.

When a bad product is widely sold into the economy it can have immense impacts on the economy and society. A great example of such a product is asbestos. Asbestos was widely used in the early part of the twentieth century for a vast number of products but was later found to be ill suited for many of the purposes in which the product was employed. At some point during this time it became obvious that asbestos products presented a health danger. *(It's debatable as to when this knowledge made its way to the manufacturers and how quickly they moved to modify asbestos usage).*

Asbestos had many positive attributes, particularly as a fire retardant, that made it ideal for use in many products especially long-lived products like ships, homes, and schools. Once society became aware of the dangers associated with asbestos, a new industry was born whose function was to safely remove asbestos from products or in other cases to oversee their safe destruction and disposal.

As an example let's consider a school built in 1960, this school was expected to last eighty years however so much asbestos was used in the school's construction that there was no choice but to destroy the school and rebuild it using current safer building materials. Your first thought might be that building a new school will provide jobs and stimulate the economy... this is true but it only takes into account part of the facts. Let's suppose that the county, in which the school was located, had a five million dollar capital budget for that year and had intended to build a community college. The county could not afford both capital projects therefore the cost of the asbestos problem to this county was local access to a community college.

When a bad product is put into the economy it tends to act as a drag on the economy. You might suggest that lawsuits against the manufacturer might, in the school example, allow the county to recover enough money to complete both projects. This would be true in the microcosm of that county but that five million dollar cost for tearing down an otherwise perfectly serviceable school would still come out of the economy somewhere. You may envision that the money is coming from some billionaire living in a luxurious mansion and parting them from their possibly ill-gotten millions is not only just but also good for the economy. While that could be the case it's also likely that the money will force the closure of a business in another county that will create economic hardship equal to or worse than the loss of the new community college.

Every society has to weigh the risks of carefully policing new products and scrutinizing existing products to make sure they are the best suited for their society. This can be a two edged sword since being too careful might inhibit innovation thereby costing society the benefit of new products, services, and technology. My point is that, it's not easy to be efficient in the process of finding and selecting the best products without considering the very human predisposition to buy based upon emotion or incomplete facts. Our goal as a society should be to recognize this weakness and avoid attempting to over regulate or under analyze our product choices.

Our goal should be to create an economic environment that keeps the door open to new products and innovations. If society chooses a regulated environment, so that entering a new product into the market requires significant resources *(be they financial, legal or something else)*, these become barriers to innovation that will hold society back as a whole. The balance between easy access to the market and protecting society from bad products will always be a delicate balance but it's one worth trying to maintain or striving to achieve.

As society becomes more sophisticated the majority of products are not as likely to come from the personal laboratories or workshops of people like Alexander Graham Bell, Thomas Edison, or George Washington Carver. While technology and innovation may, at some point in the future once again become a more personal and private affair, the situation in the early twenty-first is one where the most effective research is a costly proposition. We are now dependent upon innovation coming from large facilities and with these facilities come a great deal of bureaucracy.

The term "a culture for innovation" is a used often and is a concept that is needed in the research and development of products today. Every minute a talented inventor, possibly the next Edison, spends navigating red tape may potentially result in the loss of an innovation. As an example, if George Washington Carver were working for one of today's food manufacturers, his propensity to focus on the development of peanut based products might be considered, for fear of peanut allergy related lawsuits, too dangerous to pursue. Should that prove to be the case then innovations from his great mind would be lost. And if Edison worked for a firm where senior management thought that electric light was absolute folly his research may have been stopped before the development of the first practical electric light bulb.

While there are downsides related to large research organizations that have resulted in failures there have also been great successes. Consider the space race during the last half of the twentieth century, it produced the moon landings, the space shuttle, and the international space station, these are all products of large organized research and development initiatives. Much of this research was government funded and many of the products of this research have found their way, not only into space but, into the homes of people throughout the world. These product concepts were released into private industry and transformed into products that could be sold into the broader United States' market. These products competed in the economic marketplace some gaining acceptance and others failing but the overall result was a giant leap forward for society in numerous areas of technology.

As a society we need to foster the environment necessary for innovation if we want a better life for ourselves and future generations. We need to be aware that within society there are some individuals and organizations that have vested interests in seeing progress move in a certain direction or at a certain pace, and while this may be good for that individual or organization it's not necessarily good for society as a whole. While growing up I heard a number of my relatives tell stories where they were convinced that the large automakers had discovered a way to make an engine that used much less gas but the oil companies conspired with the automakers to suppress the technology. I doubt there is much truth to this rumor but the concept is intriguing and things like this certainly do happen when an innovation threatens profit.

Today our society is in dire need of more energy. Finding the next energy source provides a large profit potential and countless businesses, government research facilities, and universities are working hard to find new energy sources. Profit is a strong market motivation but there are also other societal factors to be considered. Regardless of whether or not you're a believer in the risks of global warming you can still appreciate the fact that adding more CO_2 to the planet's atmosphere is not a good thing therefore being able to reduce carbon dioxide emissions would be a good thing. The dilemma for researchers is how much this particular long-term issue should factor into their efforts to find alternative energy sources. Let's suppose for a second that the worst case global warming scenarios were absolute fact and that twenty years from now billions of people would die as a result; in this scenario how much effort do you think would be focused on searching for alternative energy and on finding zero CO_2 emission energy products?

The free enterprise system works well when you're choosing a better cleaning product but when peripheral aspects, such as environmental impacts, are involved the concept of the letting the free enterprise market determine which product survives may not serve us well. Returning to the evolution analogy *(and this is where the concept of intelligent design may figure in)*, when it comes to the evolution of inventions there are times when the free market needs to be guided in the right direction for the benefit of the broader community.

Many may think this means we should turn research facilities into government run organizations (like the IRS)... quite to the contrary... instead we need to use the market driven motivations that have served us so well but deploy them in a way that factors in, not only short-term profit goals but, the needs of society for generations to come. As an example, suppose the researcher (or research team,) who developed a device or production concept that decreased our carbon footprint, would earn a bonus equivalent to a percentage of society's long-term savings. I suspect that this free market based reward would spur the innovative genius needed to make progress against this potential problem.

Developing a concept that works for intelligently guiding both government and privately sponsored research innovation is well beyond the scope of this chapter and book but, in order for free market economic concepts to work, we as members of society must understand which levers can be pulled to encourage innovations. For problems like energy or growing carbon dioxide emissions, this type of approach is needed so that multiple solutions can be developed in order to compete within the free market where only the best solution(s) will survive and then those responsible for developing those solutions should be rewarded.

The risk we need to avoid is falling for any of the simple solutions such as "drill baby drill" or "just say no to offshore drilling". We as voters, and as members of our society, need to understand that the solutions to complex issues, such as energy or environmental concerns, are too complicated to be solved by simple slogans. The answer to finding the right culture of innovation is not going to fit on a bumper sticker or be simple enough for a thirty second commercial, the answer will require consideration of the facts from all sides including both short-term and long-term factors. While researching the facts recognize that proponents, regardless of their position, will have vested interests and have every reason to keep you from hearing and fully understanding all sides of the issue. And, as with all economic concepts, it's important to keep in mind that what works now may not, and most likely will not, work even ten years from now… as our society continues to develop so will the need for us to adapt. Your position today may be the equivalent of fastest Zebra on the Serengeti Plain but five years from now that same position may get you eaten by the lions of progress.

Chapter Twenty-two

(Productivity, Economics' Magic Elixir)

If there is a silver bullet amongst the workings of economics it is productivity. Productivity is the central premise that makes any process work, not work, or work progressively better. In a micro setting most people get why productivity, specifically how being productive, is essential to progress. Given the importance of the vital premise let's begin with its definition. **Productivity** *is an average measure of the efficiency of production. Productivity is a ratio of production output to what is required to produce it (inputs of capital, labor, land, energy, materials, etc.). The measure of productivity is defined as a total output per one unit of a total input.*[17]

Productivity really only has meaning when it is accompanied by a modifier such as *higher productivity* or a *loss of productivity*. As a child, when cleaning your room, your mother or father no doubt helped frame up your productivity in terms like, *"you call that a clean room?"* or *"how much longer is it going to take you to finish cleaning your room?"*. In applying modifiers to the science of economics there are a number that apply when describing productivity. The most applicable of these descriptors describe the amount of output, the quality of the output, and the fit of the output to the needs of the consumer of the output.

---

[17] http://en.wikipedia.org/wiki/Productivity

Remember back to your worst room cleaning experience as a child? That experience was probably when you were the least productive at performing this chore. Your experience may have been similar to some I recall where I was stuck in my room for what seemed like an eternity, I would spend hours looking at the mess and make repeated half-hearted attempts at progress before pleading with my parents for a reprieve from this overwhelming task. Now looking back, I know the task could have been productively completed in about a half hour or so, which would have been followed by several speechless minutes from my shocked parents then by a level of praise that I had likely never heard before in my life.

In the simplest terms being productive is being effective and timely in completing a task. In your home, if you live in a family setting, the end of a meal is an excellent example of what is relative about productivity. Anyone who has had a child or a younger sibling has certainly experienced a meal that drags on and on, sometimes several times longer than it would have had it been productively completed by everyone at the dinner table. Using our usually male chauvinistic pattern of thought, let's assume the degree of productivity is measured by the amount of time from when Mom sets down the last article of food on the table until the last dish is put away and the table is cleaned and ready for the next meal.

Let's say, in an ideal situation, the time it takes to complete the dinner cycle *(after which the family will head to the local amusement park)* takes fifteen minutes. Everyone eats quickly, is careful not to make any added mess, rinses off their own dishes, and then carefully places the dishes into the dishwasher. However this same process, with little brother or sister staring at a pile of inedible green beans and Mom having to chase down the soiled dinnerware throughout the whole process, may take two hours to complete. Clearly the productive loss to this family, and particularly Mom in this case, is a couple hours or more, time which could have been devoted to something else that could have provided greater value to Mom and/or to the entire family.

This example is the absolute essence of what is so relative in terms of what it means to be productive or not productive. In a work setting achieving productivity is the key to success and yet, as a manager, it seems virtually impossible at times to get that concept across to otherwise intelligent adults. While it's easy for people to understand that Mom standing over little sis for hours, trying to get her to eat her green beans, decreases household productivity, it's often next to impossible to get subordinates to understand how spending twenty minutes on a personal call decreases office productivity. Though daunting, my challenge in this chapter is to convey a piece of enlightenment and understanding as to how productivity, across the expanse of a great economy, determines if our standard of living rises or falls.

Our economy is a collection of resources or inputs which, when applied in the economy, yields a level of output that we as consumers have available to consume. The more productively we apply our efforts to effectively using resources the higher the standard of living we achieve. As I have attempted to do throughout this book, I will put the concept of productivity into a simpler setting in order to nurture a better understanding.

Yesterday a terrible apocalypse befell the planet Earth and today the entire population of the planet consists of two people, a guy named Adam and a girl named Eve *(pretty clever, right?)*. Clearly, in this setting, both Adam and Eve will need to stay productive if humans are once again to rule a resurgent Earth. These two people will need to focus on building a life and a family and, in order to survive; they will need to be effective in gathering and converting the resources of the planet into what they need to be successful. Obviously, in this example, we don't need to worry that our two lone survivors will spend twenty minutes on a frivolous phone call or, for that matter, that they will waste any of their time on things that don't contribute to rebuilding the quality of humankind's life… in other words this couple will be productive.

In our post-apocalyptic Earth, our two survivors will be driven to make the most of every hour of every day. The possibility that either person will sit out their life as a non-productive person is, by virtue of necessity, eliminated. Adam and Eve, absent the occasional distraction by a slithering snake, will keep their eye on the ball and their nose to the grindstone throughout their life in order to build their family which will be the nucleus for rebuilding human society.

In our current economy we are not as effective keeping everyone productive as our fictitious survivors were. In fact, listening to political pundits, you might be more inclined to believe that our standard of living has more to do with the rates of taxation or the level of government spending than with something as simple as keeping our society working productively. We have, at numerous times in this book, touched upon productivity and attempted to demonstrate how getting more done has led to improved standards of living, particularly within the setting of our Adam's Island families. It's clear and easy to understand that if the Fishers spend more time fishing *(in the right places and with effective equipment)* all the islanders will be able to eat their fill of fish. When looked at in those terms, the concept of productivity is so simple but it still consistently befuddles us on a national scale.

During the past hundred years there have been numerous times when many national economies have had ten percent unemployment and, in some cases, even higher. Within a national economy, because of the enormity of scale, we are often overwhelmed by the problem and then mystified later when the unemployment predicament goes away. When there is unemployment within a society does that mean that all the society's needs are being met or are there still needs that are going unfilled? I'm pretty sure that there are always unfulfilled needs within a society and, if these needs could be satisfied by someone from amongst the unemployed *(using a skill that they already have)* it would seem to be obvious that the economy is to some degree dysfunctional. This dysfunction is embodied by the state of chronic unemployment. At this point it's important to ignore the rhetoric that might begin to bounce around inside your mind about how this dysfunction can become the arguments for or against capitalism, socialism, and communism. You will struggle to grasp the concept we are seeking to understand if you let yourself be limited or distracted by bumper sticker slogans, slogans that are so often used to comfortably and quickly explain the causes of unemployment within society.

Unfortunately, the reasons for productivity issues are not always the same in every economy. The answer however, is almost always the same… find a way to get people working and earning wages that will drive consumption in that economy. The simple example of people starving in the cities, while food spoils on the farms, is among the clearest analogies of this type of dysfunction in an economy. Going just a step further, what if people were starving in the cities because farm workers were unemployed and food was not being grown on the farms? Looking at it this way the picture of unemployment and its impact on society becomes a bit clearer.

Continuing on, if we can convince the farm workers to work the land and produce enough food for the starving city dwellers then we have begun to lessen the dysfunction. In Communist Russia, Joseph Stalin addressed this problem by simply telling the farmers that if the city dwellers needed food he would take it from the farmers therefore, if the farmers wanted enough food for themselves, they would have to produce enough for both themselves and the city dwellers. In the United States in the 1960's, President Lyndon Johnson's Great Society program[18] established the welfare state. In this model, unlike Stalin's approach, the hungry population would receive food the government purchased from the nation's farmers. In both Johnson's and Stalin's solutions the problem of a hungry population was dealt with and, to the extent that idle farmers or farmland was amongst the symptoms, was effectively resolved.

The problem with both of these solutions is that neither leveraged the concepts of free enterprise to resolve the problem which, in both the case of the planned communist economy and the welfare state promoted by President Johnson, left their respective societies with a solution that would ultimately fail. If you're expecting a magical solution in the coming pages let me adjust your expectations now... I don't have it. Finding the

---

[18] fhttp://en.wikipedia.org/wiki/Great_Society

solution for this problem will only come to our society by our achieving a better understanding of how to leverage society's resources productively.

The Great Society programs hit upon only one aspect of the solution and that is to keep consumers consuming; long-term however, you also need more people producing. If nothing else, maybe we can at least agree that it is in society's best interest to keep people working. Having millions of society's able bodied individuals unemployed clearly reduces productivity and reduces our standard of living. In our search for an answer we should look for solutions that keep people working, making things or providing services that people want. I would further argue that we should guard against anything that takes productive people out of the workforce.

Early in the twenty-first century there was a widely publicized fight in France between unions and the conservative party government[19] which involved moving the retirement age from sixty to sixty-two years of age. Today most Americans have

---

[19] http://www.guardian.co.uk/world/2010/nov/10/french-retirement-age-reform-62

reconciled themselves to the fact that they will need to work until their late sixties, if not longer. You might wonder why keeping older workers in the workplace makes sense when so many countries are struggling with unemployment. The answer is simple arithmetic. As a society, people are living longer increasing the number of years that will be spent in retirement. In order to ensure that there will be enough money to fund retirement for society's elderly we need to tinker with the retirement age in order to make sure there is a relative balance between those working and those who are retired and, as a result, are only consuming. If we are using our own savings to fund our retirement then it clearly makes sense to us that we will need more productive years in order to save enough money to cover our longer retirement period. The same logic applies to government pension programs like social security, if people will live to be ninety then stretching the retirement age out a few years will keep more people paying into the system and will shorten the number of years the government will need to fund social security payments to retirees.

Continuing on with the issue of the retirement age in France… if the French do not raise their country's retirement age then they will need to find alternative solutions to address their collective shorter working lives. One obvious solution would be to lessen the amount of resources retirees consume. For example, if the French retirement age was five years earlier than that of an American worker but the life expectancy for both the Americans and the French was ninety years of age then, on average, Americans could expect twenty-three years of retirement and the French twenty-eight. The easy answer to deal with the dilemma of the longer retirement would be to reduce the annual retirement payment to the French by about twenty percent.

You should now be a step closer to understanding a good bit about the economics of retirement as well as the real cost of unemployment *(and other non-contributing members of society)*. In the past few paragraphs I have touched on sensitive topics to my left-of-center readers so, in an effort to equally offend my conservative readers, let's expand the discussion to include the non-working wealthy.

Often, in TV dramas, there are wealthy individuals who are portrayed to be living off their inheritance usually accompanied by some other vice, as we do love to vilify the idle rich. As a society we spend too much of our time either idolizing or criticizing the wealthy. Neither of these are productive pursuits and our focus here is more on why it's harmful to the economy and society itself to have too many of our fellow citizens sitting idle. This is particularly true when some of our brightest people are among them. As a student of economics, I'm surprised why people don't equate generations of families living off of previously accumulated wealth to citizens living off government provided welfare, the effect to the working population is largely the same, other than one is responsible for more consumption than the other.

In chapter fourteen we had the discussion about balance in terms of the inheritance tax *(estate or death tax as its critics like to call it)*. I maintain that there should continue to be the ability for a parent to pass some amount of wealth onto the next generation but there should be a reasonable limit. *(Bill and Melinda Gates self-imposed an inheritance limit on their own children providing each with only ten million from their fifty to sixty billion dollar fortune with the other 99% reportedly going to charity not to the United States government as taxes)*. As I have previously explained one benefit of providing the opportunity for citizens to leave some of their accumulated wealth to their younger relatives *(or other acquaintances)* motivates the benefactors to be more productive in their lifetimes. And again being able to motivate individuals is the key to driving talented individuals to be as productive as possible and is something we must maintain.

Every wealthy family has their own story as to how they accumulated their wealth. Every story is different and so are the motivations that drove those productive individuals to accumulate their wealth. At some point, in another book, an author might debate how many earned their wealth in productive ways as opposed destructive ways, such as those who earned their wealth through the 2008 mortgage market meltdown or one of the accounting scandals like Enron. I have seen close-up how a few people became wealthy, in some cases it was the product of bringing new found productivity into the economy but in other cases the wealth was the product of something less healthy for society. It suffices to say that the drivers leading to the accumulation of wealth are not all good or all bad and I would not hazard a guess on what percentage came via the good methods. I would however love to read a well-researched book on that subject, not sure that I would be the best author for that "tell-all-tales" project.

Our society has a plethora of examples of wasted effort or massive expenses paid for things that have not served to advance society. Most of these examples fall into the categories of being non-productive or productivity sapping efforts. Whenever I have had a conversation on the subject of wasteful projects, virtually everyone has a good story to tell on the subject. One, worth sharing, was an audit performed by our favorite "kick-around" organization, the Internal Revenue Service. The company involved was one that virtually anyone *(even those with the most rudimentary financial analysis skills)* could see was on the road to bankruptcy or some other form of financial restructuring but, despite the fact that there was no tax paying probability in this company's future, the IRS and one its agents chose to spend a year and half auditing this hapless company. The company reportedly spent nearly a million dollars in consulting fees to help get the auditor to leave them alone and used significant in house resources that entertaining *(pulling records, making copies and answering questions)* an IRS agent for a year and a half entails.

I'm pretty sure the facts in this case are pretty accurate but, for illustration purposes, let's assume they are in fact accurate. Under this assumption, what did the consumption of a million

(possibly as much as two million) dollars do for the United States'
economy or for society? The agent of course earned a salary and
another year toward his/her pension but, other than that, I am
at a complete loss as to what benefit this exercise brought to
mankind. To be fair, there are reasons why companies that are
losing money need to be audited by the IRS but, in terms of
efficiently doing this, I would argue effective IRS management
could have averted the extent of the economic loss in this case.

In addition to the IRS, the Environmental Protection Agency
(EPA) also tends to have its fair share of critics. I have had only
limited exposure to the EPA during my career, and that was
restricted to doing nothing more than completing some of
EPA's annual reporting while working for a paint manufacturer.
The EPA, like the IRS, has a largely thankless job in that their
work in the present is almost never welcomed by the company
or person under its scrutiny and its benefit is in preventing
something that could happen. Pretty much the EPA is damned
in the present and then damned again in the future whenever it
is found to have missed something in the past. Both federal
agencies have jobs that, if done well, serve to make the
economy more productive. In the case of the EPA, we know
little about what they have saved us from but we certainly know

about cases when there was not sufficient oversight, such as the Love Canal case and a host of other environmental disasters that lead to the creation of the Super Fund legislation in the 1980s[20]. We know that cleaning up these environmental disaster sites cost many billions of dollars and were funded by United States taxpayers but, what many of us don't consider, is how much money could have been saved if these hazardous wastes had been disposed of properly in the first place. In this set of examples the productivity gain to society, if the right oversight had been in place to prevent these dumpsites, would have been measured not only in terms of money saved but also in terms of improved health for those impacted by these environmental disasters.

Moving on from government's role in productivity, let's get back to the more important discussion… the private sector's role in making the economy more productive. In our quest to understand there's one question we have to ask ourselves. Why in the twenty-first century, in what is a largely free enterprise based economy, did we have so many people unemployed in the United States from 2008 to 2013? In free enterprise economies

---

[20] http://www.epa.gov/superfund/about.htm

excessive unemployment is not an infrequent phenomenon and tends to occur frequently and is often severe. Throughout this book I have, and will continue to, maintain that the free enterprise economic model is superior to all known alternatives. So given this how do I reconcile these two statements?

Unlike some who view free enterprise and capitalism akin to the stone tablets handed to Moses, I am of the belief that these concepts are great innovations. History tells us that the Ford Model T was a great car, so good in fact that Henry Ford is reputed to have resisted moving onto a new model until his competition's progress had resulted in a large loss in Ford's market share. My point on capitalism is that, like the automobile, it was a great innovation but it's not one that can be optimized without continued innovation. Unlike a car, where the skills of tens of thousands of highly trained experts consult to develop the next model, our tinkering with today's capitalism is not done in quite as an organized fashion.

If we are to take our economy to a level where it delivers a higher standard of living and one which maintains a more stable employment, our solutions to economic problems will need to be done in a setting that provides for a more studied approach.

The process of proposing improvements to our economic methods has denigrated to a process that has minimal study and virtually no tolerance for discussion. To elevate our approach more of the voting population needs to develop a higher level of understanding of economic concepts and the members of the two major political parties need to be open to considering alternatives for bringing the economy to a better place.

This means things like regulations and taxes need to be thought of as levers and used by the enlightened political leadership to develop an economy that will consistently deliver a higher average standard of living. To do this we must open the door to having meaningful discussions about why our nation is not more productive and then take actions to drive changes that will result in improved productivity. Sometimes these changes may fly in the face of what we have come to identify as America's version of free enterprise.

Let's consider one example in terms of medical care. Within the medical community there are many exceptional physicians and from amongst them the best of the best, some of whom have very specialized skills, can earn huge sums of money over a short period of time which, unfortunately, results in some choosing to retire early, well before the time when their age degrades their skills. This is certainly not true for all doctors but, to the extent that it is true, it will certainly lessen the availability a much needed skill set within our society. Here is where the economic arguments tend to break down, with some screaming socialist medicine and predicting that the very idea of discussing the problem will lead to mediocre medical care while some equally obstinate folks on the other side may want to adopt a maximum wage for all doctors, CEOs, bestselling authors, and anyone else who might, in their view, make too much money.

An informed discussion on how to keep doctors in the workforce longer, particularly those that are the most talented, can be a balanced discussion between the needs of society and how to allow for generous rewards for the best physicians. Anyone who has followed the healthcare debate can probably imagine the likelihood of an even tempered discussion on this small part of the overall economy of the United States. Some would argue that this is why the United States should have a more powerful executive branch, one that can unilaterally make changes quickly to laws and regulations without the inconvenience of gaining legislative consensus. This approach has been used in Russia for some time and the results are, at least, just as equally flawed as the more democratic methods that are in use within the United States.

Returning to the automotive analogy, consider the approach used for new model development and testing. New car models are worked up within extremely complex CAD systems which provide the project leader with good data on what to expect on the test track. And "yes" before your next new car hits the showroom floor it is tested on test tracks and sometimes ran millions of miles before it is brought out for worldwide consumption. Possibly the nation could benefit from a few economic test tracks in order work out some of the kinks in economic strategy. Obviously this is not the sole answer, for example, you could not adopt a different approach to estate taxes in the "test track" of say the State of New Jersey because people would simply move out of state or into the state to either avoid or take advantage of the concept being tested. Some things like alternative medical care concepts might, in some cases, work within this economic test track approach.

The point here is that higher productivity and the benefits that increasing productivity provides, have continued to elude us. Economics and society itself grows continually more complex every day and at some point we have to come to the conclusion that what we are doing is simply not working as well as it could. There are no easy answers and we need to recognize that economics is a complicated subject, one that deserves a calm informed debate, a willingness to try different concepts, and, based on the facts, the ability to recognize the results of deploying those concepts as being either good or bad then moving on from there.

Chapter Twenty-three

(Barriers to Entry)

One of the most significant causes of friction to the workings of an economy is barriers to entry. In chapter four we discussed import tariffs as a barrier to imported goods entering into an economy. Governments have used these barriers for a variety of reasons including protecting a local industry from foreign competitors. The tariff, in a way, acts like a fence enclosing a property which to some degree inhibits the flow of things across the property's boundary. If the fence is six inches high the effectiveness of the fence as a barrier is pretty insignificant whereas if it is twenty feet high and topped with razor wire then the fence is extremely effective as a barrier. The same concept applies to various types of barriers to entry throughout economics; some barriers are minor impediments while others are virtually impenetrable.

Many types of things can be barriers to entry, so at this point it's important to open our minds to what exactly can operate as barriers to the natural movement of resources. The tariff example is easy to understand… the more expensive you make an imported good within the importing country the less of that product will be consumed in that country therefore making the tariff an effective economic barrier. Other barriers to entry however, are not as easily recognized and their effectiveness is much more difficult to quantify. In a broader context prejudice could be a barrier to the effective flow of resources to those in need of them. In my home town *(Cincinnati, Ohio)* there are a couple high schools that are considered to be the best private schools in the area and in some cases employers, when hiring, give special consideration to graduates from these schools. You might disagree that this as a barrier to economic flow but, in the purest sense, if anything less than the best possible employee available is hired for a job then by definition the employer is not maximizing the benefits of operating in a free enterprise economy. As an example Jill and Sam are both interviewing for the same sales position, Sam went to the preeminent school but Jill did not, Jill however has a much better performance record and skill set. If the hiring manager hires Sam because he appreciates the value of having that particular high school experience, then the manager's company may suffer as Jill would have sold a thousand dollars more in gross profit per month than Sam. In this case, the school prejudice was an economic barrier that cost Sam's new employer twelve thousand dollars per year and frustrated a potential employee costing the economy an un-quantified amount.

Barriers to entry are often impacted by the regulations imposed, or not imposed, by the government of that society. For example, in the United States the only people who can practice medicine are doctors who meet certain governmentally set standards. This is a regulation but it's also a barrier to those who would seek to enter into the medical profession. It's fairly obvious that these regulations have merits but there are also economic impacts from these regulations that are not all positive. Suppose there is an individual who is extremely gifted as a medical practitioner but, because of these regulations, was unable to contribute their skills to society. If a regulatory hole existed that allowed this individual to contribute then society would benefit. This is of course ignoring the risks created by having other less competent individuals who might slip through this same regulatory crack.

Regulations are not the only barriers to entry into the medical profession, the length of time required to complete the required education and the long rigorous training rotations involved in the medical profession will deter many talented but less motivated people from choosing this field. The more challenging the barriers to entry are into a particular profession the fewer individuals will enter into that profession which will affect the supply of, in this case, qualified practitioners. Supply and demand influences costs; therefore, by constricting the supply of qualified medical professionals, the cost of medical services increases. For example, if some medical services, such as the diagnosis and treatment of erectile dysfunction, could be performed by someone with far less training than your family practitioner then this medical service could be provided at a much lower cost. I'm only using this example to make a point; it's certainly not a realistic since with erectile dysfunction, as with most medical problems, it's not safe to treat without considering the overall health of the individual. And as anyone who spends any part of their evening watching television can tell you, we are all not *"healthy enough for sexual activity"*.

If you were to examine the medical industry you would find many elements that are effectively barriers to entry into that profession. The benefit of many of these barriers may not be as clear as the benefit our society receives from the regulations that define the type of education required for those who can practice medicine. A controversial topic is the issue of medical malpractice lawsuits. Medical malpractice lawsuits and malpractice insurance make up a portion of the total cost of medical care in the United States. During my research I found a variety of numbers on the total cost of malpractice lawsuits and malpractice insurance and all the numbers were large but the following quote from Wikipedia.org on the subject seems to be as good as any. *"Studies place the direct and indirect costs of malpractice between 5% and 10% of total U.S. medical costs."* You might wonder how exactly this is a barrier to entry. The answer again goes back to supply and demand. Medical malpractice lawsuits have three fairly obvious impacts on the supply of doctors. First, the very thought of being at risk for a malpractice lawsuit will keep many potential doctors out of the profession. Second a number of doctors no doubt leave the profession out of frustration from malpractice legal issues. Finally many doctors choose to retire at a younger age rather than continue to practice medicine in the current environment which keeps them at risk of a malpractice claim.

Other industries also have barriers to entry. Consider for example the auto industry… it would be very difficult for the average Joe to go out and start up a car company. In the early twentieth century there were car companies coming and going within the auto industry on a regular basis however, as of the early part of the twenty-first century, the amount of capital required to start a new automotive manufacturing company became enormous, so much so, that competition within the industry is now largely limited to the players already in the marketplace. Numerous factors come into play to create this steep barrier to entry, two examples include the cost of designing a car model and the complexity of design required in a saleable auto in the twenty-first century *(versus the early car models)*.

In the past the cost of shipping a car made automobile manufacturing more of a local affair than it is today. In fact, in the middle of the twentieth century the vast majority of all the cars sold in the United States were manufactured in the United States. This barrier to entry largely went away in the last quarter century to the point where a good number of the cars now sold in the United States are not manufactured here. There still remains a cost benefit for cars that are sold in the United States to be made here which is why Toyota, Honda, and Mercedes Benz now have U.S. plants. This is an example of, not only the resilience of some barriers to entry but also, how the changes in taste and technology can shrink some of those barriers.

Not all barriers to entry in business are constructed by governmental entities or are products of the physical world. In some cases the freedom within a free enterprise society has naturally produced its own barriers. Consider the monopolies that developed in the late nineteenth century and early twentieth century. Among those monopolies were U.S. Steel and Standard Oil. These businesses were often castigated for their behavior, behaviors which forced the passage of regulations that broke their hold on their respective markets. In purely business terms, management within these monopolies were acting in the proper way… they were running a business and each business's stated goal is to maximize their company's value to their shareholders. Just like the wolf is not wrong for eating the rabbit, so too the company management is not wrong for working to make the most of its opportunities while following the rules of the political entity within which it operates. Realistically if John D. Rockefeller did not manage Standard Oil to perfect its operation as a monopoly it's quite likely somebody else would have. Ewing Oil could have just as easily been responsible for the evils of a monopoly as was Standard Oil. Given the legal environment at that time in history, a monopoly was destined to arise because it was the natural evolution of the most successful oil business in that period. To make this point more clear the economic environment, which includes the national laws at the time, would naturally result in having a single steel company and oil company dominating their respective markets. Expecting a different result is just as absurd as expecting the wolf to ignore the rabbit sitting a few feet away and choosing a nice patch of grass for his dinner instead.

In its unaltered state, the free enterprise system makes it simple for business people to operate in pursuit of their goal to maximize revenues and profits. While having a good value system is desired for leaders of all kinds, including business people, it's natural and expected for a business to attempt to exploit every legal means available in order to make a profit. Survival of the fittest means as much to the business world as it does to evolution of life on this planet. Businesses, as a form of survival and as a way to achieve higher profits, will naturally seek to limit competition. Since this ability to limit competition is a bad byproduct of the unregulated free enterprise system it is something that governments have chosen to regulate. There are many barriers to entry that are the natural product of free enterprise, these barriers require some form of regulation in order to keep the economy operating in a more efficient manner or in a way that is more beneficial to society.

Starting a business in the United States has always been a difficult endeavor, from the first step of developing a marketable concept through marshaling the resources needed to deliver that product or service to consumers. The statistics that highlight the importance of small businesses are real and, in our political environment, most politicians try to find ways to promote themselves as the champion of small business. Small businesses help to strengthen our communities and are therefore deserving of much of the attention they receive. Starting and running a small business includes a great deal of effort to overcome barriers to entry. Some barriers to entry are again the product of the free enterprise system itself.

One such barrier is competition. If you decided to start a lawn services company you would likely be joining a very crowded field of providers, one in which I suspect the competition is quite intense. In much of the twentieth century lawn service providers were largely local kids who were willing to mow lawns for a few bucks. In the early twenty-first century these blossoming entrepreneurs have become less of a factor in this market and have been supplanted by adults running businesses of a variety of sizes. Because of the relative ease of starting a lawn service business, and the number of competitors in that line of business, I suspect there are not many small business people running lawn service companies who are making the big bucks. In most communities there are generally a few larger players who have the aura of a bigger more profitable business and tend to service corporate entities and large personal estates. In the case of these companies they have the scale of operation that makes doing business with them more appealing to those with larger needs than doing business with Joe, the Lawn Guy who maybe has a truck with a trailer, a couple mowers, and a buddy named Bill who helps out on bigger jobs. While there are a lot of lawn care providers there are still barriers to entry into the parts of the market where size really does matters.

As a new lawn service company you would be barred from competing for the larger jobs and would have to overcome the steep competition for the smaller jobs. As a new provider these competitive marketplace barriers can be overcome by doing it better, cheaper, and doing so with a less worrisome smile on your face than your competitor has. This is truly free enterprise at its best, at least from the consumer's perspective. While there are few regulations on lawn mowing services, business that apply chemicals on lawns have to comply with governmental rules and regulations. As a result there is not as much competition in this sub-market of lawn care and the competition that exists is usually in the form of larger businesses. Consumer's need to be assured they have hired someone who will not poison the household or leave them with a permanently brown lawn.

Complying with regulations has a tendency to lessen the competition which therefore increases the price of the regulated service or product. Some regulations that hamper small business formation are necessary others are more debatable. Most of us would agree that we need regulation to manage what chemicals a lawn service provider can apply to your yard, after all… while Agent Orange may be effective in killing unwanted plants, such as poison ivy, there are a number of well documented reasons why you wouldn't want it applied to any part of your property or around the place you work. Other regulations, like labor laws, also apply to service providers. For example while in the 1960's it may have been okay to hire a twelve year old to mow your lawn, you will not see any people of this age working for the larger lawn service providers. Now we will return our focus back to Adam's Island to look at a time when the island experienced a barrier to entry that impacted its economy.

There was a time on Adam's Island when the inhabitants found a reason to regulate the island's fishing industry, this came about after a member of the Sheppard family fell ill after eating a fish caught and sold by the Farmer family. The families met to discuss how this unfortunate event had happened and what the families could do to prevent it from occurring again. The families decided that the Fisher family alone had the expertise needed to insure that only safe fish were provided for the islanders' consumption. The law was therefore made that only fish caught and sold by the Fishers would be allowed to be consumed by anyone on the island.

As time moved on, the island had no further incidents of illness brought about by the consumption of bad fish... the law *(or regulation)* had proved to be effective at doing what the families had intended when it was put in place. However the law created a monopoly for the Fisher clan and, without competition on the island, the Fishers soon implemented changes to how they serviced their market. In the past, members of the other families could go out and fish for a certain species of fish that they preferred or, in some cases, tried to catch a particularly robust specimen that would be the focal point of a celebratory meal. With the new law this was no longer an option and now any special requests had to go through the Fishers who, as one of their changes, now charged a premium for these special orders. Also, under the new arrangement even though the fish were always a safe variety to consume, the quality of the fish provided to the other families seemed to deteriorate over time. Fisher knew that their customers, if they wanted fish, would have to buy the fish they provided and could do little more than complain about any perceived decrease in quality.

The Fisher's, as the sole provider of fish, began to enact price increases so that the other island families were now not only getting less quality and less choice but were also paying more for the fish. After a time, one of the Farmer children proposed to the heads of the families that he should also be allowed to catch and market fish, arguing that he could do a better job than what was being done by the Fishers. While the family heads agreed that things were not at their best, Fisher offered some embellished stories about the dangers of consuming bad fish and the risks of allowing people unskilled in the art of fishing to catch and sell fish. Alas the heads of the families were moved by Fisher's warnings and rejected the young Farmer's pleas to enter into the fishing business.

Young Farmer however remained committed to his desire to become a fisherman and provide higher quality fish for his fellow islanders. He chose to bypass the law and pursued his new career by fishing under the cover of darkness. Young Farmer began to catch a good number of high quality fish during his nightly labors, so much so that he had more fish than his immediate family was able to consume. As you might expect, young Farmer began to offer some of his excess fish for sale to other members of the Farmer clan, carefully excluding the elder Farmer who was part of the island's leadership committee and had helped enact the fishing law in the first place.

Young Farmer's undercover fishing operations continued for a number of years during which time the elder Farmer had, on a number of occasions, dined with the younger Farmer. The elder Farmer noticed that the quality of fish served at young Farmer's house was much better than the fish she herself had been buying from Fisher. At first Farmer thought her young relative had been very fortunate to purchase such a good fish but after experiencing several meals at young Farmer's house, all with high quality fish, she became suspicious. The elder Farmer at first thought, since young Farmer had married a daughter from the Fisher clan they were being given the opportunity to select fish before the other island families. Although the young Farmer and his wife were not in fact receiving any preferential treatment, Farmer's suspicions were somewhat correct; the Fisher clan had been holding back the better fish for their own clan's consumption and selling the fish of lower quality to the other islanders.

The head of the Farmer family met with the heads of the Sheppard and Trader families and brought up her suspicion of malfeasance on the part of the Fishers. The other family heads agreed there might be some merit to Farmer's complaint and began to investigate the matter. Unbeknownst to the Fishers, the other families started to monitor the activities of the Fisher clan and discovered they were in fact keeping the better fish for themselves. However, prior to taking any action, the investigators decided they wanted more evidence and decided to wait until they caught the Fisher's giving some of the better fish to the young Farmer and his bride, the former Miss Fisher.

The newly minted island investigators kept watch at the fish market to see if they could catch the Fisher's in the act of selling the better fish to either the young Farmer or his wife. After weeks of observation, the investigators never witnessed the

Fisher family selling the better fish to this Farmer family. They did notice however, that the young Farmer family wasn't buying any fish at the market; in fact there were several Farmer families who weren't buying fish at the market. Given this turn of events, the investigators decided to question the Fisher's directly to find out how they were selling fish to these families. When Fisher learned about the investigation he was initially very angry but after getting past his anger he too started to wonder why the families in question were buying less fish. After the investigators finished their inquisition of Fisher they began to question their initial conjecture and began to consider what other means could be available to young Farmer.

The ad hoc investigation team began to observe the young Farmer family and quickly learned how he was getting his fish. Once having confirmed young Farmer's blatant disregard for the island's fishing law, he was called before the heads of the island families to answer for his actions. Young Farmer was immediately ordered to desist from his nighttime fishing but, shortly thereafter, the island council made several revisions to the fishing law. Revisions that allowed for more competition within the island's fishing industry and insured that better quality fish would be available to all families on the island.

Obviously changes in regulations occur much more quickly and effectively on Adam's Island than what typically happens in most countries including the United States. Just imagine how, in the United States, this would play out with the Fishing lobby interacting with consumer protection groups. There would no doubt be a multi-year study before there was any possibility of any meaningful reform... but we are getting a little off topic.

Keeping people from doing things, particularly those things at which they could earn a living at, are clear examples of barriers to entry. The Adam's Islanders had their reasons for erecting these barriers as do national, state, and local regulators. It's important to keep in mind that just because someone does something for a good reason it does not mean, on balance, that it's the best way to accomplish the task.

I have spent the bulk of my life working in accounting so some of the things I see are unique to my experience and of course are a source for my writing. As you may have guessed, this is a warning that we are about to embark on an example emanating from the "oh so exciting" accounting profession. Consider yourself dully warned as this might be a good time to take a caffeine break or whatever else you may need in order to remain conscious during the next couple paragraphs.

Throughout my career, as I managed the accounting for several national and marginally international companies, I found it surprising how much work it was to stay in compliance with the numerous state and local laws. Certainly complying with the various state and local laws are a challenge but one set of laws, the state sales tax laws, seemed particularly inefficient. Most states have a sales tax and within many states there are also a number of county and local sales taxes. In some states, the reporting and collection of state and local sales tax are combined and consistent while in other cases the sales tax rates and laws can vary by locality. This myriad of laws, rules, and forms all serve to become barriers to entry for companies who attempt to do business outside of their own state.

The fact that there are so many different governmental offices involved in the sales tax collection process not only makes it difficult for companies to comply but, makes it more difficult to ensure consumers and businesses are paying the correct amount of sales tax. Sales tax law is a special area of expertise, one that requires years of education and experience before one can be considered an expert, I am fairly knowledgeable of the process but I don't pretend to be an expert. Federal law in the United States doesn't make the collection and payment of sales tax any easier for companies or the states; there are, within the national legal code, an obtuse concept of sales tax Nexus which determines when a company must collect and remit sales tax in a state or locality.

Nexus is a complicated legal concept that determines who must collect sales tax on retail sales… a concept that has been made more complicated by the advent of internet sales. For example, if I am a local retailer and I set up a website to sell my products online then, by virtue of having a physical store in my state and locality, I am required to collect sales tax on the sales I make on my website to local residents. However, if people from another state make purchases from my online store I can often legally sell those products without having to charge sales tax. If an internet retailer from another state happens to carry the same products I do they may be able to sell that product to my next door neighbor without charging sales tax. Naturally, if my neighbor knows this, it is financially beneficial for my neighbor to buy that product from the other online retailer. What makes this even more illogical is, if the company doesn't collect the sales tax it doesn't mean that the payment isn't still due it just means that it is the responsibility of the individual buying the product to self-assess and pay the uncollected sales tax to the state and local governments. I can only imagine how many people actually exert the effort required to keep track of untaxed purchases and then calculate and pay the sales tax on their Amazon and other online purchases. Both individuals and companies take advantage of this sales tax loophole to avoid being responsible for collecting and paying sales taxes.

A simplified sales tax law structure, along with one centralized reporting agency, would improve the efficiency of the sales tax collection/payment process. With a centralized reporting agency, a company could report all their retail sales and would be able to collect all applicable sales tax. This would ensure that states received all sales taxes due but, more to the point of this chapter, this arrangement would make it easier for companies to comply with the sales tax laws thereby lessening the barrier that the complexity of the current sales tax rules create. We could certainly continue on with the irrational aspects of the sales tax rules but our focus for this chapter is barriers to entry. With that said, the current sales tax structure is a good example of a barrier. This barrier causes not only a loss of revenue to companies but also a loss of available products to consumers which together act as an unnecessary friction on the economy.

Complex taxation structures often cause companies to avoid certain markets within the United States as well as markets elsewhere in the world. These serve to be barriers to those markets and certainly lessen the competition in those markets. Often state and local governments tend to focus on their revenue needs and forget the needs of the businesses who are trying to serve the customers within those localities.

The basic premise behind the effectiveness of the free enterprise system is the smooth flow of resources from sellers to those who can use their products and services. No one knows how restrained the world economy is by the various barriers that restrict the effectiveness of the free enterprise system. Ideally the world would benefit by having a perfect flow of resources to where they can best be used.

Everyone knows the benefit of having a great mechanic to work on their car or a repair person to work on whatever piece of equipment might be broken in their home or building. Repair people need the right tools in order to be the most effective at making repairs. Consider for a moment an auto mechanic who needs to replace the headlight and needs a Phillips screwdriver to do so, if all they have is a worn or broken Phillips head or possibly even a flathead screwdriver available that repair might take a half hour longer than it would if the mechanic had the right or best quality of tool in their hand. Continuing on with this example, the loss to the economy from not having the best tool in the right hands results in the loss of a half hour of productivity. Whatever is keeping the best tool from the mechanic is the barrier that is causing friction on the economy. Looping back to the sales tax system example, using an inefficient system for the administration of state sales taxes is a barrier to commerce and is, in my mind, very much like the mechanic who is using the wrong screwdriver as both makes a process more difficult than it needs to be.

Earlier in the book we reviewed the problem of wasted resources in "feudal" times where many of the exceptional minds of the era were wasted because they were stuck in a society where rigid class structures kept serfs as serfs and lords as lords. Every society has that same failure to one degree or another. Even today, within the United States society, there are barriers that are the result of wealth or more often the lack of wealth.

In many middle or upper class communities it has now become uncommon for children to work while they are attending high school. The coolest kids have the nicest things and have the time to enjoy them because they are not expected to work on weekends or after school. Even parents, many of whom grew up in an environment where kids were expected to work, have now apparently bought into this new reality of children not having to earn their own money. It remains to be seen if the trend toward this way of thinking will harm or benefit society. Clearly I believe there is benefit to receiving work experience at a young age and learning the value of money. Children with a good work ethic and the desire to earn their own money now have the added barrier to doing so by the societal attitude that cool kids don't perform menial labor. Possibly missing this experience will not lessen the capabilities of future generations but, nonetheless, it is a barrier to a valuable resource flowing into the job market where employers could make use of the additional low cost labor.

Some barriers to entry in economics are more obvious than others. For example, if a bridge were out between your community and a nearby fruit farm and the fruit you wanted was rotting on the trucks then that would be an obvious barrier. This non-functioning bridge is a barrier to entry for fruit coming into your hometown marketplace. Within our society many resources are restricted by barriers similar to the bridge and the fruit in this example. In our society we are lacking trained employees who have advanced skills in math and science. At the same time there are a number of bright students who are not receiving the right training that could lessen this shortage. Many things within a society can cause this, such as growing up in a home where the parents are unable to provide an intellectually gifted child with the tools or opportunities they need in order to pursue a career that would best utilize their capabilities.

Unfortunately our country's finest colleges and universities are not always filled with the best minds in the country. This is the case because either the best minds have not been adequately prepared to attend these schools or because some less capable students gained admission through other means. It's not reasonable to assume that the best schools are going to focus solely on admitting only those with the best minds and ignore their traditions such as giving preference to the children of former graduates. Obviously wealth and social position will continue to influence who gains admission into our country's finest schools… the extent to which this occurs will vary based on the society's sensibilities at that time.

Making the most of our children's minds is certainly the most efficient path for obtaining the skills needed within our country's economy. Although the most successful societies can attract talent from other countries, the extent to which internal talent is wasted is still a drag on the internal economy… the cost to the worldwide economy is even greater. By having to go outside our country for talent, talent that existed internally but was not optimized, costs other societies the loss of their most talented individuals. Therefore the total cost to society is the productivity lost by the sub-optimized local individuals plus the cost to the societies that lost their most talented individuals. It is in this way *(pilfering the best and brightest talent)* that the failures of the United States education system became a barrier and serves to hold down developing economies.

The point of this chapter is to help you develop an understanding of the breadth of things that can be barriers to entry and to help you recognize how many of these barriers serve to make the overall economy less effective thus lowering the quality of life for all those who live within that society. Although this knowledge is valuable to anyone who operates in the economy, it is particularly important when a voter considers the platform of a candidate for political office. Having this knowledge may enable a voter to better understand concepts in the politician's platform regarding regulation, healthcare, and campaign financing. If you work as a manager, this knowledge may help you to understand why decisions are made the way they are or to at least arm you with a better understanding of what represents bad economic policy which will allow you to recognize failures that exist within our society.

Chapter Twenty-four

(Free Enterprise, Motivation & Prosperity)

All of us have a certain level of motivation, you may be highly motivated or have very minimal motivation and your motivation can have either a positive or negative effect on society. We all need motivation to get out of bed in the morning, to eat a meal, exercise, or to just flip on the TV and "veg out". Nothing happens with us, as individuals or within society, without some sort of motivation. A prosperous United States' economy is the result of a large percentage of the population being reasonably motivated to contribute their efforts to production. In a more day-to-day type comparison consider a prosperous United States' economy to be the equivalent of a well maintained home. Your home can only stay in tip-top shape by the collective efforts of everyone in the family. Kids can help out by helping with the lawn work, keeping their rooms tidy, taking out the trash, or any number of other household chores. The parents would keep the maintenance of the house current, no leaky pipes or gutters, floors would be kept swept and mopped, and anything in need of a fresh coat of paint would promptly receive one coat or more likely a second for good measure. If only one person in the household worked to maintain the home's upkeep then their home would pale in comparison to the home where it was a family effort.

Motivation is often a topic of conversation, as an example in the past forty years in the United States, we have heard about people on welfare lacking the motivation to work and their failure to contribute to society. This particular discussion is often centered on the question of what would motivate a person, who is getting money, healthcare, a place to live and food, to get out there and work for those things. The factors that have made and continue to make this an energetic discussion remain applicable today.

In our society people go to work every day, in their mind they are going to work to *(among other things)* earn a living. From society's perspective, all workers are providing some benefit that will flow to others within society. Think of it this way, if you are an autoworker the money you receive for your labors comes from someone purchasing a car. Keep in mind, it doesn't matter if the money is paid for a new car or a used car, any money paid for a car goes in some part back to the auto manufacturer and the workers in the automobile factory. Society receives value from the manufacture of an automobile as transportation and the value paid is the wages going to all the workers in the supply chain involved in making, transporting, and selling the automobile. Yes my friend even the sleaziest used car salesperson plays an essential part in this value chain.

Unfortunately we don't often consider the part we play in making our society productive since it's everyone's collective effort that determines our society's overall quality of life. It's therefore worthwhile to put a little thought and consideration into how this collection of efforts connects to makeup the lifestyle available to the society in which we live.

We can appreciate the simple connection between the service we receive in a restaurant and the tip we leave the server. In terms of effective motivation there are few better examples than that between your desire for good service, the motivation of the server, and the tip you pay. Sometimes customers make it very clear at the onset of the meal that they are a good tippers to ensure the wait staff knows there will be a reward for exceptional service. Any successful server is quick to catch any implication that the customer is likely to be a good tipper and make every effort to capture their customer's appreciation by making noticeable efforts to improve the customer's dining experience.

If every linkage between the price paid and value received were as clear and clean as the diner's and the wait staff it would be much easier to understand the levers involved in making an economy prosperous. Contrast this easily understood provider and customer relationship to that of the Internal Revenue Service workers and their customers, amid this murky relationship just who is the IRS's customer anyway? Believe it or not the customer of the IRS is the taxpayer. Those of us who have had the experience of working with the IRS would likely agree there is little about those experiences that would make you want to tip your friendly IRS employee.

Few groups of employees receive less appreciation from their customers than the IRS. I suspect this may, in part, be that the IRS employees don't recognize they are serving the taxpayer any more than we taxpayers recognize the IRS is performing an important service for us. This somewhat extreme example of the supplier and customer relationship exemplifies why effectively motivating employees to provide great customer service is so difficult. Despite that fact that the IRS provides an important service to its customers, ensuring everyone pays their fair share of taxes, *(a service that is a necessary and beneficial function to society)* the IRS's work is still not highly valued by society as a whole. In terms of a concept, the service that the IRS employees provide is not overly opaque; their work should simply be performed timely, efficiently, and without inflicting any unneeded hardship upon the taxpayers.

The measure of what would define a successful IRS could be a book unto itself but for our purposes we will keep the depth of our examination relatively shallow. I suspect as my wife proofs my writing she will agree that when it comes to shallow thinking I am the man for the job, hopefully my enlightened paying readership will, by this point, choose to disagree. I suspect ten weeks on the best seller's list will be sufficient proof of my competence. As a start, to our shallow undertaking, let's agree that the customers of the IRS comprise the entire population of the United States even those who do not have tax liabilities. If the IRS is perfectly successful in their work, all the honest taxpayers would end up paying less tax because taxpayers who would have otherwise successfully evaded some of their tax liability would end up paying their full share. If you consider this to be the goal of the IRS you would probably have a little better feeling about the agency and would wish them great success in their work. Unfortunately this concept is not readily apparent to most taxpayers who have worked with the IRS and, based upon my personal experience, is not well understood or accepted by the agents, at least not the ones I worked with.

A common problem that impacts worker productivity is that the worker often is not properly motivated to serve their customer to the best possible degree. In chapter one I discussed my early work experience at a furniture factory where evading our responsibilities as workers became something akin to an art. These workers, myself included, were no better than many of the poorly motivated IRS agents in that we were not doing our jobs in a manner that best served our customers or society as a whole. This is important because every wasted moment on the job diminishes the quality of life for society as a whole, whereas added output, either from increased efficiency or just working harder, adds to the overall quality of life for our society.

As a way to better define this element, let's consider a worker at a small business who is responsible for customer service. The worker's hours are from 8 AM to 5 PM each day. One day as the clock approached 5 PM the phone began to ring. The worker stopped before answering the phone realizing that once on the phone, the call might go past 5 PM. In this case the worker chose not to deliver service to the customer which may have cost the business money. This employee's choice also forced that customer to work harder in order to meet their needs. It's hard to blame the worker because he was most likely correct in that the call would have extended his time at work, time he probably wouldn't have been paid for. Because the economy we work within is so immense we don't consider how avoiding our work can actually decrease our quality of life. Had our customer service worker believed that by answering this end-of-the-day call it would have increased his chances of having his next late service call answered then he may have chosen to provide that extra bit of productivity at four fifty-five PM on that day.

Extra effort is something that we all are aware of, but we tend to see it in more personal terms as opposed to seeing the effect it has on a business's overall output. As an example, there's a restaurant close to my home where my family and I occasionally dine; our first couple of visits to the restaurant had not been great but one evening we decided to give them another try. On this visit we noticed almost immediately that something had changed since our last visit, not only was our server very attentive to our needs but other servers, as they passed by, would check on us too. My wife and I observed this outstanding service at the tables around us as well and we began to wonder what brought about this transformation. After some observation, we noticed that there was a new manager and, when he himself stopped by to check on us, we complimented him on the outstanding service and asked how he had accomplished it. Cutting through his modesty and deflection of credit to his staff, we discovered that he had worked with his staff establishing the expectation to deliver, not just good but, outstanding service. These changes included encouraging all the wait staff to pitch in wherever they saw an unfulfilled need. As restaurant customers, we have all seen our own server struggling to keep up with their assigned tables while others were temporarily idle. As customers we no doubt wished the other servers would give ours a hand. This restaurant manager tapped this unused capacity within his restaurant and took the overall service level up several notches. In short, we understood from the manager's brief explanation, the point he effectively made to his staff was that if collectively the restaurant delivered better service to all of its customers then everyone who worked there would benefit.

As an economic model, free enterprise is successful because it naturally provides the motivation to business owners to find ways to efficiently deliver products or services to their customers. The one person hotdog stand strives to meet its customer's needs to the extent the owner desires to make additional profit. The issue of the owner motivating the employees remains easy as long as the owner is the only employee. Anyone who makes their living as a one person operation understands that poor customer service will cost them money, so naturally the employee/owner is highly motivated to provide customers with great service. From the customer's perspective, if they find a hotdog stand that provides good quality hotdogs, fresh condiments, and great customer service then they are apt to patronize that hotdog stand on a regular basis.

While writing this book I had the opportunity to read three books related to Russia and the Soviet Union. Although none of the these books focused on the communist economic system, I did learn that the reason communism failed in the Soviet Union was not due to particular flaws in the philosophical teachings of Karl Marx or more specifically the socialist methods of running a country and its economy. The central failure of communism was something much more mundane and that trait leading to communism's demise is one quite common even in many free enterprise economies. Over time within the Soviet economy, opportunity and individual success came to have less and less to do with the capability of the individual and more to do with whom their parents were. The ability to get a good education, a good job following graduation, and promotions once hired was tied to the politics of who had connections and who did not. If my limited knowledge of the failed Soviet society is correct then the reason it failed is that individual motivation declined. More precisely there was not a clear link between capability, effort, and reward hence there was nothing to motivate the Soviet citizens to do more or to do better. Whereas outright rebellion or criminal activity in the Soviet Union would win the perpetrator a trip to the gulag, doing no more than what was required yielded the same result as working very hard.

In chapter fourteen *("Feudal" to Futile)* we discussed the Dark Ages and what may have caused mankind's lack of progress in the five hundred plus years that made up that period. The point I made was that the system in place kept exceptional people from being able to use their talents effectively stalling progress for society as a whole. In fairness to those who lived in the Dark Ages' times weren't easy; there were constant wars, the plague, and the fear of starvation all of which contributed to the lack of progress. But to some degree, the society and economic system played a large part in holding back growth… it did not provide any real opportunity for individual advancement therefore eliminating motivation.

In the communist state of the Soviet Union the society began to spiral down a path of increasing inefficiency and lack of innovation. The two pronged attack on Soviet prosperity, an unmotivated workforce and the failure to find and utilize exceptional individuals, brought the communist system down. I would argue that, if the Soviet version of communism had a more effective system of allowing the top performers to rise in prominence, the cold war may have still been going on well into the twenty-first century. This is important, not because communism could have been saved with a little tweaking in the administration but, because it's a testament to the importance the role of individual motivation plays within a society.

There is an adage in baseball that says *"the best players often make the worst managers"*. The logic behind this axiom is that, unless a player worked and struggled tirelessly in order to become a good player then he will not have the skills to guide others to be the best that they can be. This same logic may be true for motivation within the economic realm. Successful people are usually among those who find themselves in leadership positions within our economy and, by virtue of their position, are left with trying to figure out how to deal with the poor, unemployed, or underemployed. Someone who has never experienced the poverty cycle may be ill-equipped to develop a system that moves people out of the social safety net and into the middle class because they lack perspective. Certainly the most capable leaders don't have to experience all things in order to be great leaders however, regardless of how it is gained; perspective is a valuable attribute to those seeking to be an effective leader and motivator.

The amount of motivation present in any one individual is highly variable and may change greatly throughout their lifetime. Effectively motivating members of society to produce more and better products, and then pairing them with the right type of job opportunities, remains amongst the vital attributes necessary to have a productive economy. These concepts leave us with a basic premise that the economy will be the most successful when everyone is working their hardest to produce the most goods and services for others to consume. The more output we have the better off all members of an economy are... the fact that this is such a simple concept belies the fact that it is so difficult to achieve high employment, balance output to consumption, and otherwise make the economy work efficiently. While the concept is simple the complexity of the economy, particularly the interweaved dependencies of suppliers and consumers, investors, entrepreneurs, and others, result in inefficiencies like unemployment, poorly trained workers, and shortages of certain types of skilled laborers.

Since the processes are complex it's very challenging for leaders of our society to make things work. Officials in many government agencies are getting mixed directions and often these directions are tainted with politically charged concepts with right wing and left wing ideas being inserted with alternating administrations. Some economic and social programs vary between states which makes it even more challenging to fine tune the nation's economic engine.

Let's consider one common scenario where some states provide a more generous safety net than others. We will examine what might happen when two adjacent states have different approaches to providing a safety net, how the approaches differ, and how this complicates the problem of finding the most effective approach.

Suppose you are a generally lazy person and you happen to live in the State of Self-Reliance. Your state has a minimal safety net program which includes food stamps, Medicaid, unemployment insurance, and maybe a few other basic programs. Because you lack motivation to work hard, maintain a job, and otherwise provide for yourself you are often in a situation where you are without food or shelter. You're tired, hungry, and cold and on the verge of committing suicide or, worse yet, finding a job but then you hear that your neighboring state, the State of Entitlement, has many wonderful programs in place that will take care of you.

The state of Entitlement has taken, what they describe as, a very enlightened approach to taking care of their poor and unemployed. The state has generous benefits including Medicaid, extended unemployment insurance, and welfare. After learning about your neighboring states entitlement programs you realize that suicide and finding are job are not your only two options; by simply moving to the State of

Entitlement you can continue your lazy lifestyle and enjoy a better lifestyle.

You move to a nearby city located just inside the State of Entitlement and there you find a boom town of government sponsored housing. You quickly pick out a new place to live and sign up for welfare, Medicaid, and food stamps; soon you are housed, well fed, and secure in your new state. As an individual this opportunity would seem to be a great opportunity for you short-term but how will this new situation help you overcome your tendency to be lazy? The answer is, having this great package of aid programs may well encourage, rather than discourage, this personal flaw unless of course there is a clear and aggressive program to move you out of the safety net and into productive employment.

Forgetting about you for a moment, let's consider how this situation will work out for the two states *(the State of Entitlement and the State of Self-Reliance)*. Entitlement, as a result of its efforts to provide for the poor, will have a flood of new residents *(from the State of Self-Reliance)* whose sole purpose will be to consume the easily obtained *(and maintained)* benefits. Entitlement will now need to support both their own poor and *(to the extent*

allowed by its laws) the poor who have migrated into their state.
The motivated people living in Entitlement *(those who have
obtained an education and training and who work hard to maintain their
employment and incomes)* will now need to pay more taxes in order
to support the overburdened programs.

Just like the poorly motivated moved to Entitlement *(excited by
the opportunity for better economic circumstances)* many businesses and
working individuals will soon be looking to move out of
Entitlement into states where they will not be taxed so heavily.
While not everyone will move, the Sate of Entitlement and its
residents will pay the price for having a more generous safety
net than its neighboring state. You may believe that Entitlement
was doing the right thing and probably just needed to tighten up
the rules somewhat. But, even if Entitlement strikes the exact
right balance in terms of a safety net, it will still lose in the long
run because working residents and businesses will be drawn to
states where taxes are not as high.

While other countries might have more attractive social benefits
and/or tax structures, there are barriers that make it difficult for
people to easily move and take up residence in another country.
However, moving between states, counties, and cities within the

United States is fairly easy which only complicates the ability of state and local governments to establish fair tax and benefit programs. Establishing a tax and benefit structure is not simply about doing what may be ethically correct, it's also about doing what's required in order to attract and maintain a tax base *(people and businesses)*. As much as Entitlement may want to avoid having homeless and starving people within its borders, it must first think about what is economically practical in its area taking into consideration what neighboring states are doing *(or as in this example, not doing)*.

At this point in the argument many would say that "you" need to get your lazy ass out of your government apartment and find a job and, if the "bare bones" entitlement program offered in the State of Self Reliance forces Entitlement to not be so generous in the care of their poor then so be it. Did you really think it was going to be that simple? It's simply not that black and white, in fact there is plenty of gray. Often the poor, underemployed, or unemployed are not solely the product of laziness but sometimes a victim of circumstances. If you lived in a town where there was only one large business and it suddenly closed its doors, you and thousands of others could be thrown out of work. Most would agree there should be some safety net in place to help those people while they recover from an event that could potentially happen to almost anyone within our society.

The question isn't whether or not a safety net should be there but is more about being able to fine tune it in order to achieve and maintain the right balance. If your state is too generous people may be encouraged to be out of work and live off of unemployment or other social programs. If, on the other hand, your state is too stingy there is the risk of having economic misfortunes tear families apart, possibly resulting in otherwise good people taking desperate measures such as resorting to crime. Additionally, the pain of losing a job could adversely impact others in the family resulting in problems that will affect future generations. For example, if a family falls onto hard times their children are more likely to be undereducated and/or to not receive the benefit of a good parental example, both of which are more easily provided by a parent or parents who are leading successful lives. The result of not having these two beneficial environmental factors while growing up increases the likelihood that the children will fall victim to economically damaging lifestyles such as drug use, crime, or both.

Circling back to the earlier point is that we as an economy and a society live best when everyone is productive. If everyone is working then there is a greater pool of products and services to be consumed by everyone. If ten percent of the people are not working then in aggregate everyone's collective consumption will be roughly ten percent less. In other words, if only ninety percent of the people are producing and one hundred percent are consuming, there will be a ten percent shortfall in achieving the optimum output.

This adverse result seems so simple to fix when you look at it in a micro-economic setting. Let's say you are working and your neighbor is currently unemployed. You are working eighty hours a week and have no time to take care of your house and the neighbor is simply sitting around all day waiting for the next unemployment check. What if the state required that, in order to receive an unemployment check a person would have to help four neighbors by providing each with ten hours of labor per week for a total of 40 hours? In your case, it would be very helpful if you were able to come home to a house that had received ten hours of maintenance that week. On an overall basis the economy would have received more value through this type of arrangement in that the all the people are being productive. Going a step further, let's say the state comes up with a program where instead of $300.00 of weekly unemployment it will pay $400.00 per week if you perform at least 40 hours of work each week for your employed neighbors. Would you or your neighbors agree to pay, say fifty dollars week, to the state's unemployment program if you were going to receive ten hours of work from the program? Chances are likely that you would want to take advantage of this bargain priced labor as it will have the added benefit of freeing up more of your time for leisure or, if you prefer, additional time at work.

As an accountant, I tend to look at the numbers, so let's take a minute to do that. Before this fictitious program the state was paying unemployment benefits of $300 per week to one of your neighbors while collecting a total of $200 per week from you and three other neighbors. With the new program you and your three working neighbors will each pay an additional $50 per week, but will each receive ten hours of labor in return, and your unemployed neighbor will receive $400 per week from the state. Under this new arrangement the state will pay out a third less in unemployment, saving a net of $100 per week, and the economy, as a whole, will be producing more. In the real world it clearly wouldn't be this simple but, conceptually, you can see that what was once a wasted resource is now employed and is benefiting the interrelated individual economic situations of all five neighbors. This approach adds to society's economic output. The society benefits because the unemployed worker is now earning a higher wage allowing the family to live better and to more effectively prepare for a more productive future *(including the ability to provide a better education for themselves and their children)*.

One of the products of having too thin of a safety net is that, when money is short, one of the areas that often suffers is the education of the family's children. An unemployed family may not be able to properly feed or clothe their children detracting from the child's ability to learn, a little extra money each week could mitigate this. Ideally we would like a safety net that would ensure children receive an optimal level of education. I grew up in a family with nine children and, as a family, we faced several serious bouts of economic hardship so I well understand the added challenges that being poor can create for a child at school. Something as simple as having to wear used shoes to school generated teasing that at times made learning difficult. I was fortunate to have good parents who saw the value of a good education, kept me on track, and helped to offset some of the negative aspects that went along with being poor at school. I was fortunate to have supportive parents but it's easy for me to see how a borderline student could easily fall into choices that could lead toward a life of crime or substance abuse.

Another personal example, there was a family whose father and mother both had good jobs throughout their lives but this family never seemed to be able to make ends meet. This family had five children who, despite the fact that their family's income was much greater my family's, would go to school appearing to be poorer than my siblings and me. Unfortunately for these children, the cause appeared to be the result of the father's choice to overindulge in drink which put a drain on the family's finances. Additionally, both mother and father weren't motivated to keep their children focused on getting a good education and, as a result, only one of their five children made good use of their time in school, graduating with decent grades and a positive outlook on life. This one and one of his mechanically inclined brothers became solid contributors to the economy while the other three continue to struggle financially. I believe many of the people who access the social safety net on a regular basis do so because their early years lacked the necessary preparation to be good productive members of society.

Society pays a heavy price for adults, who as children, were not prepared to be productive members of society. When I talk about motivation, and how motivation affects the economy, I'm referring to long-term motivation not about having an occasional motivated or unmotivated day. Long-term motivation is where the values one holds true to throughout their lifetime are put into place or, said another way, are internalized.

Motivation impacts economics as much as having the right economic system. Earlier when I referenced the communist Soviet Union I made the point that it failed not because the system concept itself was bad but because the leadership fell into the trap of self-serving nepotism. Marx and Lenin never considered developing a system that would not utilize the most capable people. What happened in the communist society was that its leaders fell back into the same selfish shortsighted politics which, in capitalistic societies, regularly brings down companies. Human nature appears to drive individuals to selfish actions. Just like in the Soviet Union when a party leader would orchestrate the hiring of a relative for a choice position over a more qualified individual, the same flawed thinking is used when a company manager or politician chooses a less capable person for nepotistic or political reasons.

Working as an accounting person for thirty plus years I have, on occasion, seen mild examples of unwarranted favoritism in hiring decisions. I've known leaders who would only hire people who shared their background. These leaders almost exclusively looked to hire people who came through a specific public accounting firm. I say this type of favoritism is mild in that it's not blatantly sexist or racist but it nevertheless unnecessarily narrows the pool of candidates which could potentially cost the business and deny the company the best available job candidates. The economic impact from any decision, that is not made based on the pure free enterprise motivation of producing the least cost, best quality product, represents a waste of economic resources.

Rewarding the best available candidate with the job should be the obvious best answer however none of us are completely capable of keeping inappropriate factors out of our decision making processes be it in business, politics, or other areas that impact the effectiveness of our economy. It's critical to the long-term effectiveness of any economy that processes are kept as pure as is humanly possible so that the best resources will flow naturally into the roles that will best utilize those quality resources. Just as you wouldn't choose military spec parts to build a coffee maker you would not want the next Albert Einstein spending his lifetime working as a patent office clerk. Along the same lines organizations that do not hire and promote based on knowledge, performance, and capability underutilize those resources thereby making the cost of their products higher.

The objective of this discussion is not to find the most flawed players within the economy but instead to point out how important it is to economic health that proper levels of motivation are maintained. The grand concept we need to understand is that, when any organization or process wastes resources, it matters. The fact that organizations like the IRS do not deliver good value and do not use the people it hires to make the most of their abilities is waste. The negative stigma we apply to that organization and others like it do little if anything to improve the problem. What is needed is to setup organizations, like the IRS, in such a way that motivates the staff to collectively do the best job possible. This could be achieved by running the IRS like a business within the United

States government or by possibly outsourcing the work to the private sector. The underperforming IRS is a great example of why, due to an organization not having an effective means to do their assigned work, each of us has a little less than we otherwise would.

Motivation, as an element of the free enterprise system, is both a product of the system and a component of a successful free enterprise system. Organizational or process success comes when resources naturally move to where those resources produce the most value to society. Fairness is considered an element of morality but, in a perfect free enterprise system, it is a natural means by which to produce the optimum output. If every buying and hiring decision was based solely on what the business needs, then only by choosing *(without any bias)* the best available resource, can optimal output be achieved. Societies recognize that in some cases humans need help to learn and employ what are truly fair processes. Fifty years ago women and minorities were not typically placed in management or in any other position of leadership; it took many years and artificial constraints, like regulations, to move decision makers into making better use of these under-utilized resources. These artificial constraints led to a fairer society, one which better utilizes the available resources thereby making our economy more productive.

Some economists choose to believe a completely unconstrained business environment is the best means to achieve economic success. History has proven that human nature, when left on its own, does not always make the best choices for society as a whole. Instead, in this aspect of economics, we need to mix in only those regulations needed to motivate out those economically dysfunctional tendencies while retaining the motivational elements of a free enterprise economic system.

Chapter Twenty-five

(Concluding Thoughts)

We have covered a lot of ground in the previous chapters and I would like to wrap up our journey with what I will call the ten commandments of economics. Absolutely no sacrilege intended just some parting thoughts and quick overview of what was contained in the book.

I. **Free enterprise, to date, is the best functioning economic system developed by man.** Mankind should not ascribe divinity to the free enterprise system nor disregard the free enterprise concepts which have worked so well in the past.

II. **Free enterprise itself is not justification for ignoring other real facts that are available about other aspects of our society and the world in which we live.** Just because pollution regulations inhibit short-term economic growth is not an excuse to ignore the fact that, when left to its own accord, the market will likely *(as it has done in the past)* ignore the effects of pollution until it is well past the point of harming society. In some cases thoughtful regulation trumps what free enterprise would produce if left to its own devices.

III. **Thou shalt not condemn the seeking of profit for profit's sake.** Free enterprise, as a system, produces the drive for profit within entrepreneurs, business management, and others within the economy which is among free enterprise's greatest attributes. Attempting to make this drive for profit into something bad or something to feel guilty about is a disservice, not only to those hard working individuals seeking profit, but to society itself.

IV. **Seek to find the balance between what is needed to have a productive economy and what is needed to sustain a society that treats humanely its children, elderly, sick, and all others who are not fully able to compete.** The failure to manage this balance results in either a poor economy or in a society that we cannot be proud to be part of.

V. **You shall not ignore bad players who abuse the free enterprise system, those who garner unjust rewards for practices which do not create value in the economy.** You shall seek a society that aggressively strives to limit this behavior and in doing so specifically limit or, even better yet, achieve the recovery of those economic rewards received by economic abusers. Those who participate in truly beneficial behaviors that build value *(innovation, invention and hard work)* should be rewarded and encouraged but are often frustrated by those who receive rewards by abusing the free enterprise system.

VI. **You shall seek to find a quick route to help each individual in society find their optimal role within the economy.** Anyone who is not in a role where they can contribute a valuable service or valuable work to produce products is a drag on the economy. Someone consuming and not working is a drag on the economy and lessens everyone's lifestyle as a result of not being productive.

VII. **Society should seek to establish a legal environment that supports an effective economy.** Allowing an economic environment where individuals can work the margins around what is legal in order to enrich themselves steals from everyone else in society. Frustrating those who would seek to shortcut the process to wealth by taking advantage of cracks in the foundation of laws is a worthy goal, just as worthy as seeking to not frustrate producers in the economy with unneeded or ineffective laws and regulation.

VIII. **Seek the truth in what really does work in economics.** Question those who make their words sacred economic scripture; challenge their assertions and endeavor to find what will work for the circumstances at hand. In doing so, keep in mind that what works in economics can never be written in stone because mankind, technology, and society are all constantly evolving. Your role is to continuously seek what is truly working within the economy.

IX. **Do not deny the successful their rewards or waste valuable time envying their wealth.** Everyone should seek to be successful at what they do. Recognize that anyone not being productive, including you, takes something away from everyone in society.

X. **Honor the merits of trade.** There are some things your neighbor does better than you and others that you do more efficiently than they. Through trade both of you are enriched.

Keep in mind that this list is not all encompassing… it is simply a listing of ten elements that are among what I believe to be good rules for economic policy. Your ongoing role in our economy is to keep thinking and evolving your thoughts on economics; and now that you are armed with what I hope is a bit more perspective, perhaps you can help move the economic dialogue, within your sphere of influence, a little more towards an effective path. My hope is that, as a society, we can move the discussion out of shop worn rhetoric toward a discussion of which economic tools we should be employing based on the current economic conditions. If we can avert the crippling consequences of legislative gridlock and move to where we can take the right action for the economy more quickly then, when we enter into a period of economic dysfunction, our society will suffer less as a result.